*Prophetic* **Politics**

# *Prophetic* **Politics**

CHRISTIAN SOCIAL MOVEMENTS

AND AMERICAN DEMOCRACY

David S. Gutterman

*Cornell University Press* ITHACA AND LONDON

First published 2005 by Cornell University Press
First printing, Cornell Paperbacks, 2006
Printed in the United States of America

*Library of Congress Cataloging-in-Publication Data*

Gutterman, David S.
  Prophetic politics : Christian social movements and American democracy / David S. Gutterman.
     p. cm.
  Includes bibliographical references (p.  ) and index.
  ISBN-13: 978-0-8014-4138-7 (cloth : alk. paper)
  ISBN-10: 0-8014-4138-2 (cloth : alk. paper)
  ISBN-13: 978-0-8014-7338-8 (pbk.: alk. paper)
  ISBN-10: 0-8014-7338-1 (pbk.: alk. paper)
  1. Christianity and politics—United States. I. Title.
  BR115.P7G88 2005
  322'.1'0973—dc22                                        200403944

Cornell University Press strives to use environmentally responsible suppliers and materials to the fullest extent possible in the publishing of its books. Such materials include vegetable-based, low-VOC inks and acid-free papers that are recycled, totally chlorine-free, or partly composed of nonwood fibers. For further information, visit our website at www.cornellpress.cornell.edu.

Cloth printing      10 9 8 7 6 5 4 3 2
Paperback printing    10 9 8 7 6 5 4 3 2 1

*For Jennifer, Cassie, and Everett*

"The prophet is the figure of crisis."

—Paul Ricoeur

# Contents

# *Preface*

As I write, the challenges religion poses for democratic politics in the United States are profoundly apparent. The United States is led by a President who is outspoken about his born-again Christian faith and who has taken the nation into a war in Iraq that is framed as part of a national "mission" in often explicitly religious terms. During the 2004 election season, Roman Catholic archdioceses around the country refused to give communion to parishioners (including Democratic nominee John Kerry) who support the legal access to abortion. In Massachusetts, same-sex couples are getting legally married in a flurry of civil ceremonies to the delight of some religious bodies and the apocalyptic consternation of others. Meanwhile the nation awaits the Supreme Court's decision regarding whether displays of the Ten Commandments on government property are a violation of the First Amendment and religious organizations throughout the United States are poised to assert broad claims about the "essential religiosity" of the nation or about the growing condition of moral decay.

In the United States, political issues and debates are deeply entwined with religious controversies. Although this feature of American public life is widely recognized, we have developed surprisingly few ways to talk about the often contentious relationship between religion and democracy. My intention in this book is to help expand the range of ways in which to think and talk about religion and democracy in the United States. My goal, accordingly, has been to write in a way that is accessible to a broad audience, so that while my analysis is shaped by works of political theory, this book is not written for only political theorists. Indeed, religious social movements and the challenge of democracy constitute such an encompassing subject that an interdisciplinary approach is required. Writing about religion and politics, I am well aware that I am raising topics one is advised to avoid in polite company. Sacrificing politeness, I have tried to maintain an attitude of respect. The debates about religion and politics (and race, sex, gender, and economics) I broach in these pages are at the heart of deliberations about the identity of the nation and its citizens. There are all too few models or vehicles for respectful and engaged conversations about these topics in the United States, and it is my hope that this work can enhance the public space we share by encouraging such exchanges of stories, ideas, and opinions.

WRITING is not a solitary practice for me. This book is the result of conversations, and I want to thank those who graciously and generously offered me their insights, concerns, criticisms, and stories.

At Rutgers University I had the extraordinary good fortune of working with individuals willing to both challenge and encourage me as this project unfolded. Steve Bronner, Linda Zerilli, and Dennis Bathory offered intellectual guidance as well as simple kindness. Dan Tichenor has not just shared with me his critical analysis and exceedingly sound advice; he has also been a great friend as this project has evolved. Working with Carey McWilliams was a great joy; I was inspired by his vast knowledge of religion and politics, learned lessons about friendship, and found enormous pleasure in listening to one of the most magnificent storytellers I have known.

From its inception, this book has been enlivened by friendship. Mark Button (who let me drag him to Shea Stadium for a Promise Keepers event), Laurie Naranch, Karen Zivi, Jennet Kirkpatrick, Claire Snyder, Karen Shelby, Sandra Marshall, Ronnee Shreiber, and especially Jill Locke, have been thoughtful, supportive, and demanding friends of mine and of this project. Their voices and enthusiasm are a constant presence in these pages. George Shulman generously shared with me his own fascinating work on prophets and American political thought and, in addition, offered a supportive and detailed reading of this work. Lisa Disch kindly provided critical insight and encouragement at a crucial moment in the development of this project. Kim Curtis introduced me to the work of Hannah Arendt many years ago; her friendship and sharp insight have been vital to me at all the right moments.

While teaching at Willamette University, I was part of a vibrant intellectual community of students and faculty; Sammy Basu, Joe Bowersox, Seth Cotlar, Mark Conliffe, Leslie Dunlap, Richard Ellis, Steve Green, Melissa Buis Michaux, and Angus Vail each made vital contributions to this project in ways that they may not be able to recognize in these pages. I now have the great pleasure of teaching at Linfield College, where my colleagues Scott Smith, David Sumner, Nancy Cornwell, Dawn Nowacki, and Howard Leichter have provided unstinting encouragement, and where four students, Alexis Lien, Laura Penland, Danielle Regan, and especially Tiffany Scott, have worked on this book with thoughtful and thorough care. I thank Linfield College and Dean Marvin Henberg for providing crucial financial support. Beth Thompson gave the manuscript a careful read and offered astute editorial advice. Catherine Rice, Sheri Englund, Teresa Jesionowski, and Roger Haydon at Cornell University Press have been unflagging supporters of this book, and I thank them for their invaluable counsel.

Over the course of this study I have been fortunate to present earlier incarnations before a number of receptive and inquisitive audiences, including professional conferences, the Center for the Study of American Religion at Princeton University, and the Center for the Critical Analysis of Contemporary Culture at Rutgers University. Two other venues deserve special mention. First, much of the writing of this work took place at the Smithsonian Tropical Research Institute on Barro Colorado Island in Panama. Presenting my work before an international group of scientists provided a lesson in "visiting," listening, and storytelling that remains vivid and instructive. Second, in 1998 I was asked to give a public lecture at Duke University by the Department of Women's Studies. Returning to my alma mater and the domain of my dear friend and mentor Jean O'Barr to present my research on Promise Keepers and contemporary feminism was an enormous pleasure and enabled me to glimpse what this book would become.

Conversations about this work were by no means limited to academic environments; I will gladly talk with anyone who might be remotely interested in these matters. In particular, I would like to thank my family. Pamela and Joseph Johns not only enthusiastically supported my efforts but also helped with the research and fieldwork. My brothers, Andy and Glenn, and sister, Jamie, pushed me to think and write clearly and thus strengthened this project and broadened its appeal. My parents, Alan and Emily Gutterman, raised me on lessons drawn from the story of Exodus, inspiring and encouraging me to ask the right questions, to listen carefully to the voices of others, and to work for the day when "justice shall dwell in the wilderness." Their love and wisdom are to be found throughout this book.

While numerous conversations went into the development of this book, it is ultimately the work of a particular dialogue. It is not simply that Jennifer Johns has supported and encouraged me with loving patience as I pursued this project. Sometimes this work feels as much hers as mine; surely it is ours. My thinking, my writing, my imagination, and certainly my capacity to listen to the stories that are always being told have been transformed by our life together. And as this book has been written, new voices, those of our children Cassandra and Everett, have joined the dialogue and animated our shared storytelling. It is to Jennifer, Cassie, and Everett that this book and its author are dedicated.

David S. Gutterman

*McMinnville, Oregon*

*Prophetic* Politics

# Chapter One
## Prophetic Politics
## in the United States

When reading the many portions of the Scripture, including the major and minor prophets, we are reminded again and again that if we—as a nation and as individuals—obey God, He will bless us. But when we disobey Him, He disciplines us. Tragically, we as a nation have disobeyed and grieved God. I think primarily of the colossal insult to our God and heavenly Father when we betrayed Him and the trust of our Founding Fathers by removing prayer and Bibles from our schools. As a result, an avalanche of evil, crime, immorality, abortion, and drug addiction has devastated our country and broken the heart of our Lord. This disintegration of America is not news to you because, like ancient Israel, our nation has for the most part forgotten God and failed to obey His commands.
—**Dr. Bill Bright,** *The Coming Revival*

The world isn't working. Things are unraveling, and most of us know it. Tonight, the urban children of the world's only remaining superpower will go to bed to the sound of gunfire. Bonds of family and community are fraying. Our most basic virtues of civility, responsibility, justice, and integrity seem to be collapsing. We appear to be losing the ethics derived from personal commitment, social purpose, and spiritual meaning. The triumph of materialism is hardly questioned now, in any part of our society. Both domestically and globally, we are divided along the lines of race, ethnicity, class, gender, religion, culture, and tribe, and threaten to explode our divisions into a world of perpetual conflict.
—**Reverend Jim Wallis,** *The Soul of Politics*

The trouble is that factual truth, like all other truth, peremptorily claims to be acknowledged and precludes debate, and debate constitutes the very essence of political life. The modes of thought and communication that deal with truth, if seen from the political perspective, are necessarily domineering; they don't take into account other people's opinions, and taking these into account is the hallmark of all strictly political thinking.
—**Hannah Arendt,** *Between Past and Future*

These are fragile times for our nation, according to the cries of many in the American public sphere. In an era of military conflict and economic hardship, religious and political leaders adamantly speak in the language of crisis. Whether one attributes this public religious fervor to a response to the attacks of September 11, 2001, millennial hopes and fears, a sense of moral decay (generally based on either growing economic inequality or the "breakdown of the American family"), or a sign of the normal progression of the stages of history, the discourse of religious revival is increasingly prominent.[1] And, as is amply evident in the United States and throughout the world, devout declarations of religious belief in the public sphere can bring intractable passions to politics.[2]

When debates on social issues are informed not simply by temporal considerations of justice but also by the threat of God's wrathful judgment, the stakes for the nation are raised to extreme levels. We are confronted by the question of whether we can reconcile religious belief and participatory democratic politics. If democratic politics is defined by the open participation of a people representing a plurality of opinions, what happens when voices of religious conviction enter the political sphere? In the third epigraph above, Hannah Arendt articulates the suspicions of many defenders of democratic politics. Religious claims of "Truth" presumably refuse to countenance the possible legitimacy of other opinions, and as such, so the argument goes, must be considered anti-democratic. And yet, despite Arendt's claim that "our world is spiritually a secular world precisely because it is a world of doubt," religious voices continue to speak emphatically in the American public sphere (Arendt 1953, 106).[3]

My examination of Christian social movements in the United States begins by displacing the common view of the status of religion in American political culture. This project is guided neither by the question of the "separation of church and state" nor by the conviction that religion—because it consists of claims of absolute truth—necessarily leads to anti-democratic politics. Rather, I begin from the premise that religious belief and religious narratives have been central to the foundation, development, and current status of the American polity. In particular, I aim to explore different forms of "prophetic politics" in the 20th- and 21st-century United States that illuminate this tension between religion and democratic politics in America.

To explore the tense and dynamic relationship between religion and democratic politics in the United States, I analyze and compare four different illustrations of prophetic politics: an early 20th-century conservative evangelist, Reverend Billy Sunday; a central leader of the civil rights movement, Dr. Martin Luther King Jr.; the contemporary all-male conservative

Christian organization Promise Keepers; and the contemporary progressive Christian federation Call to Renewal. My analysis of these four expressions of prophetic politics involves a close textual analysis of their sermons, speeches, books, and other public documents to examine the ways they define their respective identities and promote prophetic visions for social change. In particular, I explore the ways in which each of these movements relies on retelling the resonant story of Exodus to delineate and disseminate their prophetic politics. These four case studies are preceded by an exploration of the relationship between narratives and politics.

This discussion establishes a theoretical framework for assessing what makes different expressions of prophetic politics a potential source of great vitality but also of great danger for democratic politics. Answering this question requires careful attention to the stories that practitioners of prophetic politics tell in their efforts to define the crisis in America, and whether and how these stories direct audiences to engage in public life.

## "Secular" America?

Much analysis of religion in American public life remains indebted to the "secularism thesis" that dominated 20th-century thinking in the West. This premise holds that humans are defined by their capacity to reason, and that thinking and discovery will progressively and inextricably overcome faith and belief as science and other forms of human inquiry pull back the veil of ignorance. According to this line of thinking, religion represents a "primitive" mode of belief that offers stories and rituals to ameliorate human limitations, or more generously, as a "means to engage lofty metaphysical issues like the immortality of the soul, but inappropriate for all other matters" (B. Lincoln, 2).[4] However, as human limitations are progressively scaled back, the need for religious belief will abate and once-obscured truths will come to light.[5]

Yet, even adherents to the secularism thesis find it hard to deny that religion continues to play a significant role in American public discourse. Most prominently, George W. Bush's prolific use of religious language has attracted great attention to the conspicuous role of religious language in American political discourse.[6] A 2001 survey conducted by the Pew Research Center for the People and the Press found that nearly two-thirds of Americans (64 percent) call religion very important, 43 percent attend religious services at least weekly, and 90 percent pray at least once a week.[7]

Illustrations of this religiosity among American citizens abound: athletes pointing skyward after a big (or not so big) play; the prominent role played by members of the Church of Latter Day Saints in the development of public policy regarding stem cell research; a president who declares that his favorite philosopher is Jesus; the growth of a multimillion-dollar Christian "parallel" youth culture of skateboarding, rock bands, comic books, and fashion accessories.[8]

The role of religion in American public life is of vital importance in assessing the "war on terror" abroad (and at home) and on innumerable domestic issues. If, for example, "faith-based organizations" are increasingly hailed from an array of political forces as the answer to government failures, the always complicated nexus of religion and politics in the United States may become even more delicate. If the nation increasingly turns to churches, temples, mosques, and faith-based organizations to step in where government is stepping out, what are the implications for civil society in the United States?[9] What might this say about the future relationship of religion and politics in America?

In recent years, the most resounding religious voices in the national popular discourse (including that of George W. Bush) have proffered "anti-political" lessons. Prominent Christian conservative voices such as former leaders of the Moral Majority, Cal Thomas and Ed Dobson, proclaim that, for the Christian Right, politics and government are a dangerous dead end, an enervating realm in which, at best, minimal political change is purchased at the price of sullying one's religious values.[10] Framing social ills in a personal and private manner, a manner that complements broader inclinations toward "therapeutic" solutions to both personal and societal problems, has become virtually hegemonic in an era of "feeling one another's pain." While the influence of the Christian Coalition has waned, many religious voices (especially on the right) increasingly seem to lend their powerful voices to this anti-political lesson. One of the best examples of this phenomenon is the influential open letter composed by Paul Weyrich, president of the Free Congress Foundation and longtime socially conservative political activist, in response to the failure of the Senate to impeach President Clinton. Weyrich indicted the American political system and majority of its populace as so "infected with moral decadence" that religious conservatives would do best to "quarantine" themselves from the spread of moral decay. The remaining hope, he declared, is that "remnants of the great Judeo-Christian civilization" will escape the sure apocalypse facing the nation and in turn survive into the dawning of a new era.[11]

Promise Keepers is a prominent purveyor of this anti-political message. Like many voices in civil society today, when it addresses social concerns, Promise Keepers emphasizes the importance of volunteerism and service to local (church) organizations. Recent social trends suggest an increasing detachment from political participation in the United States and a concomitant upswing in volunteerism across the nation. The implications of the decline in political activism and the rise in volunteer service have not been fully appreciated in much of the nation's popular discourse. Service organizations—secular or religious—have a powerful capacity to address individual needs, but they are almost helpless in confronting structural and institutional issues. An apocryphal story is circulating that illustrates this problem exquisitely. As reported by Kate Zemike in the *Boston Globe* on February 22, 2000: "A professor tells of a college student who had volunteered, like so many of his peers, in a soup kitchen. It was such a great experience, the student enthused, he hoped his grandchildren would get the same opportunity." As admirable as dedicating energy to treating the symptoms of social conditions may be, if the political question of what can be done to *change* social conditions is not addressed, then community service has all the makings of a growth industry (like the building of jail cells).

## The Study of Religion and Politics in the United States

Despite the limits of its predictive power, the secularism thesis has had an enormous impact on American cultural imagination. For example, by positing religious belief as an indication of backwardness or at least anti-progressivism, it has helped to simultaneously detach much of the political left from culturally resonant ideas and rhetoric and it has helped enable certain Christian groups to frame themselves as "victims" of forces of social change. The secularism thesis has also provided a narrow lens for academic analysis of religion in American political culture.[12] William Connolly laments this limitation, arguing that "secular conceptions of language, ethics, discourse, and politics . . . [are] insufficiently alert to the layered density of political thinking and judgment" (Connolly 1999, 4). Indeed, although the secularism thesis remains a cultural force, prophetic politics still retains a vibrant energy in American public life. Believers cannot be dismissed as "rubes" to preserve the realm of politics as the space for a "culture of disbelief."[13] Nor can the claims of revelation be uncritically accepted as unassailable. Rather, the visceral and conceptual power of religious narratives in American politics must be acknowledged in evaluating the impact of religious voices on the continuing challenges of democracy.

The focus in this study is on religious revivalist social movements that are—while ecumenical—primarily Protestant. Although each of the movements and "prophets" I discuss sought at times relations with Catholic, Jewish, and other religious groups, their primary political and theological visions remain within a Protestant framework. Moreover, none of these organizations and figures (with the possible exception of Martin Luther King Jr.) had an affiliation with a single "mainline" Protestant denomination as a principal theological, political, or structural force.

My primary interest lies in the retellings of the Exodus narrative, the "sacred story" that was adopted by the Puritans of 17th- and 18th-century New England as their foundational story, by leaders such as Jefferson and Franklin at the birth of the nation, by Lincoln in his efforts to give a "new birth" to the nation, by generations of slaves—in whose retelling of Exodus, America was transformed from Canaan to Egypt—and on and on throughout the history of the nation. Indeed, today the Exodus narrative still plays such a central role in the American imagination that even those immigrants to the United States from outside the Judeo-Christian tradition are portrayed as "wanderers" searching for the "Promised Land." So varied are the uses of the Exodus narrative in American popular culture that Weigh Down Workshop Inc., an evangelical organization helping people to confront obesity by coming to Jesus, has named its latest venture designed to reach overweight youth "The Last Exodus."[14]

## Paths of Religion and Politics Scholarship

Scholarship on religion and politics in the United States is both extensive and, especially within the discipline of political science, particular. Assessments of religion and politics in 20th-century America commonly work from (or against) the secularism thesis and ask two types of questions. One set of studies concerns the "separation of church and state" and explores largely legal, First Amendment questions about the threats to or, alternatively, benefits and detriments of, this "wall." The second common mode of scholarship examines the question of how religious groups continue to influence American governmental and/or electoral politics. These scholars have cogently raised awareness of the impact of religious groups in local, state, and federal government and have also shone the bright light of empirical analysis on claims of influence made by religious leaders such as Jerry Falwell and Pat Robertson.

My analysis instead falls best within a third mode of scholarship on the relationship of religion and politics in the United States. This field of inquiry might loosely be said to have its foundation in the work of Alexis de Tocqueville, who, in speaking of the peculiarity of America, famously emphasized the importance of religion in the new nation. Although my work on the surface appears to follow the path carved out by this observer of American democracy, this study addresses issues beyond Tocqueville's analysis of religion and American political culture.

Isaac Kramnick refers to Tocqueville as "he who must be quoted," and indeed, especially for those who work in the field of religion and politics, Tocqueville sits in an imposing position, as if awaiting at least a polite nod in his general direction.[15] Typically Tocqueville is celebrated among scholars of religion and politics for emphasizing the manner in which religion secures American democracy, with Protestant Christian institutions providing crucial venues for civil association and Christian beliefs guaranteeing American freedom.[16] In the second volume of *Democracy in America,* Tocqueville proclaims:

> One must recognize, whether or not they save men's souls in the next world, that [religions] greatly contribute to their happiness and dignity in this one. . . . Every religion places the object of men's desires outside and beyond worldly goods and naturally lifts the soul into regions far above the realm of the senses. Every religion also imposes on each man some obligations toward mankind, to be performed in common with the rest of mankind, and so draws him away, from time to time, from thinking about himself. (Tocqueville, 444–45)

Tocqueville's assessment that religion ("every religion") has the force of moving citizens beyond individual and materialist concerns is often cited as one of his most vital insights regarding the success of democracy in America. However, while enamored of the generic value of religion in a democratic polity, Tocqueville was not particularly concerned with the specifics of the Christian belief that dominated the American landscape in which he traveled.

This lack of concern is evident in his discussion of the many Protestant denominations in the United States:

> There is an innumerable multitude of sects in the United States . . . all different in the worship they offer to the Creator, but all agree concerning the

duties of men to one another. . . . Though it is very important for man as an individual that his religion should be true, that is not the case for society. Society has nothing to fear or hope from another life; what is most important for it is not that all citizens should profess the true religion but that they should profess religion.[17]

This functional understanding of religion in the United States is also apparent in one of the great gaps in Tocqueville's study of American culture. Despite touring America during the height of the Second Great Awakening, Tocqueville virtually ignores the religious revival in the two volumes of *Democracy in America* (and what he does say is glib and disparaging).[18] While certainly appreciating the institutional role of religion in American political culture, Tocqueville says very little about the specifics of religious beliefs and themes that are prevalent in the United States. So focused is he on the "great unity of Christian morality" that he neglects the practices and narratives that give religion in the United States its distinct texture.

Such a functional approach to American religiosity has shaped both popular and academic beliefs—a sentiment perhaps best captured by the declaration often attributed to President Dwight Eisenhower: "Our government makes no sense unless it is founded in a deeply religious faith— and I don't care what it is." The functional account of generic religion fails, however, to appreciate the rich and intricate ways—the particular flavors—in which religion informs not just government but American public life more generally.

My aim, accordingly, is not to think of religion in broad terms, but to focus on specific ways religious social movements have sought to shape American politics. Indeed, Great Awakenings and religious revivals in the United States have historically been tied to significant periods of political change. As historian William McLoughlin explains,

> Great Awakenings are the results . . . of critical disjunctions in our self-understanding. . . . Awakenings begin in periods of cultural distortion and grave personal stress, when we lose faith in the legitimacy of our norms, the viability of our institutions, and the authority of our leaders in church and state. They eventuate in basic restructurings of our institutions and redefinitions of our social goals. (McLoughlin 1978, 2)

Specific religious revivals coincided with and helped shape the struggles for abolition, for the prohibition of alcohol, for the creation of laws that protect labor, for the Cold War against "godless communism," for civil rights, for restrictions on access to abortion, and for the debates about the definition of marriage in America, to name but a few areas where religions' influence on public policy can readily be seen.

Religious revivals tend to raise the awareness of, and serve to define, the breach between "higher principles" and the lived experiences of individuals. In turn, these revivals raise similar political questions about the fissure between the nation's higher ideals and its existing social institutions. As Samuel Huntington argues, "Religion was the source of the morality that required the saving of souls on the one hand and the regeneration of society on the other" (Huntington, 160). Revivals all share a sense of acute dissatisfaction with the current social and political order, and all rely on a common set of biblical stories. However, revivals can differ profoundly both in their diagnosis of the crisis afflicting the nation and in the development of concomitant paths toward solace.

Proclaiming the presence of a particular crisis in the land and directing a path to solace are what religious voices have often done in America. Using the great tradition of the American jeremiad—a prophetic mode of expression that Sacvan Bercovitch cites as the most striking contribution of the United States to political rhetoric—religious voices have consistently provided stirring portrayals of societal sins coupled with explicit steps needed to avoid catastrophe. In *The American Jeremiad*, Bercovitch convincingly argues that the basic pattern of jeremiadic expression follows three steps: a delineation of sins, a warning of God's awful judgment, and always an offer of renewed hope for the nation should the people return like prodigal sons and daughters to a path of obedience to God's divine plan. In each generation, the definitions of the "crisis" and the necessary road to "renewal" take a particular shape and speak to specific social contexts.

The jeremiadic pattern of crisis and renewal provides a rhythm for religious social movements. The jeremiad presumes a declension in the land (and in the souls of individuals) and an "errand" to be fulfilled.[19] With this pattern as a background, revivalist movements are equipped to name the tenor of the declension and to direct the path of the errand. For example, the two contemporary Christian social movements I explore, Promise Keepers and Call to Renewal, do not merely describe the cultural landscape and the "crisis" currently wreaking havoc; they define it. The epigraphs from Bill Bright and Jim Wallis (associated with Promise Keepers and Call to Renewal respectively) illustrate how these two organizations present quite distinct depictions of the crisis in the United States, and quite different paths to solace. These jeremiads represent, in other words, particular flavors of American religiosity that a functional analysis of generic religion in America neglects.

## The Historical Narrative of Exodus

To appreciate the resonant power of a given jeremiad, it is instructive to conceive of a particular depiction of crisis as a potent religious and political narrative. Narratives shape individual and collective identities—we are born into stories, inhabit stories, and understand ourselves and others through stories. While stories provide the ground on which we walk and the light by which we see, stories can be retold with new meanings and our worlds are not defined by a single, monolithic story. That is, we each inhabit a world mediated and defined by a multiplicity of stories and interpretations.

Some narratives, however, are more significant, more world-defining, than others. In the discussion of narratives and politics in chapter 2, the notion of "sacred stories" is developed. Such stories are not quite meta-narratives because they do not serve as uncontested, fixed horizons. Nevertheless, these "sacred stories" do bear a heightened significance in a given cultural context.

Although I call such narratives "sacred,"[20] these stories should not be perceived as natural or divine. Rather, they shape what we might think of as "second natures." The definitive distinction of "second natures" is that while they construct individual and collective identity, they are also themselves constructed and thus are malleable. Moreover, any given culture (though this project focuses on the United States), is likely to have a number of "sacred stories," each of which fulfills different needs.[21] The inter-relationships of a society's "sacred stories" need not be seamless, and the import of a particular "sacred story" may vary over time. In the United States, the narrative of "liberal individualism" with its "autonomous, reasoning subject" likely remains the nation's predominant "sacred story."[22] In this book I focus on a different American "sacred story"—the narrative of Exodus.[23] While this American "sacred story" has been adapted over time from the narrative provided in the Bible, I want to review some of the key components of the story in order to set the stage for the ensuing analysis of Exodus and prophetic politics in the United States.

The original Exodus narrative contains many provocative themes—enslavement, liberation, faith, doubt, the longing for the "comforts of bondage," the creation of a polity, political leadership, principles of social and economic justice, holy wars, and many others. Not all of these themes hold an equally prominent place in the retellings of this Exodus narrative in American culture.[24] Indeed, this is the case of all retellings of narratives; no retelling is perfectly mimetic, for each retelling takes place in varying conditions (or contexts), shaped by the tellings of the narrative that precede it.

The Exodus narrative is fundamentally a political story; it is an ideological telling of a people's history—a story that in the telling not only engages in rhetoric in order to define and raise the political stakes, but also defines the identity of a people, the ancient Israelites. In his analysis of Exodus in *Moses: The Revelation and the Covenant,* Martin Buber stresses this political and rhetorical quality of the narrative. For instance, Buber notes that the narrative of bondage in Egypt is not a chronicle but a "poesy" aimed at heightening and emphasizing the suffering and lowliness of the Hebrews in order to figuratively render their liberation that much more poignant.[25]

The "basics" of the Exodus narrative are familiar in the American context. Led by "God's humble servant" Moses, the ancient Hebrews are liberated from bondage in Egypt, cross the Red Sea, and make a foundational and conditional covenant at Mount Sinai. After a generation of murmuring, purges, wandering in the desert, and the death of Moses, Joshua finally leads this "chosen people" into the Promised Land. Those who were slaves in Egypt were "borne on eagle's wings" and delivered into the land "flowing with milk and honey."

In my discussion of the Exodus narrative throughout this book, I focus on particular aspects of the story: (1) the portrayal of Moses and the collective identity of the people; (2) the construction of the setting; (3) the emphasis on memory and covenants. While other themes drawn from the Exodus narrative play important roles in my analysis, concentrating on these components enables a rich appreciation of the manner in which the Exodus narrative facilitates different forms of prophetic politics.

## Chosen People in a Promised Land, Sojourners in the Wilderness

The most common Exodus themes in the United States are the notions of a "chosen people" living in a "promised land." The early Puritan self-description as God's "newly chosen people" remains pervasive—although generally more understated—in the United States today. Likewise, the notion that God has (and continues) to particularly "bless America" is not easily dismissed from the national mind-set. With its abundance of resources, the nation appears to many to be the "land of milk and honey." This national self-understanding as God's "chosen people in a promised land" has, of course, justified both national glory and national shame.[26] Whereas the belief in America's "mission" has helped bolster the nation in its efforts to promote democracy and human rights around the world (albeit with decidedly mixed results), American triumphalism legitimated "manifest destiny" in the past and helps validate the contemporary equivalent by which the United States continues to consume a shockingly disproportionate amount of the world's resources. Belief in the nation's status as God's "chosen people" has also justified numerous collective American blind spots and a politics of exclusion. (Hence the rhetorical significance of Lincoln's delineation of America as God's "*almost* chosen people" and the inclination, particularly fervent in the African American jeremiadic tradition, to portray the United States not as Israel but as Egypt or Babylon.)

Although predominant, the familiar themes of "chosen people" and "promised land" are by no means the only themes of this American "sacred story" invested with national import. The conception of Exodus as a simple triumphalist story is significantly mitigated by the prominence of the themes of "sojourners" and "wilderness." Recall that as part of their covenant with God, the ancient Hebrews are commanded repeatedly not to oppress but to love the "sojourner," for they "were sojourners in the land of Egypt" (Ex. 22:21, 23:9, Lev. 19:33, Deut. 10:19). The identity of these "sojourners" is never specified; this is a command to the Hebrews to maintain and institutionalize a historical memory of their own oppression such that they neither become oppressors themselves nor reject or fail to reach out to whoever is the sojourner, the one who is different, in their midst. The Israelites were sojourners once and are likely to be sojourners again. The ethical principle contained in this directive is to be sensitive to the needs of others, particularly those suffering from afflictions. This principle is manifested throughout the narrative and is a central theme of the biblical prophets. The jeremiads of Isaiah, Jeremiah, and Amos, for example, repeatedly castigate the people for neglecting the poor, the widows, and the slaves among them. As Jeremiah says, "Thus says the Lord: Do justice and righteousness, and deliver from the hand of the oppressor him who has been robbed. And do no wrong or violence to the alien, the fatherless, and the widow, nor shed innocent blood" (Jer. 22:3).

This theme of "sojourners" is even clearer in light of another, related theme of the Exodus narrative and prophetic jeremiads: the lesson of the contingency of the political realm, in particular, and the human condition, in general, contained in the metaphor of "wilderness." Ancient Israel may be chosen and covenanted, but this does not enable it to transcend the fragile and contingent realm of politics; whatever "promised land" they attain, it is far from Eden. The wilderness is not simply the setting for the wanderings between Egypt and the "promised land"—the wilderness also is present in the land of Canaan. The wilderness, unknown and contingent as it is, generates fears that lead to the rise of kings in Israel and ultimately to the declension and backsliding that define the social context in which the prophets arise.

Having adopted the "sacred story" of Exodus, Americans are faced with a basic tension. How ought we to understand a people defined as "chosen" and as "sojourners"? How can we understand a land that is both "promised" and a "wilderness"? These are questions of exclusion and inclusion, of order and instability. These are questions that indelibly shape retellings of Exodus in America and, accordingly, the relation between religion and democratic politics in the United States.

## Memory and the Covenant

The other crucial theme of the Exodus narrative is the imperative of memory. If there is one message concerning human behavior contained in the Book of Exodus that serves as an umbrella over the whole of the narrative, it is the commandment to remember. From the beginning, the story of Exodus is about memory and forgetting. The new Pharaoh forgets Joseph and his brethren, initiating the conflict between the Hebrews and Egyptians (1:18); Moses and Zipporah name their son Gershom as a remembrance that they "have been sojourners in a foreign land" (2:22); God hears the groaning of Israel and "remembers His covenant" (2:24); God instructs Moses to teach God's name to Israel 'so that it will be "remembered throughout all generations" (4:15); God hardens Pharaoh's heart and sends plagues so that "these signs of mine" will be told "in the hearing of your son and your son's son" (10:1–2); the Passover rituals are established to mark and preserve the memory of deliverance (12:1–27); immediately after leaving Egypt and throughout the wandering in the desert, Moses tells the people, "remember this day, in which you came out of the house of bondage" (13:3); the memory is to be preserved in sensual terms "as a sign on your hand and as a memorial between your eyes that the law of the Lord may be in your mouth" (13:9)—as well as, of course, the circumcision of the men's "feet"; the murmurings of the people in the desert that culminate in the purge following the worshiping of the Golden Calf are a struggle between the memory of God and forgetting (16:6, 33:6 and passim); and, of course, the story of the covenant is throughout a story of memory. For example, consider "You have seen what I did to the Egyptians, and how I brought you on eagle's wings and brought you to myself . . ."(19:4), and the aforementioned and repeated commandment, "you shall not wrong a stranger or oppress him, for you were strangers once in the land of Egypt" (22:21, 23:9). The Ten Commandments, of course, open with the reminder that God "led Israel out of the house of bondage" and include the imperative to "remember the Sabbath day" as an institutional act of honoring God (20:2, 8). The Exodus narrative is clearly a story that throughout history carries the imperative of memory. Prophetic declarations are themselves acts of memory—in fact, they are acts of memory in a context defined by "forgetting." Indeed, it can be argued that the declarations of the prophets amount to the proclamation "Remember the Exodus narrative and act accordingly." In the Book of Jeremiah, for example, we read,

> The word that came to Jeremiah from the Lord: "Hear the words of this covenant, and speak to the men of Judah and the inhabitants of Jerusalem. You shall say to them, Thus says the Lord, the God of Israel: Cursed be the man who does not heed the words of this covenant which I commanded your fathers when I brought them out of the land of Egypt, from the iron furnace, saying, Listen to my voice, and do all that I command you. So shall you be my people, and I will be your God, that I may perform the oath which I swore to your fathers, to give them a land flowing with milk and honey, as at this day." (Jer. 11:1–5)

Retellings of the Exodus story—simply by virtue of the fact that they are re-tellings—inevitably raise the question of memory. It is "the task of prophecy," Walter Brueggemann argues, "to empower people to engage in history" (Brueggemann, 22). The prophet is not simply the mediator between God and the people; the prophet is also the mediator, the story-teller, who sits between past and future. The themes emphasized in any retelling of the sacred story will shape the understanding of the relationship between the past, present, and future that guides any effort for social change. Accordingly, to understand particular manifestations of prophetic politics in our time, we must analyze how prophetic movements understand history—how they mediate between memory and forgetting, between past and future.

BILLY Sunday, Martin Luther King Jr., Promise Keepers, and Call to Renewal can be viewed as representative of *social movements*. Herbert Blumer defines social movements as "collective enterprises to establish a new order of life . . . [that] have their inception in a condition of unrest and derive their motive power on the one hand from dissatisfaction with the current form of life, and on the other hand from wishes and hopes for a new scheme or system of living" (Blumer, 60). Blumer's definition provides room for an array of different conceptions of "new orders of life," motivations, and methods of pursuing social transformation and the fulfillment of hopes. Nevertheless, this mantle falls more comfortably on some than others. Martin Luther King Jr. and Call to Renewal both explicitly speak in the language of "movement," striving to use their prophetic voices to inspire and direct citizens to pursue social and political transformation. Billy Sunday and Promise Keepers, however, might well deny that they are "social movements" at all, since they are not directly focused on pursuing a political agenda, but are striving instead to move people closer to salvation. Yet despite not adopting the term "social movement," Billy Sunday and Promise Keepers are worthy of the title for the following reasons: (1) While both Billy Sunday and Promise Keepers consider themselves "apolitical," their efforts have a profound effect on the American polity. (2) Both Billy Sunday and Promise Keepers claim the lineage of previous incarnations of American revivalist movements. (3) Calling Billy Sunday and Promise Keepers simply "organizations" seems innocuous—and, in the case of Sunday, inaccurate. Likewise, calling any of these four examples of prophetic politics "interest groups" seems inappropriate, for each sought more than appealing to the government for help. (4) Religion is often—especially for those beholden to the secularism thesis—considered a mollifying force, the "opium of the people." Yet, religion has long been, and is obviously today in this era of sectarian warfare between "good and evil," also an "amphetamine of the people"[27]—inspiring and often demanding momentous acts intended to transform the world. Indeed, Aminzade and Perry offer a series of reasons religious-based social movements have distinct advantages over their "secular cousins." These advantages include "the unusual institutional legitimacy of religious-based organizations, which creates distinctive threat and opportunity structures, and the ability of religious movements to appeal to an other-worldly, transcendental ontology, which has implications for commitment processes, challenges to authority, and logics of action" (Aminzade and Perry, 158).

The social movements examined in this book are practitioners of *prophetic politics.*[28] By prophetic politics, I mean simply that each of these movements has grounded its identity and political vision in retellings of the Exodus narrative and the prophets of the Hebrew Bible. Accordingly, my analysis addresses not simply the nexus between religion and politics but also the nexus between narratives and politics.[29]

This examination of prophetic politics and Christian social movements is directed toward my concern with the *democratic politics* in the United States. Democracy is too often used as an empty signifier in popular political discourse, given that everyone favors democracy, but few bother to concern themselves with what democracy might actually mean. That work is commonly left in the hands of academics, and there the various permutations of democracy are explored and debated at great length. I do not focus on representative democracy or the structure of government per se. Rather, my discussion of democratic politics is concerned primarily with the public world shared by citizens, and the capacity in that world for different voices to speak and be heard and to enrich this shared space. Hannah Arendt, whose writing on democracy and storytelling serves as a touchstone for this study, has written hauntingly about "dark times" when the shared world of democratic politics has become pinched and diminished.

> History knows many periods of dark times in which the public realm has been obscured and the world become so dubious that people have ceased to ask any more of politics than that it show due consideration for their vital interests and personal liberty. (Arendt 1968, 11)

In the wake of September 11th, the trends in the United States regarding the shrinking of public space and the growing distrust of government have continued, if not accelerated. In such "dark times," when perceptions of threats abound, not only do people want to be left alone, but they are also actively encouraged to go home and shut the doors against the world. In these times, the public realm is shrouded in patriotic unity, dissent is often equated with terrorism, and the shared world is daily depleted. In such dark times one of the basic resources left is, one would hope, the capacity to tell and listen to stories. Arendt was partial to quoting Isak Dinesen's assertion, "All sorrows can be borne if you put them into a story or tell a story about them."[30] To respond to times of fear and potential meaninglessness, individuals must be able to exchange stories, to recognize and be recognized by others. This public and pluralistic exchange of stories is vital to democratic politics.

With these definitions in mind, there are three major questions with which this book is concerned:

1. What is the relationship between religion and democratic politics, focusing especially on whether claims of moral certainty are antithetical to democratic politics?

2. What is the relationship between narratives and politics?

3. What makes a retelling of the Exodus narrative by practitioners of prophetic politics congenial or hostile to democratic political life?

Examining this final question, as I do in greater detail in chapter 2, will entail analyzing the respective expressions of prophetic politics to see whether they encourage: (1) a disposition to politicize rather than personalize suffering, (2) a world view that emphasizes social justice rather than personal salvation, (3) an openness to difference characterized by Arendt's notion of "visiting," (4) a capacity for dialogue and a respect for pluralism, and (5) a conception of history that is open to new possibilities of both understanding the past and re-conceiving the future.

IN chapter 2, I develop more fully my understanding of the relation between narratives and politics. Indeed, this discussion of narratives ultimately serves as the analytic framework for my ensuing analysis of prophetic politics. This exploration of narratives further discusses the concept of "sacred stories" and also addresses the relationship between narratives and different approaches to history, memory, truth, and politics.

Ultimately, this examination of narratives and politics is aimed at understanding the significance of the American "sacred story" of Exodus. Because the story of Exodus is itself a narrative that lies at the intersection of religion and politics and has "sacred" status in the United States, it provides fertile ground for exploring the relationship between religion and politics in America. The ensuing chapters examine prophetic politics in the 20th- and 21st-century United States focusing on the different ways four Christian social movements retell the Exodus narrative.

In chapter 3, I take a historical turn and examine the Reverend Billy Sunday and Dr. Martin Luther King Jr., two prominent practitioners of prophetic politics in the 20th-century United States. Sunday and King provide a great contrast not simply in their political goals, but in how they conceive of citizenship, the relationship between religion and politics, and in how they emphasize personal or social salvation. My analysis links the variations in their prophetic politics to their use of the American sacred story of Exodus to portray the setting and character of America. Sunday and King also raise issues of gender, race, class, and other markers of identity, as well as "family values issues" that are so central to current debates about religion and politics. While chapter 2 provides the analytic framework for my analysis of prophetic politics in the United States, my examination of Sunday and King in chapter 3 adds the historical background for the ensuing analysis of Promise Keepers and Call to Renewal.

In chapter 4, I address the prophetic politics of Promise Keepers, one of the most vibrant expressions of religion in America over the last fifteen years. This all-male, ecumenical, multicultural, Christian social movement founded by former University of Colorado football coach Bill McCartney has been a powerful jeremiadic voice in the United States. Decrying the crumbling "moral order" in America, Promise Keepers is seeking a revival led by the "chosen men of God" to "deliver the nation" in the name of Jesus. A compelling prophetic voice in the United States, Promise Keepers has reached millions of men through events held in sports stadiums across the country. Promise Keepers has sponsored a conference of 39,000 clergy members in Atlanta, brought hundreds of thousands of men to Washington, D.C., for its 1997 Stand in the Gap gathering, and has begun to heed "God's call to go global," sponsoring events in Costa Rica, South Africa, and Mexico.

In chapter 5, I explore a wholly different expression of prophetic politics emerging in the United States today. Call to Renewal, convened and led by The Reverend Jim Wallis (editor of *Sojourners*), seeks to become an alternative voice to both the "religious right" and the "secular left" in the United States. This ecumenical, multicultural social movement has recently begun a ten-year campaign to "overcome poverty" in America. Like the other prophetic social movements under consideration, Call to Renewal generates its political identity and political vision from retellings of the American "sacred story" of Exodus.

Following this discussion of Call to Renewal, in chapter 6 I conclude by assessing the challenges posed by prophetic politics to democracy—and the challenges posed by democratic politics to those who would be "prophets" in America. Religious social movements in the United States have confronted these challenges as they seek to transform the world. In their successes, and even in their failures to realize the vision of their respective political theologies, the four Christian social movements have had an impact on American society in often far-reaching ways.

There is much at stake in assessing the course and implications of this influence. The introduction of the divine into human affairs can be remarkably beneficial and remarkably dangerous—in either case, it is often exceedingly powerful. Such results should be expected when the extraordinary is interjected into the prosaic. That this interjection takes place, despite the risks, is a testimony to the longing and hope for superhuman grace, direction, justice, meaning, and solace in a contingent, tempestuous, and all-too-human world. Moreover, the introduction of the divine can enhance the strengths and exacerbate the weaknesses of democracy. Religion can motivate and empower citizens to engage in the effort to change the world—and provide support in the face of the sacrifices that such changes generally require. But religion also can limit the necessary exchange of opinions in public life. Conversation between "believers" and "non-believers" can be so laced with suspicion that listening is disregarded; one party "knows" the other is misguided before words are even spoken. Even among "believers," conversation can be diminished as empathetic "unspoken understandings" obscure differences and limit the inclination for critical reflection. Moreover, religious commitments can often lead to impatience with the fitful and incremental pace of change that typically results from a democratic process requiring consensus.

My own conclusions about the challenge religion offers democratic politics are ultimately ambivalent. I came to this project impressed by the abiding influence of the Exodus narrative in American public discourse. I conclude it keenly aware of both the great hopes sustained by this narrative and the grave dangers to democratic public life inspired by recourse to this resonant story. Indeed, in the context in which I am writing, prophetic politics and retellings of the Exodus narrative are too often being used to legitimate and sustain anti-democratic efforts. These are fragile times to be trying to encourage proponents of democracy in America (broadly understood) to utilize the resonant imagery of Exodus.

Nevertheless, I am unwilling to cede prophetic politics, the Exodus narrative, and religion in general to anti-democrats. Not only do I think such a surrender would have detrimental political implications, but also I think that it would be to abandon vital theological and intellectual concerns. Instead, it is necessary to take the risk of seeking to enable prophetic politics to enhance democratic politics. Fears of the danger of religion to democratic politics often lead to an impossible liberal dream of an America where religion is secured in the private sphere and has no discernible role in politics other than a vague incentive to keep promises and the "ceremonial deism" Justice Sandra Day O'Connor finds in the Pledge of Allegiance.[31] Religious narratives enjoy a prominent presence in the American public sphere. The Exodus narrative still resonates strongly, and thus as a descriptive exercise, it is necessary to acknowledge and try to understand it. And then, as a normative exercise, it is vital to assess the implications of the vibrancy of religion in America for democratic politics.

# Chapter Two
## Narratives and Politics

Human narrative, through all its visible length, gives emphatic signs of arising from the profoundest need of one fragile species. Sacred story is the perfect answer given by the world to the hunger of that species for true consolation. The fact that we are hungry has not precluded food.
—Reynolds Price, *A Palpable God*

   The hunger for consolation is even more profound than Reynolds Price suggests: Humans long not just for consolation, but for meaning and hope. Consolation, meaning, and hope are all attended to by the vivifying force of narratives—and of "sacred stories" in particular. This hunger for consolation, meaning, and hope is particularly acute in contemporary America.

   The United States has never been a place that rested easily on established customs and traditions that could provide a social order with constant "food" for the longings of citizens; today the pace of change in the United States has accelerated so that the "hunger" grows more poignant every day. Even those institutions that have traditionally provided degrees of stability are either in states of transition or suffer diminished status. In the realm of politics, the partisan distrust of the Clinton years has been followed by the bitterly contested elections of 2000 and 2004 the debates about the veracity of the Bush administration's claims regarding both domestic policy and the war on terrorism. Business leaders and corporations have been riddled with public scandals and revelatory illustrations of profound greed. Mainline Protestant denominations have suffered from shrinking congregations, and the Roman Catholic Church has been rocked by scandals and the lack of forthright accountability demonstrated by many church leaders. In conditions such as these, Hannah Arendt has written, "The predicament of meaninglessness . . . and the impossibility of finding valid standards" can be addressed only "through the interrelated faculties of action and speech, which produce meaningful stories" (Arendt 1974a, 236).

Stories nourish us, satisfy our hunger—but never satiate us permanently. The hunger for consolation, meaning, and hope—like physical hunger—returns and must be re-fed; stories must be told and told again. The point is not to eliminate the hunger for meaning—this is an impossibility that we seek to "cure" at our own peril[1]—but to attend to the process of meaningful nourishment.

Stories do not just respond to our longing for consolation, meaning, and hope. Storytelling is also an act of proclamation. Storytellers seek recognition; they seek to have their particular stories heard.[2] Storytelling, in this sense, is an act of declaring one's hunger—and one's willingness to actively seek nourishment. Moreover, to the degree that storytelling demands "story-listening," the exchange of narratives—the collective effort to search for meaning, to feed oneself and one another—helps define public life and accordingly shapes the context within which politics takes place. The exchange of stories creates relationships and a narrative framework for understanding these relationships.

Such an exchange of narratives creates a public realm, a common, even if not entirely stable world. This world is defined by the plurality of stories present—a phenomenon that is particularly significant amid the vast differences that permeate the rapidly changing American polity. Arendt portrays this tension between plurality and a shared or common world as definitive of public life: "For though the common world is the common meeting ground of all, those who are present have different locations in it. . . . Being seen and being heard by others derives their significance from the fact that everybody sees and hears from different positions. This is the meaning of public life" (Arendt 1974a, 57). Central to this conception of public life, then, is not just the recognition of the storyteller, but the relationships between storytellers and vast and diverse story-listeners. The "meaning of public life," accordingly, is found when a common object or story can be seen and heard—and assessed and judged—such that "human plurality" rather than "singularity" or the "unnatural conformism of mass society" defines the shared world (Arendt 1974a, 57–58).

This type of "public life," in which the air of our common world is filled with the sounds of stories, is a crucial part of what I mean by "democratic politics." One of the vital elements of this realm of democratic politics is the conversational space for plurality, the capacity for multiple voices and perspectives to be recognized, respected, and heard. It is an understanding of democratic politics in which any citizen can declare, as Kim Curtis aptly puts it: "Here *I* am in relation to our world. I offer you an invitation, a solicitation. Join me. I provoke you. I demand of you that you countenance me as I see our world. Respond" (Curtis 1999, 120). Such a pluralist democratic realm enables, and is in turn enhanced by, an open receptiveness to the ideas, opinions, stories, and judgments of others. Plurality and openness are, of course, closely related; the willingness to hear others' stories is predicated upon the conviction that the narrative nourishment one needs can be fulfilled by different sources and perspectives.

However, to say that the common world is defined by the telling and exchange of a plurality of narratives begs the question about the content of those narratives. Do all narratives share the same status? Are some narratives more beneficial or more harmful than others? If so, can the benefits be expanded and the harms constrained? Such questions are too often elided because of the visceral exuberance stories can produce. As Arendt declares, "No philosophy, no analysis, no aphorism, be it ever so profound, can compete in intensity and richness of meaning with a properly narrated story" (1968, 22). As will be evident, although Hannah Arendt, the great theorist of narratives and public life,[3] plays a central element in my analysis, my conception of storytelling differs from hers in one major respect that is important to address at the outset.[4]

Although there is considerable ambiguity on this question in her work, Arendt tends to distinguish between the political actor and the spectator who tells stories about that actor's actions. Ronald Beiner attributes this distinction (present especially in Arendt's later work) to a commitment to promoting a Kantian "enlarged mentality" vital to the capacity for impartial judgment, in which "the world is the primary thing, not man, neither man's life nor his self" (1977, 222).

In contrast to this understanding of the distinction between political action and the retrospective narratives of a spectator, I maintain that storytelling can itself be an act of politics. Beiner argues that Arendt's conception of storytelling is an aesthetic rather than a political endeavor, and thus enables a capacity for reflective and impartial judgment. While storytelling is, of course, commonly a retrospective narration intended to delineate the meaning of past actions, narratives are often more than the product of backward glances. Storytelling is also an action, a "world-making" action that delineates identity and context of not just the past but also the present and future. In this regard, storytelling, like other political actions in the public sphere, can be "both world making and self-making"(Calhoun, 244). Storytelling, in other words, projects a conception of reality into the world. Ultimately, the exchange of narratives creates relations between people in a manner similar to, although potentially less binding than, mutual promises. Storytelling projects a vision of the identities of the participants in the exchange into the future and establishes the common language—the story itself—through which the relationship is maintained and negotiated.

## Religious Storytelling in American Politics

The positive aspects of narratives are profound, but this power of storytelling is not without danger. Quite the contrary: fascists tell stories; zealots tell stories. To say that stories generate meaning and hope is not to say that all such meaning and hope is beneficial to humanity. If we value plurality and democratic exchange, then we must consider stories and storytelling from the perspective of politics. By this I mean that even though narratives are too often told in a manner that seeks to close off critical judgment by asserting a series of a priori claims (based, for instance, on the experience of the author), democratic stories should invite and require judgment, rather than compel acquiescence to a claim of truth. Prophetic narratives and the status of religious voices in democratic America represent a compelling test case for the role of narratives in politics, precisely because they illustrate the power of stories in public life.

In the United States, many people (particularly those of a secular liberal perspective) vehemently argue that in order to have a pluralist democratic political realm, religion and religious voices need to be seriously curtailed, if not excluded altogether. Often proclaimed under the rubric of the necessity of the "separation of church and state," this line of reasoning suggests that religious arguments "seek to impose their truth" on all others and accordingly neither respect nor enhance the principle of plurality basic to democratic politics.[5] There are those, including Arendt, who would argue that any claims of "absolute truth" are inappropriate in the realm of politics. Arendt writes, "Every claim in the spirit of human affairs to an absolute truth, whose validity needs no support from the side of opinion, strikes at the very roots of all politics and all governments" (1977, 233). Such claims to "absolute truth" are disinclined to respect or listen to any voice that does not subscribe to this truth claim and as such are non-democratic. It is, of course, the very willingness of religious voices to proclaim absolute truth that makes them so appealing to those (largely conservative) decriers of "relativism," who mourn this "world without standards" where God is "no longer welcome" in our nation's classrooms and public spaces.[6]

This preemptory challenge to the democratic legitimacy of religious arguments, of course, does not sit well with many active citizens in American public life. Critics of this argument about the "wall of separation" rightly point out that the exclusion of religious voices and perspectives is itself "anti-democratic." Absent religious perspectives, the realm of politics does not reflect the plurality of American citizens and, accordingly, falls short of the democratic ideal it purportedly champions.[7]

In the United States today, unfortunately, most of the debates concerning religion and politics fall along this "wall of separation" axis. This argument with its focus on whether religious perspectives have a rightful place in the realm of democratic politics is far too narrow for assessing the complex relationship between religion and politics in the United States. Given the foundational status of the Exodus narrative in American political culture, and given the role Exodus themes continue to play in contemporary politics in the United States, we need to confront such questions as: What is the relationship between religious narratives and the creation of political identity and political vision? What makes a retelling of the Exodus narrative by practitioners of prophetic politics congenial or hostile to democratic political life? Can prophetic politics meet the challenges of democracy? Shifting this analysis away from the question of the separation of church and state and toward an assessment of the role of the Exodus story as a resonant narrative lying at the nexus of religion and politics in American culture demands a broader analysis of the manner in which narratives construct and enable democratic politics.

This chapter, accordingly, has two major aims. First, I develop an analytic framework for understanding narratives and politics, using the Exodus narrative to establish themes drawn from the American sacred story that will be central to the ensuing analysis of the four Christian social movements. Then, at the end of this chapter, I build on this discussion of the Exodus narrative and politics and raise the pivotal question of how prophetic politics can be hostile or congenial to democratic politics. Here I highlight the significance of the narrative construction of identity, setting, memory, and interpretation for analysis of the relationship between narratives and democratic politics. These issues will, in turn, shape my assessment of what makes two of the examples of the prophetic politics of Christian social movements inimical to democratic politics and two of them exemplary of the productive—though still tense—relationship between prophetic politics and a vibrant democratic public life.

## The Power of Stories

Sailing across the Atlantic in anticipation of establishing a theocratic polity in a "new land," John Winthrop delivered his sermon "A Model of Christian Charity." To define the tenor of the community, Winthrop invoked the familiar scaffolding of the Exodus narrative and delivered what amounted to a preemptory American jeremiad.

> We are entered into covenant with Him for this work. . . . [if] we keep the unity of the spirit in the bond of peace . . . we shall find that the God of Israel is among us, when ten of us shall be able to resist a thousand of our enemies, *when He shall make us a praise and glory that men shall say of succeeding plantations 'The Lord make it like that of New England.'* . . . [But] if we shall deal falsely with our God in this work we have undertaken . . . *we shall be made a story and a by-word through the world:* we shall open the mouths of enemies to speak evil of the ways of God and . . . we shall shame the faces of many of God's worthy servants. (Quoted in Miller 1956, 82–83, my italics)

Whether the Puritans kept or broke their "covenant," Winthrop declared, their story would be told. The story would be of collective unity enabling the fulfillment of a divine mission for America, or the story would be a shameful tale of the inadequacy of God's chosen people, a narrative that would please God's enemies; either way, "we shall be made a story."

The example of Winthrop's pivotal sermon exemplifies the reason why I think it is important to extend our understanding of narratives and politics beyond the Arendtian notion of narratives as simply the product of a retrospective glance. Surely, Arendt is correct to argue that narratives about the Puritans would be a reflection on the acts of Winthrop and the Puritan community. However, such a "spectator's story" is shaped by a backward reading of the story told by Winthrop. That is, Winthrop's story of the colony as a "city upon a hill" is a political act that projects a vision of identity and context onto the community itself and into the conceptual framework of future storytellers. Winthrop's political narrative sets the terms of future debate and analysis; whether future storytellers agree or disagree with Winthrop's depiction of the colony, the stories told about the Puritans would react to, or be informed by, Winthrop's narrative projection. The Puritans were "made a story" by the narrative act of Winthrop and were re-made as stories by future narrators, some of which would themselves be political acts.

Indeed, the retelling of the Exodus narrative by the Puritans has become the story of the nation's founding that reigns as the text of a nearly hegemonic national autobiography. It is the story taught to generations of schoolchildren and preached by each president.[8] Consider this passage from Lyndon Johnson's 1965 Inaugural Address:

> They came here—the exile and the stranger, brave but frightened—to find a place where a man could be his own man. They made a covenant with this land. Conceived in justice, written in liberty, bound in union, it was meant one day to inspire the hopes of all mankind; and it binds us still. If we keep its terms, we shall flourish. The American covenant called on us to help show the way for the liberation of man. And that today is our goal. Thus, if as a nation there is much outside our control, as a people no stranger is outside our hope.[9]

Of course, as Sacvan Bercovitch reminds us, "we *know* that the Puritans did not found the United States. In fact, we know that by 1690, sixty years after the great migration and a century before independence, not even the colony of Massachusetts was Puritan" (1993, 6).[10] Indeed, the retelling of the Exodus narrative in Puritan New England was but a singular facet of a multi-vocal religiosity in the colonies.[11] In Virginia, for instance, the narrative of a "chosen people in a Promised Land" informed the political identity of the colony to a much smaller degree.[12] Nevertheless the Puritan story persists everywhere in our culture[13] and its presence raises the pivotal question, what does the status of the Exodus narrative in the United States suggest about storytelling and politics?

First, we ought to be struck by the capacity of a narrative to convey meaning despite its tenuous relationship to the "empirical truth" of historical evidence. That is to say, the continuing resonance of the Exodus narrative in America ought to make us quite aware of the related powers of imagination and interpretation.[14] The national adoption of the Puritan adaptation of the Exodus narrative is, of course, part of a long line of such imaginative acts of interpretation. "We can hardly overestimate the importance of that astonishing Westward leap of the imagination," writes Bercovitch:

> It was an achievement comparable in its way to the two great rhetorical shifts on which it was built: the Hebrews' redefinition (by verbal fiat) of Canaan—territory, name, "antiquities" and all—as *their* country; and the imperialism of the *figura* or type, whereby the church fathers declared that the Old Testament, the story of Israel in its entirety, from Adam through Abraham and David to the Messiah, heir of David, really belonged to Christ. (1993, 76)

Bercovitch calls our attention to the power of stories to erase competing stories, enacting what we might think of as narrative imperialism. Moreover, in this sense, collective political identity can be understood as an act of imagination, interpretation, and self-creation through the telling and re-telling of narratives (and this process of imaginative self-creation can often, but need not, be imperialist). Storytelling of this sort is a call for collective recognition of a particular corporate identity. The stability of this identity rests in the hands of those who would hear this story and retell the narrative in affirmation of the initial declaration of "hunger."

This component of storytelling reflects the capacity of narratives to create a sense of continuity, a vital attribute of political identity. Writing about the adoption of the Exodus narrative in early America, Russell Nye asserts, "The development of a conviction of national purpose was, for Americans, a historical necessity . . . it was necessary in a new land, which possessed no cohesion, to develop some such sense of continuity" (Nye, 165). In a sense, the Puritans sought to ameliorate their profound instability by telling themselves a narrative about themselves as God's "newly chosen people" on a mission to found a New Jerusalem in the Promised Land. Without the establishment of some sense of continuity and identity, there would be no way to create a sense of order and mutual understanding in this radically new place. Winthrop's initial invocation of the Exodus narrative comes, after all, in the service of his explicit determination to instill a sentiment of solidarity among these colonists. Even amid a community of Calvinist believers in individual salvation, the emphasis in this founding sermon was on the collective "City on a Hill" they might build as a physical *place* that might last over *time* for the glory of God.[15]

Indeed, this capacity of a narrative to foster a sense of continuity does not just work synchronically but diachronically as well. Thus, while John Winthrop and Lyndon Johnson obviously had different audiences and evoked the Exodus narrative in support of different principles, a sense of connection, of continuity, persists. Narratives, particularly foundational narratives, are part of a cultural fabric—they are inherited, interpreted, and retold. If, as Max Weber teaches, we are "suspended in webs of significance" we ourselves "have spun" and, as Clifford Geertz declares, those webs can be thought of as "culture," then I would suggest narratives are the strands of these webs.[16] As such, and as we will see in the sense of continuity found in retellings of the Exodus narrative in the United States, storytelling plays a crucial role in the establishment and maintenance of both a sense of spatial and temporal "setting" and of political identity. In contemporary conditions where this sense of continuity no longer rests upon a "simple" belief in the divine nor a common acceptance of custom and tradition, the need for storytelling to provide a sense of spatial and temporal order has become more urgent.

## Narratives—Setting and Identity

Narratives, thus, are the tools humans use to define themselves (individually and collectively) and their world—tools that organize and enable life. Narratives provide the scaffolding that offers the degree of stability we create in our world. As Alasdair MacIntyre suggests: "Man is in his actions and practice, as well as in his fictions, essentially a storytelling animal. . . . But the key question for men is not about their own authorship; I can only answer the question 'What am I to do?' if I can answer the prior question 'Of what story or stories do I find myself a part'"?(MacIntyre, 216).[17] Narratives do not just describe or reflect, but rather define and give meaning to, human existence. Indeed, we are humans not simply by virtue of our capacity to tell stories, but by virtue of the stories we tell ourselves about ourselves, of the stories "of which we are a part" and which we in turn retell in the inevitable and continuing effort to create meaning and define identity in a changing and contingent world.

In such conditions of flux, we face the constant threat of being unable to discover (or create) a sense of meaningfulness for existence. Without the capacity to comprehend existence within a narrative framework, we would be faced with a sense of flux without boundary. By telling ourselves stories we construct boundaries, which, although they are human creations, nevertheless provide at least a tenuous sense of context. Sheldon Wolin has remarked that "boundaries are the outline of a context; or more precisely, boundaries signify the will to contextualize" (Wolin 1996, 33). Narratives are expressions of this will to contextualize—the "food" requisite for our "hunger." This capacity of narratives to create context or continuity is evident in two of the vital components of storytelling—the creation of "setting" and the inter-related construction of identity.[18]

The setting established by a narrative must be understood in both spatial and temporal terms. Narratives construct a sense of place or terrain within which characters take shape and the plot unfolds. Conceptions of spatiality are conveyed through figuration and description to shape the perception of the "reader." Perspectives of the spatial setting of a narrative inform our understanding of the "characters" located within that frame. The context established by narratives also consists of temporal connections and horizons. As Paul Ricoeur says: "[T]ime becomes human time to the extent that it is organized after the manner of a narrative; narrative, in turn, is meaningful to the extent it portrays the features of temporal experience" (Ricoeur 1984, 3). Narratives, accordingly, are the means by which we create and envision connections between past, present, and future.

Narrative constructions of space and time can be independent but are often inter-related.[19] Indeed, notions of time are often expressed using metaphors of space. The notion of the promised land conveys both spatial and temporal meanings. This setting is commonly thought of as a place: a locale (whether Israel or the United States) that is "flowing with milk and honey," a place that can be inhabited. But the notion of a promised land also has temporal implications. This land was "promised" by God to the chosen people in a covenant act that took place in the past, has implications for the present, and will be (or will continue to be) fulfilled in the future. The description of the land as "promised"—a verb in the past tense used as an adjective—provides a sense of temporal cohesion. To promise is, after all, to link a present commitment with future implications—linking today and tomorrow.[20] Phrased in the past tense, current expressions of the promised land link past, present, and future in a cohesive and linear manner. Within the Exodus narrative— and its application to the United States—the contrast in spatial and temporal terms between the cohesion of the promised land and the ambiguity and instability of another key Exodus trope, the wilderness, proves to be of critical importance.

The "environment" conveyed by the notion of wilderness enjoys little of the spatial and temporal predictability that is indicative of the promised land. In a setting perceived as wilderness, linear progression between past, present, and future is less assured—one simply does not know what will happen next. Likewise, the spatial definition of the wilderness lacks the clear vision of "milk and honey." The obstacles—natural and otherwise—that individuals and collectivities may encounter are profound and changing. The differences between retellings of the Exodus narrative set in a promised land or in the wilderness convey divergent political visions.

The spatial and temporal setting conveyed by narratives provides the framework within which character or identity can be established. This is not to say that setting itself constructs identity. Rather, within familiar narratives, setting conveys expectations about the fitness or appropriateness of characters: the difference, in other words, between a fish in or out of the water. Within the Exodus narrative, for example, it is the *chosen people* and not the Egyptians, Amalekites, or Canaanites who "belong" in the *promised land*—even though the latter two peoples were indeed inhabiting the place deemed the "promised land." These "non-chosen peoples" presumably told themselves quite different narratives to establish their own sense of context and identity—and then again new stories to explain their displacement.

What does this suggest about narratives and their construction of a contextual framework within which a people might understand themselves and others? Among the implications is that we might understand subjectivity—and in this case collective subjectivity—as narrative identity. Thus, rather than conceive of identity as something fixed or inevitable, identity is "produced" by stories into which "we are born" but which constantly must be retold. As Ricoeur argues, "We never cease to reinterpret the narrative identity that constitutes us, in the light of the narratives proposed to us by our culture" (Ricoeur 1991, 32–33). This is not to say that identity is simply "fiction," and thus, easily dismissed. It has long been recognized, for example, that conceptions of race are constructions rather than immutable "facts." Asserting the narrative quality of identity does not make identity unimportant in American culture (e.g., racial identity). Some narratives are quite durable. The constructedness of the context we inhabit does not make it any less "real."[21]

## Sacred Stories and Narrative Shelter

Narratives construct context by crafting the inter-related categories of setting and identity, but not all narratives move and define us in quite the same way. Stephen Crites draws an important distinction between "sacred" and "mundane" narratives. While "mundane stories are set within the bounds of a particular context," "sacred stories" serve to define and establish that context (Crites, 70). Crites explains:

> Sacred stories, and the symbolic worlds they project, are . . . like dwelling-places. People live in them . . . men's sense of self and world are created through them . . . these are stories that orient the life of people through time. . . . [Sacred stories] form the very consciousness that projects a total world horizon, and therefore informs the intentions by which actions are projected into that world. . . . [E]very sacred story is a creation story: not merely that one may name creation of world and self as its theme but also

that the story itself creates a world of consciousness and the self that is oriented to it. (Crites, 70–71)

In the United States, the "sacred story" of Exodus and the jeremiadic retellings of that narrative set the context and the horizon of cultural understanding within which "mundane stories" help provide meaning and order for everyday existence. The "sacred story" provides the identity and vision of the teller of the story (be it nation, community, organization, or individual) and "mundane stories" offer models of political practice often aimed at meeting the vision set forth by the "sacred story." Sacred stories thus provide a sense of meaning and order that make particular mundane stories possible. Mundane stories, working within the context constituted by a particular sacred story, enable the progress toward, if not the final attainment of, the vision set forth in the "sacred story."

Calling these stories sacred need not imply a belief that these stories are actually divinely authored or inspired. Rather, following Crites, certain stories are held sacred by a nation or people and thus serve as the fundamental narrative, which is invested with meaning *as if* it were divinely authorized—or at least "natural" to the community. Such narratives create something of a "second nature" for a people.[22] The point, then, is not the "truth" or legitimacy of the claim, for example, that Americans represent God's "newly chosen people," but rather the rhetorical and constitutive function of this motif in the United States. In this sense, the nation is both the subject of and the "interpretive community"[23] among whom this "sacred story" conveys a particularly resonant meaning.

"Sacred stories" are "like dwelling places," and create cultural contexts along both spatial and temporal dimensions in two ways. The initial choice and subsequent reification of a founding narrative craft the temporal and spatial context over time. For example, the Puritans surely told themselves more than one story to help define their context and establish their identity. Their choice of the Exodus narrative was but one expression of explaining the relationship between the colonies and England (and between the colonies and the peoples already present in America), but it has been adopted like none of the others in the creation of the American autobiography. Indeed, the use of Exodus as the narrative scaffolding to define the colonies as a whole is an expression of a "will to contextualize" that has a decidedly political edge given the theological inclinations of many American storytellers, who perceived the original narrative to be the holy, predictive, and proscriptive word of God.

## "Sacred Stories," Tradition, and History

Although traditions are expressed through narratives that are held as "sacred," "sacred stories" can exceed tradition. Tradition is, of course, crucial for individual and social cohesiveness. As Arendt writes: "Without tradition—which selects and names, which hands down and preserves, which indicates where the treasures are and what their worth is—there seems to be no continuity in time and hence, humanly speaking, neither past nor future, only sempiternal change of the world and the biological cycle of living creatures in it" (1977, 5). Traditions, in this way, provide us with horizons of meaning. In an early essay, even Nietzsche recognizes this sense of the importance of traditions and horizons of meaning.

> And this is a general law: every living thing can become healthy, strong and fruitful only within a horizon. If it is incapable of drawing a horizon around itself or, on the other hand, too selfish to restrict its vision to the limits of a horizon drawn by another, it will wither away feebly or over-hastily to its early demise.[24]

If traditions allow humans to extend themselves beyond mere existence, "sacred stories" allow them to find stable meaning in the world and the possibilities of change. Here we can consider Paul Ricoeur's elegant formulation that narratives work with a "flexible dialectics between innovation and sedimentation" (1995, 240).[25] Ricoeur explains that narratives that carry (even fragmented) traditions provide the sedimentation, the grounding, necessary for collective and individual stability. However, Ricoeur emphasizes that the capacity of such narratives to enable "innovation is no less prominent . . . [b]ecause paradigms created by a previous innovation provide guidelines for further experimentation in the narrative field" (Ricoeur 1995, 240). Within this "flexible dialectic," what once were "innovations" become the "sedimentation" that informs new generations of "innovation."

In other words, "sacred stories" offer not just the stability of tradition, but also the horizon within which meaningful and intelligible innovation can occur. In this sense, traditions construct meaning, but do not fully determine, fix, or delimit innovation. Innovation, in turn, is not a completely new development; change takes place in relation to the narrative sediment already existing in a given culture. Indeed, as Ricoeur elsewhere stresses:

> Innovation remains a rule-governed behavior; the work of imagination does not come out of nowhere. It is tied in one way or another to the models handed down by tradition. But it can enter into a variable relation to these models. The range of solutions is broad between the poles of servile repetition and calculated deviance, passing by way of all the degrees of ordered distortion. (1991, 25)

The tension between the need for stable meaning and the contingency of the human condition is thus addressed by Ricoeur's "dialectic of sedimentation and innovation." On the one hand, the need for a "horizon of meaning" is met through narratives that convey tradition. And on the other hand, this horizon is not so determinative that changes in context and condition cannot be addressed; innovation develops within and is, indeed, inspired by the necessary tension between the desire for stability and the need for, or inevitability of, change.

Storytelling is an imaginative act that "creates" worlds, often through the re-constructive act of expressing memory. The event (or object) is not present but rather is re-presented by a story. Indeed, Joshua Dienstag, in his excellent recent work on political theory and narrative, goes so far as to suggest, "The project of political theory is often not so much to reform our morals as it is to reform our memories" (Dienstag, 3). To take his point further, one might argue that by reforming our memories, political theory seeks to reform our morals. To be a political theorist is to be concerned with the question of what a polity remembers—and how.[26]

If, as Ricoeur suggests, time is given substance by narratives, then crucial to understanding any given narrative is appreciating the notion of temporality it conveys. Although Aristotle asserts that a narrative must have a sense of beginning, middle, and end, or it is incomplete, Dienstag suggests that for politics, the telling of such complete and unitary narratives is not just limiting, but dangerous. Complete narratives of this sort leave no space for open possibilities in the future. "To imagine a political narrative that ends may be to imagine a too-perfect satisfaction with the present and therefore an end to politics as the realm of conflict, change and growth" (Dienstag, 19). The limitations of the future of such closed narratives are in large part caused by limitations imposed on the past. Dienstag refers to these narrative approaches to history as "reconciliatory." That is, this approach seeks to "reconcile" present conditions with a fixed understanding of "*the* meaning of the past" (Dienstag,

187).[27] This reconciliatory attitude "accept[s] iron limits to our past, and, hence, equally iron limits to our future" (Dienstag, 189).

In contrast to a "reconciling" approach to the past, Dienstag commends a "redemptive" approach to history. This narrative understanding of history seeks not to "reveal *the* meaning" of the past, but to open up the past to new possibilities. Describing this "redemptive" approach, Dienstag writes, "The past is inherently mutable. It cannot be altered at will. But the meaning of an inheritance can be worked on . . . true redemption can only come from working on the past, remaking it, retelling it, until some sense, some value, has been made of it" (188).[28] This "redemptive" mode does not dismiss the role of tradition and the narratives we inherit. "Whether one embraces the traditions one is born into or rejects them, one cannot live outside of them. But Nietzsche writes, 'There is no way of telling what may yet become part of history.'"[29] Because the past is kept open for new meanings to emerge, the future is also open. This approach to "redemptive" history encourages a narrative "dialectic of sedimentation and innovation," and as such, enables an open future of possibilities, informed by, but not limited to, a given tradition.

## Narratives and Politics: Unity or Democracy?

I have been arguing that narratives—especially "sacred stories"—provide a sense of cultural context that enables the development of a relatively stable (but always necessarily fragile) sense of political identity and political vision. This relation between narratives and politics is not necessarily democratic; indeed, the Exodus narrative itself, neither in its initial telling among the ancient Hebrews nor in its retelling by the early American Puritans would be considered emphatically democratic in either content or expression.[30] If the retelling of narratives does not necessarily encourage democratic politics, then what *is* the difference between democratic and non-democratic employments of storytelling? Democratic storytelling reveals, and encourages the understanding of, the shared public world as a realm of pluralism and freedom. In narrative terms, this democratic freedom is indicative of new interpretations and imaginative possibilities that embrace the challenges created by relinquishing the pretense that there are definitive understandings of the past, present, and future. To illustrate, consider Arendt's notion of storytelling—which I take to be "democratic"—and that of Alasdair MacIntyre, which, with its emphasis on unity, I take to be "anti-democratic."

One of the great fears among many modern and contemporary theorists is that we are quickly losing the capacity to tell—and hear—stories.[31] The fragmentation of once governing social customs and the growing presence of different "languages" has resulted in a replacement of a presumed social harmony by increasing cacophony.

Alasdair MacIntyre is quite aware of these dangers. In a post-enlightenment world, MacIntyre believes that the transmission of a coherent set of principles and beliefs is all but impossible in light of the fraying of tradition.[32] With narratives no longer able to convey an enduring telos, modern societies are left bereft in a state of "emotivism." "Emotivism," MacIntyre explains, "is the doctrine that all evaluative judgments and more specifically all moral judgments are *nothing but* expressions of preference, expressions of attitude or feelings insofar as they are moral or evaluative in character" (MacIntyre, 11–12). Seeking ways to turn from the dissonant, power-laden world of emotivism, MacIntyre offers a vision of small Aristotelian communities in which narrative can once again convey a stable and homogeneous tradition. In MacIntyre's ideal Aristotelian community, there are no "barbarian" forces telling stories in other languages and individual and collective telos is readily identifiable.

Communities of this type enjoy a broad appeal in the United States, particularly as the public realm and political discussion become identified as a site of contemptuousness and derision. If we share a common story, directed toward a common telos, MacIntyre reasons, we can share a common moral firmament. Indeed, MacIntyre suggests that communities bound by unifying moral narratives would be separated from the world of modern politics, which he characterizes as "civil war carried on by other means" (MacIntyre, 253). The unity of coherent narrative identity and contexts present (so the presumption goes) in an Amish community, occupies, for those outside their collective narrative, a romantic simplicity that many want to know is possible. This longing for the solace of coherent and unchallenged principles and beliefs is evident far beyond small religious enclaves. Bill Bishop and Robert Cushing's study of the voting behavior and political identification of citizens across the United States demonstrates that the nation is increasingly becoming segregated by political affiliation; with nearly half of Americans living in "landslide counties" by 2004, individuals are less likely to speak with others who have markedly different political perspectives.[33] The very simplicity of such unified moral communities is part of their great attraction when compared to the hard work of democratic plurality.

However, for MacIntyre's vision to be tenable, narrative must be depicted as nearly determinative and singular in interpretation. This particular vision of narrative interpretation must struggle against not only "multiculturalism," in which a plurality of incommensurable "sacred stories" meet,[34] but also the capacity of interpretations of a given narrative to exceed the tradition they convey (the source of "innovation" in Ricoeur's dialectic of narrative). MacIntyre's emphasis on "narrative unity" limits the consideration of multiple interpretations of a common narrative and subsumes resistance to governing narratives and their unitary meanings to the realm of emotivism. "The unity of a virtue in someone's life," MacIntyre writes, "is intelligible only as a characteristic of a unitary life, a life that can be conceived and evaluated as a whole. . . . Thus personal identity is just that identity presupposed by the unity of the character which the unity of a narrative requires. Without such unity there would not be subjects of whom stories could be told" (205, 218). If, as MacIntyre suggests, narratives shape all aspects of our lives and also are unitary, then a governing narrative serves as a nearly hegemonic, determinative force in our lives.[35] MacIntyre's narrow conception of the way narrative shapes identity offers a vehicle for resolving the problem of emotivism, but this resolution comes at the cost of the democratic pluralism. The very lack of a definitive narrative identity is precisely what Arendt sees as attractive—although challenging to be sure—about democratic politics.

The ideal, for MacIntyre, is a community with a definitive telos, clearly delineated by a shared and coherent unifying narrative, into which members of the community are born. Arendt recognizes the weight of the narrative webs of signification into which one is born but is far more concerned with plurality and freedom than MacIntyre. Accordingly, she is not just concerned with tacit consent to a community's stories, but also (or more so) "dissent." Writing about freedom and American politics in *Crises of the Republic*, she declares, "Dissent implies consent, and is the hallmark of free government. . . . Consent as it is implied in the right to dissent—the spirit of American law and the quintessence of American government—spells out and articulates the tacit consent given in exchange for the community's tacit welcome of new arrivals, of the inner immigration through which it constantly renews itself" (1972, 88). As concerned as Arendt is with preserving the general continuity needed for free and democratic politics, this continuity *includes* the space for dissent, and as such the space for "innovation" within the scaffolding provided by the sedimentation of a polity's narratives and institutions.

Like MacIntyre, Arendt is interested in the potential hazards of the fragmentation of tradition. Arendt is concerned in particular that the narratives that once conveyed traditions, and in so doing helped bridge the gap between past and future, have become untenable in modernity. As she writes:

> That this tradition has worn thinner and thinner as the modern age progressed is a secret to nobody. When the thread of tradition finally broke, the gap between past and future ceased to be a condition peculiar only to the activity of thought and restricted as an experience to those few who made thinking their primary business. It became a tangible reality and perplexity for all; that is, it became a fact of political relevance. (1977, 14)

This is not to say that Arendt seeks to "retie the broken thread of tradition or to invent some newfangled surrogates with which to fill the gap between past and future"; rather, she pushes us to think about how to negotiate the possibilities and dangers that exist in this gap.[36] Instead of seeking the solace of such small bounded communities, Arendt develops a conception of the role of storytelling amid the political pluralism she cherishes. Arendt suggests that without the stable boundaries provided by coherent traditions, we in modernity are "fragile—brittle, if not already broken" (Curtis 1997, 28).[37] As such, Arendt seeks paths in which narratives enable us to engage in the plurality of democratic politics.

Arendt's notion of "representative thinking" offers one path toward being able to tell and listen to stories in a plural polity. In "Truth and Politics," Arendt writes:

> Political thought is representative. I form an opinion by considering a given issue from different viewpoints, by making present to my mind the standpoints of those who are absent; that is, I represent them. This process of representation does not blindly adopt the actual views of those who stand somewhere else, and hence look upon the world from a different perspective; this is a question neither of empathy, as though I tried to be or feel like somebody else, nor of counting noses and joining a majority but of being and thinking in my own identity where I am actually not. The more people's standpoints I have present in my mind while I am pondering a given issue, and the better I can imagine how I would think and feel if I were in their place, the stronger will be my capacity for representative thinking and the more valid my final conclusions, my opinion. (1977, 241)

Representative thinking requires "imaginative reflection," the capacity to put oneself in different positions, and in so doing imagine the stories that inform other perspectives. It is crucial to Arendt's notion of "visiting"—a concept that is central to the vision of "democratic politics."

Arendt develops her notion of visiting most fully in her *Lectures on Kant's Political Philosophy*. Sympathetically quoting Kant, Arendt describes "representative thinking" as a mode of "'view[ing] the object afresh from every side and so to enlarge [the visitor's] point of view from a microscopic to a general outlook. . . . 'It is accomplished . . . 'by putting ourselves in the place of any other man.'" Arendt continues, "Critical thinking is possible only where the standpoints of all others are open to inspection. . . . [B]y the force of imagination it makes the others present and thus moves in a space that is potentially public, open to all sides. To think with an enlarged mentality means that one trains one's imagination to go visiting" (1982, 42–43). The visitor shifts perspective and adopts different standpoints in a public space open to all sides.

"Visiting," Lisa Disch explains, "involves constructing stories of an event from each of the plurality of perspectives that might have an interest in telling it and imagining how I would respond as a character in a story very different from my own. It is a kind of representation that arrives at the general through the particular" (Disch 1996, 158). In this sense, visiting allows us to recognize the constructedness of our own and others' governing narratives—and still be able to engage in politics. Indeed, the "disorientation" that results from visiting—the capacity to become familiar with others' "sacred stories" and concomitantly to have one's own "sacred stories" defamiliarized—enables us to become more fully aware of the "dialectic of sedimentation and innovation" offered by narratives.[38]

Arendtian visiting is neither an act of "tourism" in which one looks at another from the comfortable familiarity of his or her own perspective, nor an act of "assimilation" in which one "forcibly . . . make[s oneself] at home in a place that is not [one's] home by appropriating its customs" (Disch, 159). Nor is visiting an act of what might be called "assimilating the other," in which one presumes the inexorable validity of one's values and simply projects the "visitee" into one's own world. "Visiting is a temporary change of place, a liminal state that is at once exciting, disorienting and uncomfortable, because it is an encounter with the unfamiliar" (Disch, 168). In the realm of a plural democratic politics, visiting is thus crucial to the capacity to express and hear beliefs and opinions—other ways of making sense of the world. Indeed, it is the essence of democratic, as opposed to authoritarian, political communication.[39]

Through visiting we put ourselves into the narrative scaffolding of the sacred stories of others. We can perceive the world created by these stories. Perspectives other than those created by the stories into which *we* are born are made available to us if we attentively "listen" to and "inhabit" this new world. Describing "visiting" as "being and thinking in my own identity *where* I am not," Arendt is careful to cast the effect created as a liminal sensibility (1977, 241, my emphasis). The (sacred) stories of others create a setting—and I would suggest that "where" is only partially adequate, since setting is a composition of time and space. If visiting were intended as more than a liminal experience, the "I" would be more prominently affected. Within narrative structure, setting shapes identity. Therefore, if one stayed "too long" in the narrative scaffolding of a story different from one's own, one's identity would change. This is the problem of assimilation. This is not to say that visiting has no changing effect on an individual. Rather such changes occur on *reflection* after the fact. Visiting enhances representative thinking—and representative thinking enriches one's ability to engage in impartial judging. "Impartiality," Arendt writes, "is obtained by taking the viewpoints of others into account; impartiality is not the result of some higher standpoint that would then actually settle the dispute by being altogether above the melee" (1982, 42).[40]

The capacity of impartial judgment, Arendt writes, "is one, if not the most, important activity in which this sharing-the-world-with-others comes to pass." (1977, 221). Judging requires that individuals make decisions with a focus on the public world, not the private self.

> The power of judgment rests on a potential agreement with others . . . such judgment must liberate itself from the "subjective private conditions" . . . but which are not fit to enter the market place and lack validity in the public realm. And this enlarged way of thinking . . . cannot function in strict isolation or solitude; it needs the presence of others "in whose place" it must think, whose perspective it must take into consideration, and without whom it never has the opportunity to operate at all. . . . [J]udgment, to be valid, depends on the presence of others. (1977, 220–21)

The impartiality produced by the process of visiting encourages us to make judgments that take a broader understanding of our "public" life "into account." Our sense of the world we share is illuminated by the perspectives of this world conveyed by the many stories we have heard— and by the various interpretations of a sermon or similar story we might encounter as our imagination goes visiting. The enlarged mentality created by "listening" to others' stories is indicative of a broad appreciation of plurality. Always keeping the context of the world we share in mind, judgments so conceived invigorate a democratic public realm. As such, we must remember that however impartial such judgments may aspire to be, they are not fixed or universally valid. As Curtis argues:

> To be [so] unresponsive to the world's contestation and flux is the essence of irresponsibility and corrodes the validity of judgments. Thus judgments are always contestable and relative, if by "relative" we mean that because plurality is the law of the earth, we must be responsive to, must continually rethink our judgments on the basis of changing worldly events and opinions. (1999, 122)

Despite our best intentions toward impartiality, our capacity for representative thinking is inevitably limited. As such, our judgments remain particular—enlarged but particular nonetheless, and thus open to contestation. Judgments are best conceived as not final but as invitations to more exchanging of stories and more imaginative visiting.[41]

In contrast to MacIntyre, Arendt's notion of storytelling offers not near-determinative, unitary narratives, but a mode of appreciating a plurality of stories and also the capacity of a single story to engender an array of interpretations. Visiting with others, then, is a critical step in the struggle *against* the very type of unitary, hegemonic narrative that MacIntyre seems to espouse. Visiting allows us to re-member, re-tell, and refigure governing historical narratives in order to derive opinions and beliefs more "representative" in the Arendtian sense. The "disorientation" and "defamiliarizing" of one's own "sacred stories" that result from visiting permits one to re-imagine one's own sacred stories. In so doing, one becomes a more capable teller and listener of stories, and hence a more vibrant participant in the plurality of democratic politics.

We can then think of a participant in the realm of democratic politics as a "visitor." Arendt seems to suggest that such an individual maintains a clear sense of self, even as the enriching experience of the visit can lead to change. This clarity of self-understanding is over-stated, I think; indeed, visiting can be exceedingly disruptive to an individual.[42] Encountering a provocative story, seeing the world from a heretofore neglected or disregarded perspective, and perhaps especially countenancing how one's self features in another's story can provide a potentially shattering challenge to an individual's sense of self. One of the great appeals of homogenous MacIntyrian communities is that they promise insulation from such an encounter with different perspectives, that is, with the stories of others. There are less extreme ways of mitigating the disruptive capacity of visiting. Multicultural education, for example, is intended to expose individuals to the stories and perspectives of others in a relatively controlled environment. Such educational designs have the potential of "domesticating" difference so that the productive challenge of visiting is contained (and potentially diminished), but at their best, multicultural curriculums help teach individuals the importance, and process, of visiting. By encouraging people to become "visitors," multicultural education (and other comparable public programs) helps reveal the shared world for individuals, even as it disrupts their comfortable hold on reality.[43]

Arendt sometimes describes such individuals—indeed describes herself—as "not quite at home in the world."[44] This phrase is often read in despairing terms as indicative of an unassailable discomfort, an impossible longing to be at home in the world. There is a tincture of tragedy about such figures. However, I think this impression misses the fruitful and dynamic implications of the phrase. Arendt, after all, tends to talk about those not quite at home in the world with a sense of admiration.[45]

Rather than simply a product of a keen longing for an unreachable home, I take this idea of not being quite at home in the world as an embrace—even if an often exhausting embrace—of mobility. It speaks of an identity as a visitor—never quite at home—traveling amid other travelers. In the language of Exodus, it suggests a sense of being a "sojourner in the wilderness" far more than a "chosen person in a promised land." To be sure, one's mobility can vary depending on circumstances. The wilderness is rarely an easy place to travel and one can lose oneself traveling in such a setting for too long. Yet, home can be enervating; one risks growing stolid, content, unchallenged and unchanged—and neglectful of the exuberant pleasures of freedom.[46] As Arendt writes in *On Revolution*, "public freedom consisted" of actions concerned with the shared world and offered those who engaged in such expressions of public freedom "a feeling of happiness they could acquire nowhere else" (1990, 119).

Arendt recommends the position of a "conscious pariah," a figure seeking the perspectives available on the margins of society.[47] As Disch explains (quoting Arendt):

> Being at home in the world means having a teleological conception of one's life history: "If we feel at home in this world, we can see our lives as the development of the 'product of nature,' as the unfolding and realization of what we really were." In contrast, not being at home in the world means being ill at ease with what is taken for granted there. . . . Not being at home in the world is a characteristic of the conscious pariah who does not identify totally with any group or place. . . .[48]

The conscious pariah embraces visiting in a particularly dynamic way. Not only do conscious pariahs move from margin to center and back again seeing the world from different perspectives, conscious pariahs also seek to compel others (at both the margin and center) to engage in visiting. The status of the conscious pariah, of the figure at the margins of society, is of particular concern for the study of prophetic politics for two reasons. First, the biblical prophets are fundamentally liminal figures, beginning with Moses who, among many other indicators, camped on the edge of the ancient Hebrew community (Ex. 18:5ff.) and wore a veil to cover his shining face from the people (Ex. 34:29ff.). Neither fully in or out of their communities, the prophets maintained an insider/outsider status, a position from which they could offer a challenging critique of the social order.[49]

Second, modern practitioners of prophetic politics, especially as representatives of social movements, also seek to move and speak from this place on the margins. Seeking to transform the world, they share the intent to challenge people to displace themselves from the corrupting forces at the center of a given culture or community. Where modern practitioners of prophetic politics differ, however, is how and where they direct their listeners to move from this liminal space. Some counsel retreat from the corrupting world (an approach, as I discuss below, that offers "worldlessness" as a response to "homelessness"). Others direct people back into the world, promoting vital reforms that would dramatically alter public life. This direction is supported by the invitation to move back and forth from margin to center so that both critique and engagement can be maintained.

## Worldliness, *Sensus Communis,* and Wooing

Unfortunately for a proponent of such a vision of democratic politics, so much in our world generates a fear of visiting and instead promotes a call to "go home." To this point, much of this discussion of narratives has referred, if implicitly, to the power of stories to inspire efforts to transform the world. Narratives, of course, can also generate a different visceral response; they can construct a less mobile and deeply entrenched type of shelter. Stories, as tellers of jeremiads know well, can evoke fear. The terrifying images of Jonathan Edwards' great sermon "Sinners in the Hands of an Angry God" are still causing shudders in students across the United States. Prophets speak from marginal positions and use fear to motivate listeners to turn away from the corrupting influences afflicting the world. But the direction of this turn can, as I have suggested, vary. In the balance is the realm of politics, a locus Arendt describes as the "in-between," the place of public life.

> The world lies between people, and this in-between . . . is the object of the greatest concern and the most obvious upheaval in almost all the countries of the globe. . . . More and more people of the countries of the Western world, which since the decline of the ancient world has regarded freedom from politics as one of the basic freedoms, make use of this freedom and have retreated from the world and their obligations within it. . . . [W]ith each such retreat, an almost demonstrable loss to the world takes place; what is lost is the specific and usually irreplaceable in-between which should have formed between this individual and his fellow men. (Arendt 1968, 4)

When this retreat from the world occurs, the context in which individuals define themselves is privatized rather than publicized; the focus of concerns is on the self rather than the collective. This shift toward worldlessness results in the evisceration of politics. Arendt, of course, is calling us back to engagement in the world, to develop what she refers to as *sensus communis,* which draws us out of ourselves and inclines us to engage in "imaginative reflection" about the lives and perspectives of others.[50] "In Arendt's view," writes Melissa Orlie, "the perception and actuality of commonality is impossible if plurality, and the innumerable perspectives it represents, is absent or inconceivable" (Orlie, 85). Listening to the stories that permeate the public realm, our attention is directed to matters of social justice rather than concern for personal well-being or salvation.

In this light, we should consider the role of storytelling in the political process that Arendt (quoting Kant) called "woo[ing] the consent of everyone else."[51] For Arendt, the importance of the phrase "woo the consent of everyone else" lies not with the object "consent" but with the verb "to woo."[52] The point is less about agreement and more about engagement. Storytelling begins with and requires the continuance of plurality. The best democratic political storytelling enhances relationships and engenders appreciation of the shared world. Consent may be a crucial objective of storytelling, but the process of sharing narratives is of immediate and profound concern—especially in dark times when worldliness, the necessary precursor to political consensus, has shrunk.[53]

It is crucial to recognize that Arendt speaks here not of marriage or weddings—but of wooing. Wooing is never successful if one party talks and the other listens but does not respond. Wooing is a process of enticement and exchange. Wooing is a process of recognition—one party hears another and lets the other know that it has been heard by responding. Wooing creates relationships that must be carefully tended to over time. Wooing is not fixed or guaranteed. Wooing is like cultivating a garden—a fertile ground is created between people. Wooing is a process that leads to friendship—or at least to worldliness.

Ultimately, Arendt suggests that worldliness is the "point" of storytelling, at least with regard to politics. In dark times, individuals are too often seduced by the promise of truth, settling for one story with a fixed meaning. In such times, the relationships created by wooing—by the exchange of stories—appear less vital than a narrative that promises closure and mastery. In her essay on G. E. Lessing in *Men in Dark Times*, Arendt warns us of what happens when narrative becomes ideology: worldliness, and humanity itself, is diminished.

Distinguishing between stories and ideology (and here she is writing in a context of examining Nazism in post-war Germany), Arendt explains that a narrative enters the world and "there it can live on—one story among many" (1968, 22). The storyteller who seeks to remember and offer a path to meaning, but not to master the meaning of an action or event, recognizes that the story being told is "one among many." The listener to a story likewise can and should recognize that the story is one among many—and is itself open to reinterpretation and retelling. Every story, she argues, is an effort to reveal meaning that must be considered with other stories and interpretations.

Arendt offers one other crucial piece in this essay on Lessing that provides a link to my concern about worldliness. That is, in valorizing Lessing, particularly Lessing's inclination to sacrifice truth for friendship, Arendt also discusses the limits of narrative. Any story "should be sacrificed to humanity or friendship in case a conflict should arise" (1968, 28). Arendt makes this point as a vehicle for assessing Nazi ideology as something that (as an ideology) was not sacrificed before humanity or friendship. Friendship stands against ideological claims of truth and for a process of understanding that values and cultivates the relationships between people, nurtures a valorization of the common humanity. Lessing, Arendt writes:

> rejoiced in the very thing that has ever . . . distressed philosophers: that the truth, as soon as it is uttered, is immediately transformed into one opinion among many, is contested, reformulated, reduced to one subject of discourse among others. Lessing's greatness does not merely consist in a theoretical insight that there cannot be one single truth within the human world but in his gladness that it does not exist and that, therefore, the

unending discourse among men will never cease so long as there are men at all. (1968, 27)

Instead, and in keeping with the lessons of Lessing, Arendt argues that narratives—in their telling and being heard—must contribute to worldliness or they become mere expressions of ideology and must be sacrificed.

## Stories, Democratic Politics, and Social Transformation

Stories define the world and the people who inhabit it. Stories are also vital in changing the world. Since this is a study of social movements, we do well to reflect on the types of stories likely to be told by practitioners of prophetic politics. The aim of social movements is not simply the redress of grievances, but the transformation of the world. The need for such transformation and the path toward change are defined in the narratives told by social movements. The narratives thus delineate the spatial and temporal context in which the struggle for change will take place. Moreover, the narratives that animate and direct such efforts are thus told from a position of a righteous victim or sufferer in a hostile world, from the margins. Accordingly, these narratives will define the identities of the participants in the contest over social transformation. The crafting of setting and identity in turn informs the process through which change will be sought and pursued.

To say that prophetic politics calls for social transformation is not to assert that such transformations are "democratic." Indeed, from a secularist perspective, the expectation is that prophetic politics will necessarily be antithetical to democracy. To evaluate this presumption, let us keep the requirements of a robust democratic politics at the center of our attention and use the narrative scaffolding of the Exodus story to guide us, drawing from the discussion of narratives and politics ways by which we can assess the commensurability of prophetic politics and democracy. In the effort to use narratives to enable social transformation, how do practitioners of prophetic politics deal with the capacity of stories to define identity, establish temporal and spatial context, and engage with the stories of others?

We tend to think of identity as an act of proclamation—of telling a narrative that definitively projects who we are. Within the framework of the Exodus narrative, the claim "we are chosen people" delivers a different message than "we are sojourners." But narrative identity is not simply a product of one's own utterance; it is also crafted by virtue of the position one takes as a listener to the stories of others. The assertion "we are chosen people" thus situates one's respondents as the "unchosen," establishing an exclusivist identity as both teller and listener of stories. In contrast, the narrative identity of "sojourner" is crafted in inclusive terms, inviting others to hear one's story and then share their own stories as fellow travelers in return. Democratic politics in Arendtian terms, of course, requires this inclusive position of invitation. As Melissa Orlie writes, "As we enlarge our perspective to take others into account, we may find our opinions changed. According to this view, thinking may be a solitary activity, but the force of imagination makes others present. Imagination makes the presence of other perspectives matter by abstracting from our 'subjective private conditions'" (Orlie, 156).[54] Listening to and countenancing the perspectives of others comes far more readily to those who think of themselves as sojourners rather than the "chosen." The willingness to be a visitor, or to adopt the identity of the conscious pariah, prepares one to engage in public life as a critic and political participant.

The development of narrative identity is shaped by the temporal and spatial context established by the narrative. Concepts of time are conveyed by stories, but also exceed the bounds of the narrative and shaped the broader attitude toward time and history of those who tell and hear the story. The past is not something that can be created whole cloth by the "prophet" situated in the present (or at least such a whole-cloth creation will not resonate in a democratic political realm in which there are multiple stories). As Joshua Dienstag states:

> We are in a story that is of a piece. Each chapter must follow from those previous. If the earlier chapters are reinterpreted in the writing of a new chapter, it must be done in such a way that the consistency between past and future is retained. If not, the new interpretations will not stick in our minds—it will be forgotten as quickly as a dream. More than this is needed, of course, for a plot to succeed, but such consistency is a necessary starting point. Who would alter the future must begin with the past. But his is an opportunity as well as a burden. (Dienstag, 132–33)

This sense of temporality and history is central to Exodus, a narrative in which memory is a central and recurring theme. The question is not just what to remember, but how. We must assess what lessons practitioners of prophetic politics draw from the Exodus narrative. Is Moses a humble figure, slow of speech, or a fierce presence dashing the stone tablets in disgust? Is the focus on liberation from bondage in Egypt and the difficult path toward freedom, or on walking behind the fiery cloud of God as enemies are drowned in the Red Sea? Should we stress the purging of those who dance around the golden calf or the lessons about how to justly treat strangers? Just as important as what lessons a practitioner of prophetic politics chooses to emphasize is the attitude toward time and history conveyed in the retelling of the narrative. Is ancient Israel merely a precursor to the newly chosen people of the United States? Is the inhabiting and securing of the promised land guaranteed— or is it conditional on human fulfillment of the covenant? In other words, does a practitioner of prophetic politics encourage a reconciliatory approach to history, to the linear and definitive links between past, present, and future? Or does a social movement utilize and promote a redemptive view of history? Is the Exodus story open to reinterpretation and contingent futures? Differences in conception of temporal contexts will directly inform a social movement's inclination to engage in the open, contested realm of democratic plurality.

Likewise, the spatial context delineated by retellings of the Exodus narrative also establishes an attitude toward democratic politics. There is, as I have mentioned, a sharp difference regarding the fluid and sometimes dangerous world of democratic politics if space is conceived of as a settled promised land or as a wilderness. Telling a story from the margins of society that contains such pivotal metaphors of place, practitioners of prophetic politics readily use the Exodus narrative to define the attitude of a social movement toward the world. Moreover, the retelling of the narrative also provides a sense of direction to their listeners—go back into the world and seek transformation, or retreat from the world and seek the security of home as a private refuge. Such lessons about spatial context directly shape a social movement's attitude toward public life and the exchange of narratives. Is visiting, so vital to the conception of democratic politics, to be encouraged or dismissed? Is the open pluralist realm of politics to be embraced or feared? Does an expression of prophetic politics expand the "in-between" and aid the struggle to resist the seductive safety of worldlessness? Does it emphasize social justice or personal salvation?

The Exodus narrative is at once an American sacred story of a chosen people and sojourners, of a promised land and a wilderness. These categories of identity and setting are both in conflict and bound together. In the ensuing chapters, I examine how practitioners of prophetic politics in America retell this story. I will "visit" with them, seek to hear their stories and understand their visions of and for the nation—and in analyzing their stories assess their congeniality or hostility to democratic politics. The narratives told by practitioners of prophetic politics refine and maintain the figurative scaffolding within which we understand ourselves and develop visions of our polity. The resonant retellings of these sacred stories shape our shared public life in the United States. They feed our hunger.

# Chapter Three
# Twentieth-Century American Prophets: Rev. Billy Sunday and Rev. Dr. Martin Luther King Jr.

Almighty God, our Heavenly Father, we thank Thee and rejoice that through faith in Thee and Thy word this Government was built upon that foundation. We thank Thee that the compact signed in the cabin of the Mayflower by our ancestors was for democracy, liberty, freedom, and the right to worship Thee according to the dictates of our own conscience. . . . We thank Thee that we are Americans and live beneath the protecting folds of the Stars and Stripes.
—**Reverend Billy Sunday,** Opening Prayer, House of Representatives, January 10, 1918

And don't let anybody make you think that God chose America as his divine messianic force to be a sort of policeman of the whole world. God has a way of standing before the nations with judgment and it seems that I can hear God saying to America, "You are too arrogant. If you don't change your ways I will rise up and break the backbone of your power, and I will place it in the hands of a nation that doesn't even know my name. Be still and know that I'm God."
—**Reverend Dr. Martin Luther King Jr.,** 1967, in *Citizen King*

To assert that religion is central to American identity is to make a claim that is bland in tone and modest in reach. To indicate that this religiosity often takes on a prophetic cast helps clarify this assertion. To illuminate the diversity of prophetic voices in American political culture demonstrates the complexity of the role of religion in America.

As a storyteller, situated between a people's past and future, the prophetic figure takes on the role of defining the identity and vision of a community or nation. Interpreting and retelling the history of a people, the prophet articulates the "crisis" of the present moment and the promise as well as the dangers of the future. Rhetorically claiming a marginal position, the prophet preaches as a critic of the injustice, moral decay, or sinfulness that he or she perceives to be threatening the fulfillment of a just world, if not a divinely inspired vision of the "kingdom of God." The prophet is thus poised to charge listeners with a mission to transform the world.

The definition of the crisis, the interpretation of history, and the delineation of identity and context pose possibilities and challenges for democratic politics. As figures who speak from a position of alienation from a failing society, prophets often represent "pariah peoples," those who have been forced to (or sometimes consciously opt for) the margins. Such figures are often, in Arendt's phrase, "not quite at home in the world." Pariah peoples suffer from a "radical loss of the world" (1968, 13). Living in such conditions of worldlessness results in what Arendt refers to as the "atrophy of all the organs" humans have for responding to the world (1968, 13). These tools, which are necessary for democratic politics, for engagement in an open and pluralist public realm, and for representative thinking and visiting, are sometimes championed but at other times are neglected by practitioners of prophetic politics. The degree to which prophetic figures seek to enhance these capacities or revitalize these organs in their listeners is a measure of whether an expression of prophetic politics is congenial or hostile to democracy, of whether their narratives generate active engagement in public life or represent an anti-political withdrawal from the world.

In this chapter, I examine the prophetic politics of two vital and quite different figures in the history of religion and American public life in the 20th century. The Reverend Billy Sunday is widely recognized as the most influential evangelical preacher during the first quarter of this century, and Dr. Martin Luther King Jr. is often thought to be the most influential minister in the last half of 20th-century American politics.[1] I focus on the sermons, speeches, and writings of Sunday and King in order to assess the role that the Exodus narrative played in their respective prophetic politics.[2]

The differences between Sunday and King are quite stark, because they pursue quite distinct political visions, they are rooted in different theological traditions,[3] and they emphasize different aspects of the Exodus story. However, Sunday and King are united in their common appreciation of the Exodus narrative as a "sacred story" in American political culture. That they stress different tropes and use the Exodus narrative to support and generate quite different political identities and visions exemplifies Ricoeur's assertion that some narratives convey a dialectical tension between "sedimentation and innovation." The key break between Sunday and King with regard to their understanding of the Exodus narrative—and in turn their prophetic politics as a whole—lies in their divergent understandings of history, identity, and context as expressed in the different Exodus tropes through which they convey their political theologies.

The respective prophetic politics of Sunday and King rely on resonant tropes drawn from the Exodus narrative. Within this narrative framework, each raises issues of race, gender, and class as well as the tension between the private and public realms that are central to the intersection of religion and politics in the contemporary United States. Thus, the exploration of the political theologies of Sunday and King is aimed at setting the stage for the analysis of the prophetic politics of Promise Keepers and Call to Renewal that is discussed in subsequent chapters.

## Exodus Gendered: Rev. Billy Sunday, God's Apostle of Masculinity

Billy Sunday began his career as an evangelist in 1893. Prior to his life as a preacher, Sunday was a professional baseball player who, although he never hit for a great batting average, was a slick fielder and said to be the fastest man in the majors.[4] In the spirit of the prophets whom he sought to emulate, Sunday portrayed his conversion as a transformative moment in which he heard the call of heavenly voices and never looked back.[5] As he loved to tell his audiences, one afternoon while carousing with his teammates in Chicago, he heard a group singing hymns on a street corner. Leaving his friends in front of a saloon, Sunday followed the singers to the Pacific Garden Mission where he committed himself to Jesus and "bid [his] old life good-bye" (quoted in Bruns, 44). Ultimately forgoing his baseball career for evangelizing, Sunday worked first for the YMCA and then apprenticed under the revival minister John Wilbur Chapman before finally striking out on his own in January 1896. After leading his first revival in Garner, Iowa, Sunday was never without requests for his preaching services until his death in 1935.

For the first twenty years of his ministry, Sunday led revivals in increasingly larger towns and cities and with a growing geographic range, culminating in a ten-week revival in downtown Manhattan in 1917. By the end of his life, Sunday had preached to millions of listeners (all without the aid of public address systems) and won thousands of souls for Jesus.[6] Although his popularity and appeal waned in the postwar years, Sunday was never out of the public eye. Widely credited with revolutionizing revivalism in America, he created a legacy that is evident in the ministries of Billy Graham and the generation of televangelists that includes Jerry Falwell, Oral Roberts, and Pat Robertson, as well as organizations such as Promise Keepers.[7]

Like his forebears in the tradition of the American jeremiad, Sunday built the narrative framework of his ministry on delineating the crisis in the United States and the necessary path to solace. Without question, the era in which Sunday's evangelism took shape was a time of great change in American culture. The fluidity of American society—the vast impact of industrialization, the exponential growth in immigration, the rapid expansion of cities, the "great migration" of African Americans northward, the creation and movement of wealth (made possible in part by a shift in the foundation of the currency)—fundamentally altered and unsettled the nation. In an era marked by dynamic change, the stability of accepted mores—including, for example, normative sex and gender roles—faced significant challenges. As John D'Emilio and Estelle Freedman write in their study of the history of sexuality in America,

> Between the 1880s and the First World War, the pace of economic and social change seemed to accelerate, transforming the context that had given rise to the civilized morality of the middle class. As growing numbers of working-class women left the home to work in factories, offices and retail establishments, and as middle-class women entered college and pursued professional careers, the separate spheres that underlay nineteenth-century sexual codes disintegrated. Simultaneously, the economy moved beyond the stage of early industrialization, in which habits of thrift, sobriety, and personal asceticism won plaudits. Instead, the emphasis in American life was shifting toward consumption, gratification, and pleasure. . . . In the process, working-class forms of sexual practice, previously beyond the ken of the middle class, were projected outward into society. Massive immigration from southern and eastern Europe, as well as the movement of blacks from the rural South to northern cities, added to this development by making these alternative cultures of sexuality far more visible.[8]

Mainstream Protestantism was also being unsettled. The increasing public presence of Catholics and Jews in America, the emergence of theological schools of "higher criticism" (which offered new interpretive lenses for reading the Bible), and the growing influence of the left-leaning theology of the Social Gospel movement that demanded active commitment to socio-economic justice in this world, all contributed to upsetting the religious status quo. No force, however, challenged conventional religious wisdom more than the growing influence of Darwin's theory of evolution.[9] In this atmosphere, Sunday emerged as a prophet whose jeremiads articulated a diagnosis of the "crisis in America" and offered an old-time religious solution.

In utilizing the familiar themes of the Exodus narrative to reach an audience dealing with forces of tumultuous change, Billy Sunday relied heavily on the resonant tropes of "chosen-ness" and "promised land" in his articulation of the crisis in America—so much so that they serve as generally unspoken presumptions in his sermons. However, I want to begin my analysis of Sunday's sermons by discussing a relatively unconventional use of the Exodus narrative. I do so not simply because of the content of Sunday's message, but to illustrate both Sunday's gifts as a storyteller and how the Exodus narrative, as an American sacred story, is open to a wide array of interpretive uses.[10]

In his sermon "Motherhood" (a sermon in many cases delivered to assemblies of women), Sunday uses the framework of Exodus to tell a story not just about his conception of the special calling of women[11] but ultimately identity itself. Sunday begins: "The story of Moses is one of the most beautiful and fascinating in all the world. It takes a hold on us and never for an instant does it lose its interest, for it is so graphically told that once heard it is never forgotten."[12] From this invocation of the story of Exodus, Sunday goes on to preach about motherhood, developing his narrative of Moses' mother to illustrate his message: "Moses' mother was a slave. She had to work in the brickyards or labor in the field, but God was on her side and she won, as the mother always wins with God on her side." Sunday speculates on the care Moses' mother took in the construction of the basket that served as Moses' ship, the prayers she uttered, the tears she cried, and above all the faithfulness with which she trusted in God. Sunday also reflects on Pharaoh's daughter, who, although an infidel, had "feminine curiosity" and a "woman's heart" and, as we all know, "when a woman's heart and a baby's tears meet, something happens that gives the devil cold feet." Indeed, Sunday concludes, it was her "woman's heart . . . made her forget she was the daughter of the Pharaoh" (1965, 231).

Sunday not only naturalizes motherhood as the highest calling for women (a theme common in his sermons), but also makes clear that motherhood trumps national and political identity. "Look at [the] work of [Moses' mother]! It is the greatest in the world; in its far-reaching importance, it is transcendentally above everything in the universe. . . . If you want to find greatness, don't go toward the throne; go to the cradle." Raising a child—a potential Moses—is for Sunday "so important that God will not trust anybody with it but a mother . . . [t]he launching of a boy or girl to live for Christ is greater work than to launch a battleship."[13] But then what, we might ask, is the status of Moses? "Moses was a chosen vessel of the Lord and God wanted him to get the right kind of start, so He gave him a good mother" (1965, 233). In other words, Moses was the battleship his mother launched. Moses is the faithful servant and prophet of God, and "where did Moses get his faith? From his mother" (1965, 235).

Of course, if mothers are responsible for every Moses, they are also responsible for every Judas. As Sunday rhetorically asks, "Who knows but [that] Judas became the godless, good-for-nothing wretch he was, because he has a godless, good-for-nothing mother" (239)? Mothers thus have a choice: raise a Moses or a Judas; a prophet and servant of the Lord or a traitor; a leader or a wretch. In an era in which industrialization was destabilizing normative conceptions of the proper spheres of gender, in which more and more women were leaving the home out of desire or economic need,[14] Sunday's veneration of the mother of Moses as an example of the divinely ordained role of women as nurturers was a none-too-subtle reassertion of normative sex roles. That Sunday tells this story within the resonant narrative scaffolding of Exodus illuminates the crucial role of the home within his broader message of the status of America as a promised land.

There is another point about the construction of identity to be made about Sunday's retelling of the story of Moses. In his desire to venerate Moses' mother, Sunday concomitantly emphasizes the birth and very early years of Moses' life as most crucial to his character. This rhetorical move is odd not simply because most tellers of the Exodus narrative (including the original) have little to say about the young Moses and instead stress the mature adult who, after personal trials and tribulations, leads the ancient Hebrews out of Egypt and toward the Promised Land. (As we shall see, King certainly emphasizes the mature Moses.) Indeed, the Bible tells us and Sunday readily declares that Moses' mother served as his "wet-nurse," but that Moses was raised in the house of the Pharaoh.[15]

Sunday's stress on the earliest years of Moses' life has at least two intriguing implications. First, despite his assertion that Moses learned determination and discipline as an infant at his mother's breast, Sunday's Moses seems to *inherit* strength, suggesting a biological or naturalized cultural identity. Indeed, similar to the naturalizing of gender identity (women as mothers), individual identity as a whole is largely naturalized and can only be enhanced or corrupted by social forces. Second, and more importantly, if Moses' birth and experiences as an infant comprised the critical facets of his identity, then Moses takes on pre-millennial characteristics appropriate for Sunday's "anti-political prophetic politics." That is, what Moses learned from his mother is how to persevere as a slave, how, in other words, to live in Egypt. The crucial quality of Sunday's Moses is his armored soul that endures and can wait on the margins for deliverance. For Sunday, Moses is thus a man of faith who waits on God,[16] rather than a leader who challenges the central powers of Egypt, helps deliver the Hebrews out of Egypt, and forms them as a people on the way to the Promised Land.[17] In Arendtian terms, the Moses of Billy Sunday is less a conscious pariah or political figure transforming the world and more a servant guiding God's chosen people away from the corrupting world.

## Stories of Home in the American Promised Land

In his day, Sunday had few equals as a religious and political story-teller. Provocatively speaking to the American people in a common vernacular that was shocking coming from the pulpit, he reached millions as much as an entertainer as a preacher.[18] Animating his tales with his skills as an actor, Sunday would deliver sermons by changing his voice and posture to bring various characters to his stage.[19] In his revivals, Sunday told story after story, interweaving American neighbors, biblical figures, world leaders, Jesus and Satan in a manner that collapsed temporal and spatial distance into a familiar American landscape.

While Sunday was willing to make unconventional uses of the American sacred story of Exodus, he commonly used the resonant narrative in more traditional ways, enthusiastically joining the tradition of framing Americans as a chosen people in a promised land. As McLoughlin notes, Sunday

> assumed that the American way of life in which he had grown up and which was exalted in all of the sermons and public orations he had heard was the way of life approved by God for all men . . . Sunday saw the United States as a nation divinely guided by God, who [Sunday claimed] "kept this country hid from the greedy eyes of monarchs 3000 miles away" until it could be settled by "God-fearing" people who would bring it to a state of power and perfection from which it could save the world. (McLoughlin 1955, 131)

This was the particular mission of America: "Americans were 'a peculiar people;' they were God's chosen people: 'We are citizens of the greatest government on earth and we are not afraid to admit it'" (quoted in McLoughlin 1955, 131). In fact, "admitting" to the anointed status of the nation was a necessary step in developing the "vim and vigor" required to set the example of American Christianity that the world needed to see.

It was Sunday's belief that not only was the United States God's chosen nation, but God's particular chosen people were those representatives of middle America who, in contrast to the burgeoning immigrant population, were intended to be God's examples for the world. While Sunday never explicitly said that only middle Americans could count as God's anointed, his xenophobia made the boundaries of that category quite clear: "Any man or woman who wants to come here and assimilate to our way and conditions and live beneath the stars and stripes [was welcome, but] . . . if they don't like it here, let 'em go back to where they were kenneled" (quoted in McLoughlin 1955, 148). Sunday's vehement Americanism reached its zenith in the wake of the nation's entry into World War I, where his concern for national and individual boundaries became the most pronounced.

Sunday's particular portrayal of the American promised land is crucial. A child of the American heartland, Sunday tended to depict the United States within the rosy template of the agrarian ideal. Despite the growth of industrialization and the demographic shifts that fundamentally altered the state of the nation, Sunday remained committed to a vision of the American breadbasket. This vision did not have merely metaphorical implications, but shaped his understanding of social and economic issues. For example, convinced of the infinite possibilities available in agrarian America, Sunday commonly portrayed farming as a cure for the poverty of the cities. His congregations would hear this type of advice for those who were impoverished: "Go back to the farm and study expert dairying and help the lives of 200,000 babies that die every year from impure milk that is sold. . . . Go out west and study and be a horticulturist" (Sunday, quoted in McLoughlin 1955, 136). Of course, not just the poor heard this message; such simplified solutions to economic need were directed primarily to the middle class that made up the majority of Sunday's audience. The cure for poverty, Sunday taught, was not reckoning with the structural changes wrought by industrialization, but the personal effort to achieve a nostalgic ideal.

If the fertile farmland of an idyllic middle America characterized the landscape of the American promised land, the heart of this promised land lay in the middle-class home. In his jeremiads, Sunday tended to locate the crisis in America in the decay of that most crucial and cherished American institution. For example, as he declared in his famous "Booze" sermon,

> I tell you, gentlemen, the American home is the dearest heritage of the people, for the people, and when a man can go from home in the morning with the kisses of his wife and children on his lips, and come back at night with an empty bucket to a happy home, that man is a better man, whether white or black. Whatever takes away the comforts of home—whatever degrades man or woman—whatever invades the sanctity of the home, is the deadliest foe to the home, to church, to state. (1970, 60)

Sunday makes two related rhetorical moves in this part of the sermon. First, he links home, church, and state closely together as key social institutions. And second, he suggests that of the three, it is the *home* rather than church or state that serves as the moral foundation of the country. In using Lincoln's language—"of the people, for the people"—Sunday shifts the strength and defining characteristic of the nation from its government to its homes, and as such from its public institutions to its private ones. In so doing, Sunday, of course, also reasserts the ideal of the heterosexual, middle-class family. Furthermore, he establishes the home as being under siege from those forces (booze, but also other immoral temptations such as card-playing and dancing, as well as broader social-economic forces challenging the "traditional" integrity of the home), which would undermine this ideal standing at the core of the nation. Figuring the home as the center of American power and as the nation's greatest resource, Sunday thus portrays the private realm as the heart of the promised land and thus of America's global mission for God.

Not surprisingly, then, it is the home—this core of American civilization—that serves in Sunday's jeremiads as both the spatial context of the nation's greatest crisis and, ultimately, the source of its solace. It is the threat to this core of American civilization that concerned Sunday the most. All manner of vice and licentiousness were undermining the "rampart walls" of the home: card playing and dancing, gossip and striving for social status, adultery and prostitution, and most especially alcohol. As a leader of the temperance movement, Sunday decried the saloon and whisky interests as opponents of everything good and sacred. In "Booze" (or "Get on the Water Wagon"), Sunday depicts the enemy this way, and I quote at length to give the full effect of Sunday's rhetoric—and I recommend reading it aloud in order to appreciate its rhythm.

I tell you it strikes at night. It fights under the cover of darkness and assassinates the characters that it cannot damn, and it lies about you. It attacks defenseless womanhood and childhood. The saloon is a coward. It is a thief; . . . it robs you of your manhood and leaves you in rags and takes away your friends, and it robs your family. It impoverishes your children and it brings insanity and suicide. It will take the shirt off your back and steal the coffin from a dead child and yank the last crust of bread from the hand of a starving child; it will take the last bucket of coal out of your cellar and the last cent out of your pocket, and will send you home bleary-eyed and staggering to your wife and children. It will steal the milk from the breast of the mother and leave her with nothing with which to feed her infant. It will take the virtue from your daughter . . .

The saloon is a liar. It promises good cheer and sends sorrow. It promises health and causes disease. It promises prosperity and sends poverty. It promises happiness and sends misery. Yes, it sends the husband home with a lie on his lips to his wife; and the boy home with a lie on his lips for his mother; and it causes the employee to lie to the employer. It degrades. It is God's worst enemy and the devil's best friend. It spares neither youth nor old age. It is waiting with a dirty blanket for the baby to crawl into the world. It lies in wait for the unborn.

It cocks the highwayman's pistol. It puts the rope in the hand of the mob. It is the anarchist of the world, and its dirty red flag is dyed with the blood of women and children. It sent the bullet through Lincoln; it nerved the arm that sent the bullets through Garfield and William McKinley. Yes, it is a murderer. Every plot that has ever been hatched against the government and law, was born and bred, and crawled out of the grog-shop to damn this country.[20]

In this justifiably famous sermon, Sunday again locates all of the social ills in America squarely with the faults of personal behavior. Poverty and alienation, prostitution and hunger, changes in the structure of the family and the diminishment of religion in the nation, anarchism, socialism and political unrest, hatred and insurrection, all are caused by alcohol. If such is the personal, private nature of the crisis in America, the path to solace is equally simple: curbing private immorality and dedicating one's life to Jesus. Assassination and poverty, murder and theft demand the same cure—is commitment to Jesus and rigorous self-discipline. The context of the home shapes the identity of Sunday's adherents as well as their path to solving the crisis in America: private individuals closing their lips to alcohol, their minds from corrupting and illusory efforts for social transformation, and their doors to the outside world.

## Sunday's Chosen

While Sunday wholeheartedly maintained that America was a promised land, he also argued that there was a crisis in the land, a moral decay infecting God's chosen people. This "Christian nation" had drifted away from God and into the filth of the city streets. In Sunday's eyes, the breakdown was most apparent in two developments: the rise in poverty and the loss of clear gender roles. While each of these developments might suggest social analysis, for Sunday the answer lay clearly not with cultural or political developments, but with individuals. Social ills were a distraction from (and a reflection of) the primary issue of personal salvation—a distraction that could still be solved through individual conversion.

Emphasis on the personal is sharply evident in Sunday's preaching on poverty and economics. Sunday tended to link economic poverty with spiritual poverty.[21] As William McLoughlin points out, "Sunday's sermons on 'The Forces That Win,' 'Hot Cakes off the Griddle,' and 'How To Be a Man' were eloquent recitals of the American success myth and virtually equated failure with sinfulness" (1955, 134–35). Conversion and self-discipline could cure poverty and its handmaiden, drunken idleness. On the whole, poverty was not a social concern but a sign of individual fault. As Sunday told the crowd gathered at his New York tabernacle on June 17, 1917: "The world is full of failures, not from lack of opportunities but because people have drifted on without incentive or aim."[22] Solace was not to be found in "social services," even those sponsored by Christian organizations. "The trouble," Sunday declared, "with the church, the YMCA, and the Young People's Societies is that they have taken up sociology and settlement work but are not winning souls to Christ" (quoted in McLoughlin 1955, 138).

If Sunday was suspicious of the activities of what today would be called "faith-based organizations," he was even more adamant about the dangers posed by the nascent American labor movement. As Roger Bruns states, "[Sunday] had always considered himself a friend of the working-man, the 'dinner-pail' American. And yet, he mistrusted organized labor and ridiculed the pro-labor efforts of left-wing political groups. They were, he said, unnecessarily interfering with traditional American institutions. The answers for the laboring man were not in agitation and striking but in finding God" (131). Sunday was often accused by those on the political left of being a puppet of moneyed interests, providing an opiate for the masses.[23] Sunday was indeed sponsored by John Rockefeller and other leading industrialists, though it is not plainly evident that Sunday perceived himself as doing their bidding. Sunday was not a great celebrator of the accumulation of wealth for the sake of wealth. As he argues in his sermon "Under the Sun," such an attitude is illustrative of mere vanity that leads neither to happiness nor salvation.[24] Rather than celebrating capitalism for its own sake, Sunday's interest was supporting capitalism as *American.* Sunday saw himself as doing God's bidding, regarding labor unrest (much like material greed) as a discordant voice in this promised land.[25] After all, Sunday firmly believed, "We are the happiest people in God's world. . . . I do not believe there are any people beneath the sun who are better fed, better paid, better clothed, better housed, or any happier than we are beneath the stars and stripes—no nation on earth" (quoted in Ellis, 361). Anyone unhappy in this promised land was a suffering sinner who need only come to Christ and work harder to live chosen under the stars and stripes.

## American Woman

The disciplined Christians who belonged to Sunday's vision of the chosen people were not simply industrious—they were also "real men" and "real women." If the home at the heart of the American promised land was the site of both the nation's gravest crisis and its greatest strength, the husbands and wives, mothers and fathers who inhabited these middle-American homes were Sunday's target audience. Sunday's profound fear was that in the "dangerous times" in which he lived, the dominance of these real men and women was giving way to the adulteration of sex roles. Many of Sunday's stories were designed to reinvigorate and reaffirm what Sunday took to be the appropriate callings for men and women.

In his story of Moses' mother, we have already seen the immense value Sunday placed on the role of motherhood. If his similar stories about George Washington's mother did not inspire the women in his audience, or the stories of drunken women whose children died from neglect or tales of young women who forfeited their virtue on the dance floor,[26] did not sufficiently strike fear in their hearts, then Sunday was also willing to forego his tales and move directly to the moral of these stories. Perhaps the finest example of his didactic proclamations on women and their duties as wives and mothers is his sermon "A Plain Talk for Women."

Beginning by giving advice to women in his audience on what to do "when some young fellow . . . asks you the greatest question you will ever be asked next to the salvation of your own soul," Sunday delivers a sharply tendentious sermon on the glories of marriage and mother-hood.[27] The problem in America, according to Sunday, lies squarely at the feet of women who have neglected to devote themselves to the core of the nation—the home. "Our homes," said Sunday, "are on the level with women. Towns are on the level with homes. What women are our homes will be; and what the town is, the men will be, so you hold the destiny of the nation." And yet, in America today, Sunday bemoaned:

> The average girl . . . no longer looks forward to motherhood as the crown-ing glory of womanhood. She is turning her home into a gambling shop and a social beer-and-champagne-drinking joint, and her society is made up of poker players, champagne, wine and beer drinkers, grass-widowers, and jilted jades and slander-mongers. . . . She is becoming a matinee-gad-der and a fudge-eater. (1970, 111)

In contrast to these fudge-eating society girls neglecting their duty to God and nation, Sunday told his congregants of "angel[s] in heaven that would be . . . glad to come to earth and be honored with motherhood if God would grant [them] that privilege" (1970, 109). Women, Sunday suggested, had a basic choice: to live as God intended or to live a life of sinful selfishness. Framing the choice in the classic madonna/whore dual-ism, Sunday asserted, "I believe a good woman is the best thing this side of heaven and a bad woman is the worst thing this side of hell. . . . I think she is the most degraded on earth or the purest on earth" (1970, 110). The stakes of this choice before women were not simply their own salvation; the stakes were the salvation of the chosen nation and its mis-sion to save the world.

> All great women are satisfied with their common sphere in life and think it is enough to fill the lot God gave them in this world as wife and mother. I tell you the devil and women can damn this world, and Jesus and women can save this old world. . . . What paved the way for the downfall of the mightiest dynasties—proud and haughty Greece and imperial Rome? The downfall of their womanhood. The virtue of womanhood is the rampart wall of American civilization. Break that down and with the stones thereof you can pave your way to the hottest hell, and reeking vice and corrup-tion. (1970, 112–13)

Madonna or whore, saint or sinner, heaven or hell, national saviors or destroyers of civilization, the choices and stakes of self-discipline for "real women" in Sunday's Manichean world were hardly subtle or ambiguous. Identity was not something to be explored, something that might change given different circumstances and experiences, or something that even allowed for a degree of nuance; identity was fixed within clear boundaries.

## "Be a Man!" Sunday's Muscular Christianity

As concerned as Billy Sunday was about securing the place of "real women" in the American home, Sunday is even more famous for his espousal of "muscular Christianity" and his delineation of proper Christian manhood.[28] Wherever Sunday preached, he explicitly challenged the manhood of his (male) listeners. Typical is this passage from a sermon delivered during his New York City revival of 1917: "Oh, do you want to know why you are not a Christian? You aren't man enough to be a Christian! You haven't manhood enough to get up and walk down the aisle and take me by the hand and say, 'I give my heart to Christ.' . . . It takes manhood to be a Christian, my friend, in this old world" (quoted in Frank, 193). Determined to dismiss the purported effeminacy of Christian piety, Sunday provided his followers with a Jesus who was courageous enough to sacrifice his life for his followers. Sunday's Christianity was no place for "weak-kneed intellectuals" or "sissy fellows" who object to "plain talk":

> Many think a Christian has to be a sort of dish-rag proposition, a wishy-washy, sissified sort of galoot that lets everybody make a doormat out of him. Let me tell you, the manliest man is the man who will acknowledge Jesus Christ. . . . You never become a man until you become a Christian. (1970, 92, 90)

Interestingly, the standards of these manliest men were not always consistent with the attributes of masculinity generally prized in American society. Sunday's ideal of masculinity, for example, went beyond more typical American anti-intellectualism and bordered on an attack on reason in general. For Sunday, "When the Bible says one thing and scholarship says another, scholarship can go plumb to the devil" (1970, 204). This derision of the mind was enhanced by his celebration of a physical and emotional Christian masculinity. Indeed, the challenge posed to men to live up to such physical and emotional standards was embodied in the prophetic figure of Sunday himself. A famously acrobatic speaker who punctuated his sermons with dramatic leaps and dives around the pulpit,

Sunday, in the charismatic role of "God's Apostle of Masculinity,"[29] bragged openly about his own physical prowess, daring Satan to fist-fights on the altar to the end of his life. Using his own story and persona as a model and inspiration, Sunday commonly made proclamations such as: "Before I was converted I could go five rounds so fast you couldn't see me for the dust, and I'm still pretty handy with my dukes and I can still deliver the goods with all express charges prepaid. . . . So you don't have to be a dish-rag proposition at all" (1970, 91).[30] Indeed, like Sunday, Jesus himself "was no dough-faced, lick-spittle proposition. Jesus was the greatest scrapper who ever lived" (quoted in McLoughlin 1955, 179).

Jesus might have been the greatest scrapper, but Sunday frequently also used figures from the Old Testament as his models of masculinity. In his sermon "Show Thyself a Man," for instance, Sunday extols the masculine model presented by Moses who had "manhood enough to enrich the whole world." The determination of Moses leading the children of Israel out of Egypt and into the Promised Land was a crucial lesson in manhood taught by the story of Exodus—a lesson learned by David and in turn taught to Solomon. As Sunday explained:

> David wanted Solomon to reach the mountaintop . . . he didn't want him to be an old woman and a sort of sissified proposition, he wanted him to be a man with knotted muscles and a great big heart and plenty of gray matter in his brain. . . ."Be a Man!" Don't simply be a frame to hang a suit of clothes on as is the case with a lot of walking machines that pass for men and ought to be arrested for going around disguised as men.[31]

The lesson in turn taught by Sunday to his audience is not simply one of self-discipline and resolve, but also clarity of identity. Be a Man—not an old woman or a machine—or you do not belong as a citizen in this promised land.

If the calling of "real women" for Sunday was to be wives and mothers who served as the "rampart wall" of American civilization, the calling of Christian men was to protect this virtue and guard the border around the chosen people flourishing in the American home. With Moses, David, Jesus, and Sunday himself serving as models of "God's warriors," the theology of "muscular Christianity" demanded clarity of identity and purpose among the nation's men. In his focus on the reassertion of traditional gender roles as a measure of one's character both as a Christian and as an American (categories that were almost synonymous for him), Sunday reestablished standards of judgment and self-evaluation in a world in which such norms were threatened by

instability. Contesting such norms was thus a violation of religious principle and patriotic duty—indeed, in Sunday's jeremiadic exhortations, it
became the responsibility of American Christian men to stand up to such
"foreign" agitation. The role for "muscular Christians" was patrolling
the boundaries, protecting against insurgency at the edge of America's
shores and at the doors of the home with one's family tucked securely
inside. This conception of Christian men as defensive soldiers in the
army of God's chosen nation animated Sunday's outspoken "Americanism," an attitude that grew increasingly nativistic throughout his life.

## Christian America for American Christians

Critical of the growth of immigration from the early part of his career
as an evangelist, Sunday become more xenophobic during the war years,
and by the 1920s he went so far as to seek the support of the Ku Klux
Klan during a circuit of revivals through the South. Sunday's common
attacks on the "infidels" were often thinly disguised invectives against
citizens who were newly arrived on the nation's shores—especially those
who sullied this promised land with socialist politics and encouraged
labor unrest. As Roger Bruns notes in his biography of Billy Sunday:

> In early 1920 on his way to Norfolk, Virginia, Billy took time to lavish
> praise on the Justice Department and its raids on left-wing radicals around
> the country. "I would stand every one of the ornery wild-eyed I.W.W.'s
> anarchists, crazy socialists, and other types of Reds up before a firing
> squad and save space on our ships," he declared. He would later pro-
> nounce his own sentence on Nicola Sacco and Bartolomeo Vanzetti, Ital-
> ian anarchists convicted of murder in 1921: "Give 'em the juice. Burn
> them if they're guilty. That's the way to handle it. I'm tired of hearing these
> foreigners, these radicals, coming over here and telling us what we should
> do." At one rally hundreds of listeners hurled their hats into the rafters . . .
> when the evangelist called for the government to close the mouths of those
> who preached "their dirty European doctrines in the land of the free and
> the home of the brave."[32]

The onset of World War I provided the setting for Sunday's most influential ministry of "Americanism." His celebrated revival in New York City
began the day after the United States entered the war in April 1917. By
the end of his ten weeks in New York, Sunday, who during this period
"asked God to 'strike down in his tracks' any man failing to register for
the draft"—had led thousands to sign up for enlistment and spend their

"booze money" on war bonds instead (Bruns, 214). Sunday's merging of Christianity and patriotism often led him to end sermons with the Bible in one hand and the flag in the other and conduct altar calls to the strains of the national anthem. Invited to deliver the opening prayer before a session of Congress on January 10, 1918, Sunday told a narrative that figured the United States on a divinely ordained mission to fight the forces of evil on earth. On the floor of the House of Representatives, Sunday proclaimed,

> Almighty God, our Heavenly Father, we thank Thee and rejoice that through faith in Thee and Thy word this Government was built upon that foundation. We thank Thee that the compact signed in the cabin of the *Mayflower* by our ancestors was for democracy, liberty, freedom, and the right to worship Thee according to the dictates of our own conscience. . . . We thank Thee that we are Americans and live beneath the protecting folds of the Stars and Stripes . . . We thank Thee for our happy homes. We thank Thee for our wives and little ones. . . . We thank Thee that as a Nation we have never gone to bed hungry nor scraped the bottom of the flour barrel. . . . Thou knowest, O Lord, that we are in a life-and-death struggle with one of the most infamous, vile, greedy, avaricious, bloodthirsty, sensual and vicious nations that has ever disgraced the pages of history. . . . We pray Thee that Thou wilt make bare thy mighty arm and beat back that great pack of hungry, wolfish Huns whose fangs drip with blood and gore. We pray Thee that the stars in their courses and the winds and waves may fight against them. . . . And Lord, may every man, woman and child . . . stand up to the last ditch and be glad and willing to suffer and endure until final victory shall come . . . and when it is all over we will uncover our heads and lift our faces to the heavens and sing with new meaning—"My country, 'tis of thee, Sweet land of liberty, Of thee I sing . . ."[33]

This prayerful jingoism makes clear that for Sunday, World War I represented another battle in the ongoing war between good and evil, a war that will finally end with God's judgment and Christ's return. If the Mayflower Compact represented the true meaning of the past[34] in its expression of the American mission, and the future contained the fulfillment of that mission in the glory of God's—and America's—victory over evil, the present historical moment was a battle between red blooded American men and those Huns and Reds, saloon keepers and intellectuals, "evolved monkeys" and draft dodgers who were in league with Satan; for Sunday the stakes could not be higher.

Once again, we find in Sunday's political theology a sense of where the battle lines must be drawn and what the nation is fighting for—the home that lies at the core of the American promised land. In the history lesson Sunday offers on the floor of the House of Representatives, the foundational Mayflower Compact with God leads directly to the creation of "our happy homes . . . our wives and little ones . . . our bountiful harvests." The middle-American family lies at the foundation of Sunday's vision of an America without want or hunger. The home—this American Eden now threatened by the "wolfish Huns"— must be preserved by Americans under God. Still bound by its covenant, America will rise to save the nation's source of strength and consequently its divine mission. To rally support for America's role in this international conflict, Sunday repeatedly sounded these themes. In a sermon in New York City the previous spring, for example, Sunday motivated the men in his audience the best way he knew how—by challenging them to prove their masculinity in defending their homes and their nation.

> You belong to America and when America calls, you should go. You belong to your country just as much as you belong to your family. If a band of murderers surrounded your home some night and tried to break in to murder the whole bunch and then set the house afire, what would you do, sneak out and hide somewhere while your brothers were fighting in defense of your home; and then when it was all over, and the smoke of the battle had cleared away, you'd come back in and enjoy the liberty others had won for you. You have no business in this country if you are not willing to fight for it.[35]

Home and country: the Eden in the heart of the American promised land is the contested and hallowed ground in the United States.

Of course, the emphasis Sunday placed on the depiction of this idealized setting of the promised land was matched by his careful delineation of the characters that would inhabit this sacred place. Presuming a naturalized home, divinely ordained and taught through Scripture, Sunday defines the crisis as that which threatens this idealized "family." Sunday cannot see the structural problems within the polity as the cause of this very crisis, because he depicts America as God's chosen nation. Failure reflects a default of personal responsibility to fulfill one's natural role and results from a lack of faith in God. Recall that while Moses' mother "was born a slave," her faith in God and her fulfillment of her maternal responsibilities led to the transformation of her social status from a condition of oppression to one of freedom. As if drawing on the model created by his notions of Moses' mother, Sunday instructed his congregations that the solution to the crisis afflicting the idealized American home was not through political action or structural analysis, but was reached by following the path of faith and duty. The threat to the American home lay in those forces "foreign" to America—be it whiskey, socialism, Germany or another of the many infidel forces. These forces were the work of Satan, and Sunday saw himself as God's warrior, raising an army of Christian men to fight a holy war.

Sunday's belief that the United States was the promised land God kept preserved for his chosen people was the rhetorical basis for his political theology that bound the nation with "God's design." Linking the commitment to God and country, Sunday proclaimed, "God's warrior must first be God's worshipper and Uncle Sam's soldiers must first be Uncle Sam's citizens."[36] In Sunday's political theology, these categories often were confused. To be a citizen of the nation meant to worship the nation and ultimately to fight and be willing to die for the nation as any member of God's chosen people should be prepared to do. Though he spoke often of American freedom, such freedom simply meant that American citizens were free to choose to act in the one way God intended; individuals were to fulfill their roles as Christians and as Americans. Variation was a violation of God's plan, the nation's mission and the Christian's proper path. "No man who swerves in the slightest degree from absolute loyalty should be called an American citizen. . . . America is not a country for a dissenter to live in" (quoted in McLoughlin 1955, 278). That Sunday could extol America for its commitment to freedom and at the same time unabashedly preach a vision of the ideal nation as free from dissent is an illuminating sign of his conception of this promised land and its chosen people.

This constrained sense of uniformity is borne out in the stories Sunday tells and the characters that people his jeremiads. The emphasis on clarity of identity, the exuberance with which Sunday (or as he liked to call himself, "God's mouthpiece") would damn people to hell, the fervent vision of Christian manhood patrolling the borders of home and nation against discordant infiltration and agitation, illuminate a prophetic politics that repudiated pluralist voices in a democratic public sphere. For Sunday, the rationale for the exclusion of divergent belief and opinion was quite simple:

> I do not believe in this twentieth-century theory of the universal fatherhood of God and the brotherhood of man. . . . You are not a child of God unless you are a Christian. . . . [A] man will be a Christian if he is decent, and if he is not a Christian, he forfeits any claim to decency. (Quoted in McLoughlin 1955, 137)

Only decent Christians had any merit to membership in God's chosen people, to citizenship in this American promised land. And decent Americans understood Christianity in the same Manichean way as Sunday himself did—a political theology of "real men" and "real women" who faced a basic choice: conversion to Jesus Christ and salvation of self and nation, or turning their backs on the cross and going to hell, taking civilization with them. As Sunday said in his "A Plain Talk to Men," "No one is living in ignorance of what will become of him if he does not go right and trot square. He knows there is a heaven for the saved and a hell for the damned, and that's all there is to it" (1970, 89). There was nothing to discuss or debate for Billy Sunday; he just presented the choice as dramatically as possible, raised the stakes as high as heaven and as low as hell, and challenged people to decide.

Although Sunday told stories that crossed time and space and recognized the presence of different perspectives, his narrative travels are far from the democratic model of Arendtian visiting. For Arendt, storytelling is crucial to democratic politics because it enables disorientation and openness to hearing beliefs and opinions of others. Sunday's encounters with others never allowed for such space for unfamiliar perspectives. As he says in his sermon, "Nuts for Skeptics to Crack":

> Oh, they have the light of nature in China, the light of nature in Hindustan, the light of nature in Ceylon, the light of nature in India. They have mountains and flowers in India; they have stars and the sun. They have lances to cut . . . filth to smear, excrement to daub on their bodies—but they have no happiness. . . . You have to choose between the teachings of old Confucius, the 'isms' and 'schisms' of infidelity, or the Holy Bible. . . . I will take the Bible, I will take God, I will take Christ, I will take heaven, I will take salvation. . . . (1965, 109)

Clearly, his narrative encounters with difference are nothing more than tourism, as Sunday is unwilling for a moment to take off the familiar lenses with which he views the world. Sunday never begins to locate himself in the culture or belief system of differently situated individuals; rather, he constantly seeks to assimilate others into his vision of American Christianity. His push for uniformity sought to impose his middle-American agrarian ideal as a model for the nation's urban and immigrant populations. Sunday's depictions of biblical figures all reflect this desire to impose American Christianity across time and space. Moses' mother becomes a model of American womanhood, and Jesus, that great scrapper, becomes the pinnacle of American manhood.

Thus while Sunday's popular theology was surely political in its implications, it can hardly be considered an expression of democratic politics. Preaching closed narratives of rigidly defined characters, enlisting muscular Christian soldiers to guard the borders of home and nation, Sunday disparaged the disorientation and subsequent openness to representative thinking that is the hallmark of visiting and the engine of democratic politics. Rather than seek to expand the pluralist "in-between," or enhance the *sensus communis* vital to a vibrant realm of democratic politics, Sunday's evocations of the Exodus narrative limited admittance to the promised land to God's chosen people. Sunday's goal was not the reanimation of atrophied organs necessary to resist the seductive comforts of worldliness, but the pursuit of personal salvation of individuals in the comfort of their homes. Though Sunday had a significant impact on public life in the United States, his vision of social transformation was beholden to an emphatically "anti-political prophetic politics."

## "He is the Leader! He is the Moses!": Martin Luther King Jr.'s Prophetic Vision

If there is any figure in the contemporary American cultural imagination that is widely perceived as an "American prophet," it is Dr. Martin Luther King Jr. This elevated status is at once a testimony to King's own life and to the capacity of the American imagination to contain one of its most radical sons.[37] Recalling the struggles he encountered within the civil rights movement—especially after the watershed year of 1963 that included the successful confrontation in Birmingham and the March on Washington—King's status as an American prophet is even more intriguing.[38] By the end of his life, King began to criticize the nation's political leaders with increasing vehemence such as in his 1967 sermon at the Riverside Church in New York City, in which he declared that his government was "the greatest purveyor of violence in the world today"[39] (1986, 233). And yet, King also was often perceived (and perhaps perceived himself) as sometimes on the margins of the very struggle for racial justice that he obviously had helped generate over the preceding ten years. Recalling DuBois' sense of "double consciousness,"[40] within his lifetime King almost had a "quadruple consciousness"—outside two different communities yet still speaking to each in the language and strategies he had learned from the predominant discourses of both American electoral politics and social movements of resistance. King, as such, is a striking example of the interstitial figure of the prophet, the conscious pariah who moves between margin and the center.[41]

In this sense of "outsider-ness," King was a very different sort of American prophet than Billy Sunday. Yet we should also recognize the common threads of their stories. Neither was born into great power—although of the two, King's place in the black middle-class world of his family's church was—even in the Jim Crow South—a site of greater.personal status than Sunday's impoverished childhood on his grandparents' small farm in post-Civil War Iowa. Both were blessed with certain oratorical gifts that they honed as a means to their wider influence. Both quite emphatically identified themselves as American citizens—although they maintained distinct understandings of what citizenship meant.[42] Both moved in and out of favor with the governing forces in Washington politics. Both, of course, were ministers of the Gospel, and yet their understanding of the paths of Christianity led them toward very different forms of prophetic politics.[43]

My discussion of the prophetic politics of Martin Luther King Jr. focuses on close readings of his sermons, speeches, and writings between 1957 and 1968, highlighting his use of Exodus tropes. King emphasizes two elements of the Exodus narrative that do not figure prominently in most traditional American employments of this sacred story—the notions of wilderness and sojourners.[44] That is, in contrast to Billy Sunday's depiction of America as (an albeit troubled) promised land and the good American Christians in its midst as a chosen people, King never speaks in the exclusive terms of chosen-ness and never directly talks about America as a (once) *realized* promised land, but always in terms of "not yet."

King's prophetic politics were determinedly "this-worldly" and social in their focus.[45] His writings and actions speak of engaged institutional analysis of social conditions, particularly those pertaining to race and class. Unlike Sunday, for whom political activism amounted to calls for military enlistment, support of burgeoning capitalist economics, and the fight against private sins and whiskey interests, King's religious calls for political involvement amounted to a direct engagement with formal and informal social institutions. Indeed, in his jeremiads, King depicts this crisis in America (and the hope for solace) in social, public, and communal terms. As Clayborne Carson and Peter Holloran state in their introduction to the collection of King's sermons, *A Knock at Midnight:* "He devoted less attention to individual redemption and salvation than to the social message of Jesus. King's version of the Christian message applied to the affairs of this world as well as to the afterlife. He conveyed God's judgment of contemporary institutions, especially churches and political institutions" (1998, xiii). From the Oval Office to the steps of the Lincoln Memorial, from Freedom Rides and bus boycotts to voter registration, King's prophetic politics were aimed at the realization of temporal social justice, not individual salvation.

## In the Tradition of Moses

King's status as a modern Moses was conferred on him early and repeated often.[46] During the 1963 struggle in Birmingham, King's best friend and comrade Rev. Ralph Abernathy introduced him to one particular audience, crying out that "He is the leader! He is the Moses" (Branch, 1988, 801). *Jet* magazine had long before conveyed this same message, putting the young King on its cover in 1956 under the caption "Alabama's Modern Moses" (185). While King's status as a Moses on a national scale is quite distinct—only Harriet Tubman has been a comparably perceived figure—the central status of the Exodus narrative in African American religious and political cultures has long been established. Albert Raboteau, in his study *Slave Religion*, writes:

> Slaves prayed for the future of deliverance to come, and they kept hope alive by incorporating as part of *their* mythic past, the Old Testament exodus of Israel out of slavery. The appropriation of the Exodus story was for the slaves a way of articulating their sense of historical identity as a people. That identity was also based, of course, upon their common heritage of enslavement. The Christian slaves applied the Exodus story, whose end they knew, to their own experience of slavery, which had not ended. Exodus functioned as an archetypal event for the slaves. The sacred history of God's liberation of his people would be or was being repeated in the American South. (Raboteau, 311)

Raboteau here speaks to the manner in which a sacred story is used to create a sense of collective identity. What is unclear in Raboteau's statement is what exactly the slaves "knew" as the end of the ancient story of Exodus. The entry of the ancient Hebrews into Canaan is ambiguous at best, especially in light of the books of the prophets.[47] If the "end" Raboteau refers to is the liberation from Egyptian bondage, then this "end" is a crucial—but early—step in the whole of the Exodus narrative. What is quite clear in Raboteau's formulation is that African Americans, whether as slaves or as "free but unequal" people did not consider the United States a promised land.

In *Conjuring Culture: Biblical Formations of Black America,* Theophus Smith carefully explores the relationship between the Puritan theological figurations and the venerable status of the Exodus story in African American culture. Smith notes that the shift in the figuration of America from Israel to Egypt in the predominant black adaptation of the American jeremiad still leaves prophetic politics within the imaginative constraints of the Exodus scaffolding.[48] Smith is well aware of the dangers of the Exodus narrative leading to an exclusive triumphalist political vision, but he also speaks of the subversive potential in African American adaptations of the story:

> Here it is sufficient to posit a difference in worldview between the two traditions: A Puritan American tradition that projects its figural identity and destiny monolithically, as an unambiguous representation of biblical examples, and an African American tradition that is cognitively predisposed to view its reality (its tortuous past, blighted present, and foreseeable future) as simultaneously tonic and toxic. (Smith, 76)

Tonic and toxic—here is the tension of the Exodus story in the African American cultural imagination. The Exodus narrative bears toxic threats as a triumphalist *American* sacred story and offers a tonic of possibilities as model of hope and perseverance as an *African* American sacred story. If, as the eminent scholar of black liberation theology, James Cone, argues, "almost all blacks in America—past and present—have identified Egypt with America, Pharaoh and the Egyptians with white slaveholders and subsequent racists, and blacks with the Israelite slaves,"[49] then how are we to understand the political and religious vision of a figure such as King, who always stressed his American-ness, his commitment to his "beloved country"?[50] Is there no avoiding the profoundly conservative vision of American triumphalism, even when the story is told by "prophets" decrying the social injustice of the national status quo?[51]

I acknowledge the constraints of the sacred story of Exodus in the American context, while also maintaining the possibility for considering the innovation present in certain retellings of narratives. If we analyze King's use of the Exodus narrative in contrast to that of Sunday, the capacity of the Exodus narrative to serve as a tonic—not just for African Americans, but for democratic politics more generally—is illuminated. Although there are undoubtedly conservative elements in King's reformist vision, I highlight the innovations he provided in his use of the American sacred story of Exodus to shape and guide his vision of prophetic politics.

The difference between these two models of prophetic politics lies in the rhetorical and political possibilities enabled by reading the Exodus narrative in a manner that is unconventional in the American context. Rather than simply following in the tradition of "white Protestant" portrayals of Americans as a chosen people in a promised land, King uses the resonant sacred story of Exodus, but emphasizes alternative tropes— those of the wilderness and sojourners.[52] These tropes engender an innovative prophetic politics in large part by opening up this American sacred story to speak to a different conception of time and space, that is, by retelling the Exodus narrative informed by a redemptive approach to history.

Covering this terrain is tricky in large part because of the manner in which King has both been adopted by mainstream America as a prophet *and* is associated with his last, prescient sermon in Memphis in which he famously declared, "I have been to the mountaintop; I have seen the promised land. . . ." The resulting association blithely figures King as an American cheerleader triumphally claiming Americans as a chosen people in a promised land.[53] In many aspects King held conservative beliefs[54] and did pronounce his vision of and for America in an American vernacular, but a careful re-reading of King's sermons will illustrate that his employment of the Exodus tropes of chosen people and promised land was hardly conventional.

## Not Quite Chosen,
## "Not Yet" in the Promised Land

To appreciate the distinctions between King's use of the Exodus narrative and that of more conventional practitioners such as Billy Sunday, it is vital to examine how King conceives of those most typically American Exodus tropes of chosen people and promised land. The promised land is not merely figured as a geographical location, but also a place of clarity with regard to the identity of that realm's "proper" inhabitants.[55]

Not only were these two tropes closely associated but also, as we saw in the preaching of Billy Sunday, they taught a joint lesson about borders. That is (especially prior to the widespread acceptance of the waves of European immigration), the image of the chosen people in America bore a particular cast. As Roger Bruns asserts,

> Billy [Sunday] believed that America was the one true Christian nation in the world, that God was using this country to restore faith. . . . Mistrusting

foreigners and immigrants, he lamented the waning influence of the country's heartland; he stood for the rural ethos against the sin-stenched morality of the metropolis, was suspicious of social reform movements, and
stood four-square for "100% Americanism," an old-fashioned patriotism
of flags and fireworks and lemonade on the Fourth of July. (Bruns, 275)

In proclaiming a vision of the chosen people that did not include Americans such as Sacco and Vanzetti, Billy Sunday was dramatically expressing and producing a conventional middle-American conception of God's
anointed.[56] Middle America did not include immigrants from east or
west, Catholics (for the most part), Jews, or the urban poor (the rural
poor—at least the white rural poor—generally made the grade). Race,
religion, ethnicity, and ideology collapse in the construction of the categories, chosen and "non-chosen."[57]

King inherited this tropic scaffolding—indeed he could not help but be
aware of the sediment that lay at the ground of religious and political
discourse in the United States. But he, not surprisingly, was an uneasy
heir to these conceptions of chosen people and promised land, for he
also inherited alternative tellings of the Exodus narrative that subverted
these conventions. In black Christian tradition in America, the typology
shifted: the normative American chosen people became the forces of the
Pharaoh; the promised land became Egypt. How then does King adopt,
adapt, and use these tropes?

To begin, the centrality of the status of chosen-ness all but drops out
from his political theology, and where it is present, the category chosen
(often transformed into "special") is neither exclusively drawn nor a
product of divine selection. From his earliest political sermons during the
Montgomery bus boycott, King is careful to diffuse the rigid categories
of chosen and "not chosen." His categories are universally drawn even
amid the struggles against segregation.[58] The struggle as King portrays it
is not between different types of people, but between justice and injustice. As he told his audience in Montgomery, in April 1957:

Let us fight passionately and unrelentingly for the goals of justice and freedom, but let's be sure that our hands are clean in the struggle. . . . My
friends, our aim must be not to defeat [Senator] Engelhardt, not to defeat
[Commissioner and White Citizens' Council member] Sellers and [Mayor]
Gayle and [Commissioner] Parks. Our aim must be to defeat the evil that's
in them. And our aim must be to win the friendship of Mr. Gayle and Mr.
Sellers and Mr. Engelhardt. We must come to the point of seeing that our
ultimate aim is to live with all men as brothers and sisters under God and
not be their enemies or anything that goes with that type of relationship.[59]

This emphasis on the proper way to conceive of the opposition in a political struggle was central to King's fundamental commitment to nonviolence. As he explains repeatedly in his sermons:

> The nonviolent resister seeks to lift or rather to change the opponent, to redeem him. He does not seek to defeat him or to humiliate him. . . . Now the method of violence seeks to humiliate and to defeat the opponents, and therefore it leads to bitterness. . . . But the method of nonviolence . . . seeks to win [the oppressor's] friendship and his understanding.[60]

Virtually nowhere does King claim for black people the mantle of chosen that was so emphatically denied them in conventional (white) American uses of the Exodus trope.[61]

While King frequently drew the links between the "children of Israel" and those suffering from racial and economic oppression in America (and colonialism abroad), he was careful to declare that any special status held by black people comes not through anointing by God but by virtue of their historical experience of suffering. That is, the analogy King draws between the ancient people of Israel and black people in the United States is based explicitly on a common history of suffering. "Let us be those creative dissenters," King writes,

> who will call our beloved nation to a higher destiny, to a new plateau of compassion, to a more noble expression of humaneness. . . . We are superbly equipped to do this. We have been seared in the flames of suffering. We have known the agony of being an underdog. We have learned from our have-not status. . . . We . . . have a passion for peace born out of our wretchedness and . . . misery.[62]

Indeed, in sharp contrast to those who used the Bible to justify the inferior status of black people in this country as based on a divine mandate stemming from the "curse of Ham,"[63] King disputes not only this Scriptural interpretation, but also any biblically based assertion that would attribute divine grace exclusively to a particular chosen people.[64] For King, chosen-ness is thus a marker of marginality, of being relegated to the status of a "pariah people."

King does not frame black people as chosen in the traditional sense, nor does he portray Americans as chosen more generally. Despite his commitment to his "beloved country," King—in distinct contrast to the American triumphalism of Billy Sunday—is far more apt to discuss what the United States could learn from other nations than to portray America as a shining beacon.[65] From the earliest of his political speeches to his emphatic critiques of America's engagement in the Vietnam War, King challenged the "special" status commonly ascribed to the nation by its own citizens.

For example, in a remarkable 1957 sermon, "The Birth of a New Nation," delivered at his home Dexter Avenue Baptist Church in Montgomery, King uses the Exodus narrative to celebrate the emergence of Ghana from its "enslavement" as a British colony.

> This nation was now out of Egypt and had crossed the Red Sea. Now it will confront its wilderness. Like any breaking aloose from Egypt, there is a wilderness ahead. . . . *There is always this wilderness standing before you.* . . . It's going now through the wilderness, but the promised land is ahead. . . ." (My italics)

Speaking in a country that has always thought of itself as God's "newly chosen people," speaking in particular to a congregation of black parishioners who had adapted the American sacred story and saw *themselves* as the modern equivalent of ancient Israel, King challenges the exclusive attribution of both these traditions by figuring Ghana into the template of Exodus. Not content to merely open up the Exodus narrative to an inclusive casting of people bound for the promised land, King furthermore challenges American self-righteousness by expounding *not* on the lessons that Ghana can learn from the United States, but rather the lessons the United States can learn from Ghana's enactment of the Exodus narrative.

> Ghana has something to say to us. It says to us first that the oppressor never voluntarily gives freedom to the oppressed. You have to work for it. . . . Freedom is never given to anybody, for the oppressor has you in domination because he plans to keep you there, and he never voluntarily gives it up. . . . Freedom only comes through persistent revolt, through persistent agitation, through persistently rising up against the system of evil. The bus protest is just the beginning. Buses are integrated in Montgomery, but that is just the beginning. . . . [Ghana] says to us another thing. It reminds us of the fact that a nation or a people can break aloose from oppression without violence. . . . Ghana reminds us that whenever you break out of Egypt, you better get ready for stiff backs. You better get ready for some homes to be bombed. You better get ready for some churches to be bombed. You better get ready for a lot of nasty things to be said about you, because you're getting out of Egypt. . . . That's the long story of freedom, isn't it? Before you get to Canaan you've got a Red Sea to confront; you have a hardened heart of a pharaoh to confront; you have the prodigious hilltops of evil in the wilderness to confront. And even when you get up to the promised land you have giants in the land. . . . The road to freedom is a

difficult, hard road. . . . Finally, Ghana tells us that the forces of the universe are on the side of justice.

The story of Exodus may have sacred status in the United States, King reminds us, but this story is not exclusively American in its applications, expressions, or lessons. The legacy of the people of ancient Israel falls on all people who are enslaved or oppressed and yearn for freedom and sovereignty, wherever they may be.[66]

King ends this poignant sermon with a meditation on this lesson of universality and inclusivity found in his innovative (in the American context) reading of the Exodus narrative. Concluding his retelling of the Exodus narrative by citing the biblical retelling of this narrative found in the words of the Hebrew prophets, King declares:

> Then I can hear Isaiah again, because it has profound meaning to me, that somehow, "Every valley shall be exalted, and every hill shall be made low; the crooked places shall be made straight, and the rough places plain; and the glory of the Lord shall be revealed, and all flesh shall see it together."
>
> That's the beauty of this thing: all flesh shall see it together. Not some from the heights of Park Street and others from the dungeons of slum areas. Not some from the pinnacles of the British Empire and some from the dark deserts of Africa. Not some from inordinate, superfluous wealth and others from abject, deadening poverty. Not some white and not some black, not some yellow and not some brown, but all flesh shall see it together. They shall see it from Montgomery. They shall see it from New York. They shall see it from Ghana. They shall see it from China . . .

Clearly, this is an open and inclusive vision. All people will be able to see this vision of justice and freedom (begun to be manifested in the emergence of Ghana). Rather than grounding a vision of chosen-ness in the words of the prophets, King invokes Isaiah to express a message of universal justice.

> God grant that we will get on board . . . because we got orders now to break down the bondage and the walls of colonialism, exploitation, and imperialism . . . to the point that no man will trample over another man, but that all men will respect the dignity and worth of all human personality. And then we will be in Canaan's freedom land. . . . And it's there waiting with its milk and honey, and with all of the bountiful beauty that God has in store for His children. Oh, what exceedingly marvelous things God has in store for us. Grant that we will follow Him enough to gain them.[67]

The promised land that King envisions is open to all and defined by equality and freedom.[68] This utopia lies in the future, King acknowledges, but it is there. The possibilities of the promised land always await "if we follow Him enough to gain them."[69]

In this early sermon, then, King not only reconfigures the central American trope of chosen-ness but also reframes the metaphor of promised land. No longer contained by the nation's borders (as was the case with Billy Sunday), this promised land is essentially without borders at all. It is a place of "universal brotherhood," a home for the "beloved community." More significantly for our purposes, the promised land remains to be realized in the future. This always deferred status of the promised land is of critical importance in reassessing King's prophetic politics and his reliance on the sacred story of Exodus.

Unlike Sunday—and indeed unlike most proponents of the American jeremiad—King adamantly depicts the promised land as a future hope never realized.[70] In a classic sermon on this Exodus theme, "The Death of Evil upon the Seashore," King builds his lesson on the deferred and precarious status of the promised land from what is on its face a triumphal moment in the biblical text: "And Israel saw Egypt dead upon the seashore" (Ex. 14:30). Beginning with a customary application of the Exodus scaffolding to the history of black people in the United States, King declares:

> The Emancipation Proclamation did not, however, bring full freedom to the Negro, for although he enjoyed certain political and social opportunities during the Reconstruction, the Negro soon discovered that the pharaohs of the south were determined to keep him in slavery. Certainly the Emancipation Proclamation brought him nearer to the Red Sea, but it did not guarantee his passage through parted waters. . . . In the great struggle of the last half century between the forces of justice attempting to end the evil of segregation and the forces of injustice attempting to maintain it, the pharaohs have employed legal maneuvers, economic reprisals, and even physical violence to hold the Negro in the Egypt of segregation. Despite the patient cry of many a Moses, they refused to let the Negro people go. (1981, 82)

Despite this hopeful crossing of the Red Sea, however, King takes great pains to remind his listeners and readers that this passage reflects but a moment on the path from bondage to the promised land. As King pushes to the point of this sermon, he substitutes the expected phrase "promised land" with the "Kingdom of God." In making this switch, King highlights his assertion that despite conventional American depictions, the

United States is not the promised land—indeed, the promised land as Kingdom of God has never been and may never be, realized (at least in a sustained way) in this temporal realm.

> All progress is precarious. . . . The Kingdom of God as a universal reality is *not yet.* Because sin exists on every level of man's existence, the death of one tyranny is followed by the emergence of another tyranny. . . . Although man's moral pilgrimage may never reach a destination point on earth, his never-ceasing strivings may bring him closer to the city of righteousness.[71]

If we are not in the "city of righteousness," if the promised land remains tantalizingly in front of us, beckoning as we move toward the future, then where does that leave us in King's retelling of the Exodus story? For King, the setting of this narrative, the setting of his prophetic politics was an alternative Exodus trope—the wilderness.

## Sojourners in the Wilderness

In a public address titled "Give Us the Ballot—We Will Transform the South" delivered May 17, 1957, on the steps of the Lincoln Memorial during the Prayer Pilgrimage for Freedom marking the third anniversary of *Brown v. Board of Education,* King declared: "I conclude by saying that each of us must keep faith with the future. Let us realize that as we struggle alone, but God struggles with us. He is leading us out of a bewildering Egypt, through a bleak and desolate wilderness, toward a bright and glittering promised land" (1986, 200). In this example of his use of the narrative of Exodus, we have a vivid expression of the spatial and temporal setting of King's jeremiad. With the end of legally sanctioned segregation, the nation has moved out of Egypt and into the wilderness, heading toward the promised land. For King, the Exodus narrative is not complete and indeed has never been complete.[72] There is a past of oppression, a present moment in the wilderness that is transient, and a future that is promising but not assured. In the meantime, King suggests, we must learn how to live in the wilderness so that we move on that journey toward the promised land; we must seek to create the Kingdom of God on earth.

The theme of the wilderness was, as I alluded to earlier, not new to the American jeremiad. In the 19th century, the wilderness most often became figured geographically as the expanding American frontier. But with the development of this territory, the presumption that the promised land existed and was expanding *into* the wilderness was normalized. Dislocating the promised land from a spatial framework to a temporal condition of the future, King replaces the (at least once) achieved status of the promised land with the always present condition of the wilderness. As noted, King maintained quite simply that, "There is always this wilderness standing before you." As such, what we should strive for is to direct our wanderings toward the deferred promised land. This theme is evident in many of his sermons (even in his last sermon in Memphis, he has not entered the promised land but has only reached the mountaintop and "*seen* the promised land") but is perhaps best illustrated by King's discussion of the American Dream.[73]

For King the American Dream was best expressed in the foundational words of the Declaration of Independence. If Billy Sunday can be fairly accused of mixing Christianity and Americanism in a blend of patriotic xenophobia, King's tendency to link the ideals set forth by Jefferson and the Kingdom of God runs the risk of traveling the same triumphalist terrain. The differences, as I have been arguing, are still quite acute: Sunday portrayed the United States as a promised land, whereas King suggests that the nation's founding ideals—the American dream, as yet unrealized—are consistent with the principles of the Kingdom of God—also as yet unrealized. As King proclaimed to the students of Lincoln University in his 1961 commencement address:

> For in a real sense, America is essentially a dream, a dream as yet unfulfilled. It is a dream of a land where men of all races, of all nationalities and of all creeds can live together as brothers. The substance of the dream is expressed in these sublime words, words lifted to cosmic proportions: "We hold these truths to be self-evident, that all men are created equal, that they are endowed by their creator with certain unalienable rights, that among these are life, liberty and the pursuit of happiness." This is the dream.
>
> One of the first things we notice in this dream is an amazing universalism. It does not say some men, but it says all men. . . . And there is another thing we see in this dream that ultimately distinguishes democracy and our form of government from all of the totalitarian regimes that emerge in history. It says that each individual has certain basic rights that are neither conferred by nor derived from the state . . . for they are God-given. . . . The American dream reminds us that every man is heir to the legacy of worthiness. (1986, 208)

Until this dream can be fulfilled, until the promised land can be realized, Americans—all Americans—find themselves in the wilderness, facing the temptations of selfishness, of feelings of superiority, of apathy, obstacles that keep the dream from being realized. Indeed, King offers a direct link between the spatial context of the wilderness, the temporal context of an open future, and the inclusive identity of those who might yet realize the "American dream."

King, of course, picks up on this theme in his most famous public address, the "I Have a Dream" speech delivered at the March on Washington in 1963. King begins this speech by challenging the status of the United States as a promised land, distinguishing between the "promise" of Lincoln's Emancipation Proclamation and the reality faced by "Negroes" in America. Decrying the failure of the nation to "rise up and live out the true meaning of its creed," King portrays the nation as what might be termed a "broken-promise land" (e.g., "America has defaulted on this promissory note"). Yet, the United States is not simply a "broken-promise land" for its black citizens, King asserts: "The destiny [of white people] is tied up with our destiny . . . their freedom is inextricably bound to our freedom." The nation is a wilderness for all its people. The "dream" King delineates is, yes, "deeply rooted in the American dream" expressed by Jefferson, but also rooted in his prophetic vision of the Kingdom of God—including the passage from Isaiah previously cited ("I have a dream that one day every valley shall be exalted . . . the glory of God will be revealed and all flesh shall see it together"). In terms of Exodus, the March on Washington can be described as a call for the nation to keep its promise, to meet the conditions of its covenant, and then, accordingly, to emerge from the wilderness of segregation and racial injustice and—as a nation—move toward, and perhaps even reach, the promised land.

Interestingly, in this pivotal address, King speaks not just in terms of wilderness but in the language of *exile*: "the Negro is still languished in the corners of American society and finds himself in exile in his own land" (1986, 209). The difference between the metaphors of wilderness and exile is significant. Wilderness in the pattern of the Exodus narrative implies a status of not yet having entered the promised land. Exile, however, is a condition temporally located in the time of the prophets and conveys a sense of having once entered the promised land but thereafter having seen the "nation" decay as the conditions of the covenant go unfulfilled.[74] Despite the familiarity of the exile metaphor in the American sacred story, King rarely employs this language. That he did so on such a large stage is a fitting indication of the pervasiveness of conventional American versions of the Exodus narrative and (perhaps) King's willingness to speak in the more pro-American vernacular in the midst of this largely critical speech before his largest national audience. In any case, the phrase "exile in his own land" *does* illustrate the mobility and marginality conveyed by Arendt's depiction of "conscious pariahs" as "not being quite at home in the world."

King came to recognize that America remained—and probably would remain—a wilderness. In his sermon "Unfulfilled Dreams" delivered five years later and one month before his death, King addressed the political and spiritual questions that follow from the recognition of the seeming permanence of the wilderness. Beginning with a passage from I Kings 8 in which God tells King David that his dream of building the temple will not be fulfilled in his lifetime, but "it is well that it is in thine heart," King goes on to discuss the importance of intentions and effort in the face of unrealized goals. "The dream may not be fulfilled, but it's just good that you have a desire to bring it into reality. (Yes) It's well that it's in thine heart. . . . Life is a continual story of shattered dreams" (1998, 194).

King is in no way criticizing or backtracking from these dreams, but he recognizes that his vision may not be met in his lifetime. If the dream is to reach the promised land, to transform America into a promised land, then the sermon is a tacit acknowledgment that King will always remain a wanderer, that the nation will remain in a condition of wilderness. If, indeed, "life is a continual story of shattered dreams," then in the language of King's Exodus narrative, the conclusion, once again, is that as individuals and as a nation, "there is always this wilderness standing before you." What is crucial as a standard of judgment is not the failure to reach the promised land, but the intentions one has during the journey. As King says in this sermon, "Salvation isn't reaching the destination of absolute morality, but it is being in the process and on the right road" (King 1998, 196). Rather than despairing of unceasing wandering, King instructs his audience that the true measures of success are intentions and effort, not final attainment.

As the setting of the American sacred story shifts from the conventional, from the promised land to King's wilderness, the characters of the story also are transformed from chosen people to sojourners. As with the shift of setting, the shift of identity carries moral and political implications. Not only is the nation in the volatile state of the wilderness, but also its citizens are defined by metaphors of transience. The theme of sojourners is central to the biblical Exodus story. Conveying not merely a physical sense of mobility, sojourners captures a broader sense of flux—of identity, of morality, of political power, of stability in the course of individual and collective life stories. The Hebrews are instructed to remember that they were sojourners in Egypt, that they are sojourners in the desert and that they ought to treat other sojourners justly. The prophets pick up on this theme, expounding both on the impermanence and fragility of the social and political orders as well as the connection between the metaphor of sojourners and matters of social justice. In emphasizing this trope in his own retelling of the American sacred story, King similarly seeks to remind the American people of this central but neglected Exodus theme.

King employs this trope of sojourners throughout his political ministry. For instance, in his 1957 speech announcing victory in the Montgomery bus boycott, King's primary theme is "to keep on keeping on; keep on moving." In the midst of this speech, King recites the Langston Hughes poem "Mother to Son"[75] and uses Hughes' image of moving up a splintered staircase as a vehicle into the story of Exodus.

> Well, life for none of us has been a crystal stair, but we've got to keep going. . . . Prodigious hilltops of opposition will rise before us but we will keep going. Mountains of evil will stand in our path but we will keep going. (Yes) Oh, we have been in Egypt long enough (Well) and now we've gotten orders from headquarters. The Red Sea has opened for us, we have crossed the banks, we are moving now and as we look back we see the Egyptian system of segregation drowned upon the seashore. (Yes) We know that the Midianites are still ahead. We see the beckoning call of the evil forces of the Amorites. We see the Hittites all around us but, but we are going on because we've got to get to Canaan. (Yes) We can't afford to stop. (Yes) We've got to keep moving.[76]

In his prophetic last sermon in Memphis, the manner in which King uses the Exodus narrative to develop the theme of soujourners is illustrated in perhaps its most poetic and rhetorically rich form. The key to King's construction of this identity of sojourners lies in the manner in which he couples his retelling of the Exodus narrative with the story of the Good Samaritan. Themes of traveling and motion link the stories—fleeing Egypt, wandering in the desert, struggling through the wilderness, walking toward the promised land, negotiating the "bloody pass," moving from the ethereal heights of Jericho to the complex city life in a Jerusalem occupied and governed by a colonial force. These themes are brought to America by reference to the bus boycott in Montgomery, the freedom riders, marches in Montgomery, the 1963 March on Washington, the "great movement" in Selma. Through these metaphors, King draws tight the connection between the Exodus of the Hebrews, the path of the Good Samaritan, and the courageous journey of those struggling for justice in America—struggles that culminated in the marches in support of the sanitation workers' strike in Memphis. But the identity of the sojourner garners its vitality from a still stronger bond between the stories of Exodus and the Good Samaritan. For King, the Exodus narrative has at its heart a *conditional* covenant; God will fulfill God's promise if the people of Israel follow the commandments. The prophets speaking from the position of either exile from, or the decay of, the promised land explain the tenuous state of the Israelites precisely in terms of the Israelite's failure to meet the conditions of the covenant. The future promise of hope is dependent upon the willingness of the Israelites to redeem themselves and their history, to renew their commitment to the covenant made at Mount Sinai. But this covenant runs the danger—a danger often repeated in the history of its political retellings—of leading to an exclusivist ethic based on the emphasis placed on the trope of chosen-ness.

King mediates this problem by pairing Exodus with the story of the Good Samaritan and its lesson about the importance of identifying with other sojourners, encouraging us to "project the 'I' into the 'thou' . . . to be concerned about [one's] brother." King continues,

> The first question the priest asked, the first question the Levite asked, was "If I stop to help this man, what will happen to me?" But the Good Samaritan came by, and he reversed the question: "If I do not stop to help this man, what will happen to him?" That's the question before you tonight. (1986, 284–85)

The conditions of the covenant King is drawing out for his audience require the willingness to "love thy neighbor as thyself," to identify with and be willing to risk one's comfort and perhaps one's life for the other. "If I do not stop to help the sanitation workers, what will happen to them?" (1986, 285). Finally, it is once again critical to note that the stakes of fulfilling—or failing to fulfill—the conditions of this covenant are not personal salvation.[77] Notice that King does not ask the rhetorical question, "If I do not stop to help the sanitation workers, what will happen to *me?*" The status of an individual's soul is peripheral. The stakes for King's prophetic politics are—as always—the creation of a nation that fulfills the "true meaning of its creed." Indeed, King moves from this pairing of Exodus and the Good Samaritan to an all-too-common refrain that in its consistent presence illustrates the political focus of King's vision: "And let us move on in these powerful days, these days of challenge to make America what it ought to be. We have an opportunity to make America a better nation" (1986, 285).

## Redeeming Exodus, Remembering America

The Exodus story that King tells, with its emphasis on wandering in the wilderness toward the promised land, is consistent with what Paul Ricoeur refers to as a "theology of history." Ricoeur argues that such a theology is not

> centered on a given present, [but rather] is a history directed toward a fulfillment. In that sense history is itself the hope of history; each achievement, each fulfillment, is understood as the reinstatement of a promise—the "not yet" of the promise that gives its tension to history. (1995, 204)

This sentiment is central to King's stunning 1963 Thanksgiving sermon in which he uses a question raised by the prophet Elijah ("Is it well?") to help make sense of the feeling in the United States following the assassination of John F. Kennedy.

> It's midnight in human relations. . . . If you don't believe it's midnight, go with me if you will to Jackson, Mississippi . . . to Birmingham, Alabama . . . things are not too well there. The Negro is still dominated politically, exploited economically, segregated and humiliated. The Negro is still a thing to be used rather than a person to be respected. No, things are not too well, but this morning I want to thank God that it is as well as it is. . . . We've broken loose from the Egypt of slavery. We've moved through the wilderness of separate but equal and now we stand at the promised land of integration. I'm here to tell you this morning that we're gonna get in. There have been some sent over to spy the land and they are worried. They're telling us there are giants in the land . . . saying we can't make it in. There *are* giants in the land. Giants of vested interest . . . giants of old political dynasties . . . giants of economic power structure. But thank God, Caleb and Joshua came back with a minority report. They are saying we *can* possess the land. Thank God it is as well as it is. Atlanta is a better city today than it was three years ago. We can go places now we couldn't go one year ago. We have jobs we didn't have five months ago. Thank God it is as well as it is. God has brought us a long, long way. We've been to the mountain tops and [were] able to see the promised land. . . . Though there are trials and tribulations ahead, thank God, it is as well as it is. Even though America has a long, long way to go before she realizes her dream, thank God it is as well as it is. Even though we have met the storms of disappointment and the jostling winds of hatred are still blowing and the mighty torrents of false accusations are still pouring on us, thank God, it is as well as it is. Even though we do not know what tomorrow will bring, thank God it is as well as it is. Even though we do not know what the future holds, we know who holds the future. Thank God it is as well as it

is. Even though we are burdened down by the agonies of life, even though
we can't understand, even though we cry out my God, my God, why?—
Thank God it is as well as it is. This morning it is well with my soul, that is
what we can cry out on this Thanksgiving morning.[78]

In this fully developed use of the narrative scaffolding of Exodus, King
takes his listeners on a sojourn from Egypt to the wilderness to the
mountains overlooking the promised land and then—with hope and
trepidation—back to the wilderness.[79] The metaphorical context is
defined by the shifting sands of the desert—a context palpable in a
despondent nation in November 1963. Progress is at best precarious
and the promised land is perpetually deferred—but always there is
hope; on Thanksgiving morning we can cry out, "Thank God it is as
well as it is."

In dislocating the privileged status of America in general and some
Americans in particular, King not only emphasizes a radically inclusive
equality in his rendering of the sacred story, but also paves the way for
enacting another significant theme from the Exodus narrative. Given the
impermanence and fragility attendant with the metaphors of sojourners
in a wilderness, King's re-tellings of the Exodus story stress the important theme of memory. Speaking from the position of those who have
been "overlooked" by normative American jeremiadic accounts of the
nation's history, King declares emphatically, "We were here." King made
this point often, as in his sermon "Remaining Awake Through a Great
Revolution," which he delivered at the National Cathedral in Washington on March 31, 1968, and in which he announced his plans for a Poor
People's March on Washington.

> We are coming to engage in dramatic non-violent action, to call attention
> to the gulf between promise and fulfillment; to make the invisible visible.
> . . . Before the pilgrim fathers landed at Plymouth, we were here. Before
> Jefferson etched across the pages of history the majestic words of the Dec-
> laration of Independence, we were here. Before the beautiful words of the
> Star Spangled Banner were written, we were here.
>
> For more than two centuries, our forbears labored here without wages.
> They made cotton king, and they built the homes of their masters in the
> midst of the most humiliating and oppressive conditions. If the inexpress-
> ible cruelties of slavery couldn't stop us, the opposition we face now will
> surely fail.
>
> We're going to win our freedom because both the sacred heritage of our
> nation and the eternal will of the almighty God are embodied in our echo-
> ing demands. . . . [80]

Coming from King, the proclamation bears striking rhetorical weight. He is not simply reminding the nation of the story it likes to tell about itself, but about the history of slavery it prefers to ignore. King's message is then not simply about memory but about "redemptive history." The lessons of slavery are still to be defined. The future is still to be determined, and it will be shaped by the interpretation of this past, of the "sacred heritage" of the nation. By opening up the past and the future to reinterpretation—albeit in the resonant terms of the Exodus narrative—King invites listeners to visit, to hear familiar stories told in unfamiliar ways. Encouraging reanimation of the "organs" necessary for engagement in democratic public life, King retells history in a way that expands the "in-between," that places new chairs at the table from which individuals can gain new perspectives regarding national identity.

To recall the first section of this chapter, I began my discussion of Sunday's prophetic politics by discussing his 1918 prayer on the floor of the House of Representatives in which he quoted the song "My County 'Tis of Thee." In the best known of his own expressions of prophetic politics, King also quoted from this dedicatory anthem, although to quite different effects. When King concludes his speech at the 1963 March on Washington by singing, "My country 'tis of thee, sweet land of liberty; of thee I sing; land where my fathers died, land of the pilgrim's pride; from every mountain side, let freedom ring," he is reminding the nation that it is the country of the African Americans too, that black fathers and mothers died—and died horribly—in this land. As Martha Solomon concludes, "The language of the song assumes 'new meanings' because it highlights blacks' participation in the government ('my country') and the good faith sacrifices they have made to sustain their part of the covenant ('land where my fathers died')" (Solomon, 73). In other words, in claiming "My Country 'Tis of Thee," King is redeeming history so that he might tell a story that projects a new vision of the United States into the future. His own conclusion to the song is, quite simply, "[I]f America is to be a great nation, this must come true"—if the wandering in the wilderness is to cease, if America is to be a promised land, its history must be redeemed. For "freedom to ring . . . from every village and hamlet, from every state and city," all Americans must recognize and respect the historical (and political) claim of each person—"all God's children," "all flesh"—must sing "my country," and when that happens, the nation will have a "new" anthem: "and . . . sing in the words of the old Negro spiritual, 'Free at last, free at last; thank God Almighty, we are free at last'" (1986, 219–20).

A redemptive conception of history suggests that because our understanding of the past is open to creative analysis, the future too is open to an array of possibilities. Rather than conceiving of a future that must meet the fixed meaning of history (the "reconciliatory" approach to history) with a redemptive attitude, there is, in Nietzsche's words, "no telling what may yet become part of history" and as such, no telling what may yet become the future. The meaning of the past, the direction of the future—at least in the temporal realm of the wilderness—is not dictated by God but open to human creativity. Such an attitude demands active human engagement in the making and remaking of history—and, in turn, a concerted grappling with the political process.

So often, religious voices in America have taught a detachment from politics, preferring (as with Sunday's Moses) to wait on God rather than create social and political change. King's redemptive approach to history confronts this tension directly in his sermon "The Answer to a Perplexing Question." Beginning with the very Niebuhrian axiom, "man by his own power can never cast evil from the world," King proceeds to use the framework of Exodus to teach a lesson about the importance of immediate and continual political engagement, despite the limits of human power (1981, 129).

> When Moses strove to lead the Israelites to the Promised Land, God made it clear that he would not do for them what they could do for themselves. "And the Lord said unto Moses, Wherefore criest thou unto me? Speak unto the children of Israel, that they go forward." [ . . . ]We must pray with unceasing passion for racial justice, but we must also use our minds to develop a program, organize ourselves into mass nonviolent action, and employ every resource of our bodies and souls to bring an end to racial injustice. . . . No prodigious thunderbolt from heaven will blast away evil. . . . Man is no helpless invalid left in a valley of total depravity until God pulls him out. (1981, 131–32)

"Human salvation," King says elsewhere, "lies in the hands of the creative maladjusted," lies, in other words, in the hands of those who are not willing to accept historical patterns and political hegemony, but who instead are eager to rewrite history and challenge conventions (1981, 27). King's political vision sought to meet this challenge in an increasingly systematic fashion. Aiming not just for personal salvation, but human salvation, King sought answers that reached beyond individual behavior to social structures. This is a far cry from Sunday's conclusion that all individual struggles result from sin and personal irresponsibility (and thus can be cured by conversion to Christ); King argues instead that the problem of black self-hatred, of low self-esteem and fear was a direct result of the history of slavery and then-present conditions of segregation. This theme is sounded clearly in his "Letter from a Birmingham City Jail":

> When you suddenly find your tongue twisted and your speech stammering as you seek to explain to your 6-year-old daughter . . . that Funtown is closed to colored children, and see the depressing clouds of inferiority begin to form in her little mental sky, and begin to distort her little personality by unconsciously developing a bitterness toward white people . . . when you are harried by day and haunted by night by the fact that you are a Negro, living constantly at tiptoe stance never quite knowing what to expect next, and plagued with inner fears and outer resentments; when you are forever fighting a degenerating sense of "nobodiness"; then you will understand why we find it difficult to wait." (1986, 292–93)

This "degenerating sense of nobodiness" is the condition of a pariah people from the perspective of the center of society. Nobodiness is a product of a fundamental lack of recognition in the world. King's response is the embrace of the difficult work of the "conscious pariah"—the figure who recognizes his or her status and turns back toward the world in the effort to upset the easy comforts of those at home in the world. Consider the emblematic signs worn by civil rights protesters that simply proclaimed, "I AM A MAN." This act is that of a conscious pariah. It is a declaration that says: Your laws treat me as less than human. You would prefer that I stay hidden on the margins, "living constantly at tiptoe stance." But here I am proud, walking on your public streets—my public streets—and you must countenance me. You must recognize me. You must listen to me. And if it makes you uncomfortable, if it unsettles your sense of place and identity, good. Because only when you are unsettled, only when you too are not quite at home in the world, can democracy begin.[81]

## Visiting and Democratic Politics in Dark Times

After 1963, King realized that the state of integration was no simple promised land—that the end of the strange career of Jim Crow did not lead to conditions of political and personal equality. As his political vision became more radical between 1963 and 1968, King began to sharpen his critical analysis and explore the links joining racial injustice, economic inequality, and violence. Ultimately, King sought not just integration, but what he called a "revolution of values."

This shift is evident in the change in the manner in which King understood and used the story of the Good Samaritan in his political ministry. As noted earlier, King saw in this story a message about the responsibility each individual sojourner has to reach out to other sojourners lying on "life's roadside." By the end of his life, King pushed the message of this parable further and saw a lesson about structural values.

> A true revolution of values will soon cause us to question the fairness and justice of many of our past and present policies . . . we are called to play the good Samaritan on life's roadside; but that will be only an initial act. One day we must come to see that the whole Jericho road must be transformed so that men and women will not be constantly beaten and robbed as they make their journey on life's highway. . . . A true revolution of values will look uneasily on the glaring contrast of poverty and wealth. With righteous indignation, it will . . . say: "This is not just." (1986, 240–41)

This revolution in values is not merely a call for personal change, but clearly demands a commitment to pursuing structural and institutional transformation. King's political analysis extended beyond the confines of domestic policy (where he promoted a guaranteed annual income, among other policies). In the last years of his life, King became an outspoken opponent of the American engagement in the Vietnam War. In stark contrast to Sunday's vociferous support of American militarism, King extends his espousal of non-violence to foreign policy.

In his 1967 sermon at New York City's historic Riverside Church, "A Time to Break Silence," King links the war in Vietnam with domestic indifference to systematic racism and economic inequality. What is striking about this sermon (beyond even his harsh remarks about the unjust violence of the United States, assertions that understandably further alienated King from the Johnson administration) is the manner in which King's political analysis is rooted in democratic visiting. King's political analysis is founded on his willingness to engage in representative thinking—in this case, in imagining how the United States looks from the perspective of a Vietnamese peasant.

> What do the peasants think as we ally ourselves with the landlords and as we refuse to put any action into our many words concerning land reform? What do they think as we test our latest weapons on them, just as the Germans tested out new medicines and new tortures in the concentration camps of Europe? . . . What do they think of us in America when they realize that we permitted the repression and cruelty of Diem which helped

bring them into being as a resistance group in the south? . . . How can they trust us when we now charge them with violence after the murderous reign of Diem and charge them with violence after we pour every new weapon of death into their land? . . . They question our political goals and they deny the reality of a peace settlement from which they will be excluded. Their questions are frighteningly relevant. . . .

Here is the true meaning and value of compassion and nonviolence when it helps us to see the enemy's point of view, to hear his questions, to know his assessment of ourselves. From his point of view we may indeed see the basic weaknesses of our own condition, and if we are mature, we may learn and grow and profit from the wisdom of the brothers who are called the opposition.[82]

King's willingness to engage in this type of visiting was central to his political analysis throughout his life as a "prophet." As early as 1957, he declared to the activists gathered at the Highlander School that one of the basic problems in the South was that:

The channels of communication between whites and Negroes are now closed. Certainly this is tragic. Men hate each other because they fear each other; they fear each other because they don't know each other; they don't know each other because they can't communicate with each other; they can't communicate with each other because they are separated from each other.[83]

The emphasis on communicating across experiential and ideological divides—the essence of Arendtian visiting, and the key to open and participatory democratic politics—remained at the heart of King's prophetic vision even as his appreciation of the complexity of inequality in the United States grew. Thus, in 1961, he sounds this theme, asserting:

The world in which we live has become a single neighborhood. . . . In a real sense, we must all learn to live together as brothers or we will all perish together as fools. We must come to see that no individual can live alone; no nation can live alone. We must all live together; we must all be concerned about each other." (1986, 209)

King here articulates a clear and definitive understanding of the need to expand the "in-between," to cultivate the *sensus communis* vital to robust democratic politics. The true "revolution in values" he sought would be a product of citizens visiting with one another in this vibrant, pluralist public realm. In his democratic rendering of Exodus, all people are sojourners in a fragile and tempestuous wilderness; no voice should be automatically privileged or dismissed. The path to the promised land requires representative thinking.

THE contrast between the prophetic politics of Billy Sunday and Martin Luther King Jr. enhances our understanding of the relation between religious narratives and politics in the United States. While conventional uses of the sacred story of Exodus have built substantial sediment of self-understanding for a growing nation, the narrative structure also allows considerable room for innovation. Sunday's use of the Exodus framework to develop a theology of muscular Christianity is a remarkable innovation. However, this rhetorical development ultimately serves as merely a new wrinkle in a nostalgic religious vision of American Christian triumphalism. Employing Exodus tropes to reaffirm national, familial, and individual borders, Sunday's prophetic vision is essentially "anti-political" in that it encourages no dissent, no discussion, no representative thinking, no visiting with those who espouse different beliefs or the legitimacy of divergent conceptions of history.

As powerful as this traditional use of the Exodus narrative in America may be, Martin Luther King Jr.'s political ministry instructs us that the sacred story need not be put to conservative, nostalgic, or triumphal ends. Dislocating the conventional jeremiadic tropes of chosen people and promised land, King's innovative use of the Exodus story portrays a different cast of characters in a different setting. In his hands, the American sacred story tells of sojourners in a wilderness. Such a shift engenders redemptive history that reminds much of the nation of what it has forgotten, an approach that brushes history against the grain. This redemptive approach to history is a central component of a critical and systematic social analysis and concomitant political activism.

The differences between these two visions of prophetic politics are apparent in their respective attitudes toward worldliness. Sunday never sought to develop such a *sensus communis,* nor enhance his listeners' capacity for representative thinking. Nor did he embrace the hard work of the conscious pariah in a manner akin to the prophetic politics of King. Sunday at once valorizes the private sphere on the margins of public life and simultaneously locates that safe home at the center of the country where it "belongs." Indeed, Sunday was concerned with the "moral decay" in America, but he never portrayed his fellow Christians as pariahs; they were the salt of the earth, the bedrock of the nation, not its outcasts. Faced with the challenge of "not being quite at home" in a changing nation, Sunday encourages his listeners to choose "worldlessness" over "homelessness."

King, in contrast, was dealing with a "pariah people," second-class citizens suffering under the heat of segregation and injustice. Yet, rather than accept the worldlessness imposed by disenfranchisement and the culture of white supremacy, King, to the consternation of many of his fellow ministers, directed the "pariah people" back into the world. He helped them become "conscious pariahs," teaching and encouraging people to re-animate their "atrophied organs" that enable engagement in public life. The civil rights movement was designed to re-create a robust "in-between"; the revitalized *sensus communis* was required for the success of the movement. Indeed, the difficulty of maintaining the momentum of the civil rights movement is a testimony to the difficulty of sustaining the development of this "in-between" over time. We thus must consider both the claiming of the status of a "pariah people" and, more importantly, if and how Promise Keepers and Call to Renewal respond to the threat of worldlessness. What efforts do these more recent prophetic social movements make toward the difficult task of revitalizing the "atrophied organs" of citizens in an era of dark times for democracy?

## Chapter Four
## Promise Keepers: Delivering Brothers from Democracy

God told Moses to "send some men to explore the land of Canaan, which I am giving to the Israelites" (Num. 13:1). . . . During the preceding year those people had witnessed the most spectacular signs of God's favor that any nation could ever hope to see. God humbled Pharaoh through the various plagues and the Passover. He then parted the waters of the Red Sea and later destroyed the army of Egypt as he closed those same waters. The Israelites had seen God provide water in the desert and had eaten manna, the daily proof that He had not forgotten them. Now God wanted to keep His promise to Abraham and fight for His children as they entered the Promised Land. This was the moment of God's favor.

When the scouts returned from Canaan their report left no doubt in the people's mind that the land was, indeed, very good. . . . One would think that now they'd rejoice in the goodness of God and seize the land of promise. But they didn't.

Out of fear of their own inadequacies, they doubted the will and power of God to triumph through them. . . . By failing to seize the moment they sealed their fate. . . .

The time has come! . . . While we have been asleep in our routines, the enemy has attacked relentlessly, cutting away at the spiritual heritage of America. If we don't respond, time could run out! . . . We're in a spiritual war. . . . There can no longer be any doubt or confusion about what is required. [Here] is our trumpet call. [Here are] our marching orders!
—**Randy Phillips,** *Seven Promises of a Promise Keeper*

Throughout the decade of the 1990s the United States was torn by the "culture wars." Debates about abortion, poverty, sexuality, crime and punishment, pornography, political correctness and other issues split the nation. Once the Berlin Wall came tumbling down in 1989 and the Cold War came to an abrupt end, citizens and public figures in the United States quickly turned inward—and the spirit of celebration evaporated and was replaced by a sentiment of stinging critique. From the controversy surrounding the nomination of Clarence Thomas to the Supreme Court to the Clinton-Lewinsky scandal, from Newt Gingrich's Republican "Contract with America" to the bitter conclusion to the Bush-Gore presidential race in 2000, the public realm in the United States was marked by a decade of accusation, threats, reprisals, and disgust; the hopefulness of 1989 gave way to despair and "dark times" for democracy.

Promise Keepers was both a manifestation of and a response to these culture wars in the American public realm. Preaching a jeremiad consistent with Pat Buchanan's prominent declaration at the 1992 Republican Convention in Houston that there was a "religious war going on for the soul of America," Promise Keepers sought to enlist men to be holy "warriors" to fight in this grand battle.[1] Unlike Buchanan and other more conventional political figures, Promise Keepers offered an innovative battle plan—a response to "crisis" that was issued by men, for men, calling them to join a Christian social movement that sought to transform the world not through governmental action but through prayer, accountability groups, and the reclamation of the American home. Promise Keepers joined the religious war with an approach that utilized the language and symbols of sports and the military to make religious piety more palatable for men and reeducated men to help make them safe for religion. And Promise Keepers captured the therapeutic impulse in American culture, discovering and developing a niche in the flooded market of dysfunctionality by focusing on issues facing men in a society undergoing significant change on many levels, but especially in terms of gender roles and economic relations. Similar to the way it overcame the effeminizing attributes of Christian piety, Promise Keepers' masculinist ethos also made the intimacy of self-help accountability groups safe for "real men."

Promise Keepers was founded in 1990 by Bill McCartney, then University of Colorado head football coach. Impassioned by the idea of gathering together a stadium full of men in the name of Jesus, McCartney and a group of his friends and associates started praying and planning. Forty-two hundred men attended the first Promise Keepers event held at the University of Colorado basketball arena in July 1991. In the ensuing 14 years of its existence, Promise Keepers has organized more than 170 stadium and arena conferences and claims to have reached more than 5 million men through these events.[2] Promise Keepers has sponsored special conferences for religious leaders, including "the world's largest gathering of Christian clergy," in which 39,000 ministers, pastors, chaplains, and priests gathered in Atlanta's Georgia Dome.[3]

Promise Keepers also strives to reach men through "weekly radio and television broadcasts, the Internet, 16 CDs, more than two dozen books, Bible studies and multi-media resources, plus outreach to local churches."[4] Inspired by the success of Promise Keepers, conservative Christian women's organizations such as Promise Reapers, Heritage Keepers, Women of Faith, and Suitable Helpers have arisen to help women find effective ways of supporting their "soldiers of God" as these men march toward the ideal of "Christian masculinity."

Promise Keepers is most widely known for its October 1997 Stand in the Gap event in Washington, D.C. Hundreds of thousands of men (and by some estimates more than 1 million) gathered on the Mall in the nation's capital to atone for their sins, reassert their beleaguered masculinity, and pray for the "deliverance of the nation."[5] Especially during the period surrounding the Stand in the Gap event, Promise Keepers reaped remarkably positive public exposure.[6] It continues to be celebrated by leading national politicians and small churches all across the land.[7]

Although Promise Keepers has clearly declined in size, resources, and influence since the peak of its stature in 1997–98, it remains an active and vibrant organization with 70 paid staff members, countless volunteers, and significant financial resources, affiliations, and aspirations. It continues to sponsor stadium and arena events across the United States (18 such events in 2004 and 20 more planned for 2005) and has international outreach efforts in Canada, the United Kingdom, Australia, New Zealand, South Africa, Thailand, and the Philippines. In 2003, Promise Keepers launched its "Platoon Challenge"—an ambitious endeavor to bring one million men to Christ in two years. In short, the sense that Promise Keepers is in decline must be measured against its extraordinary success; many social movements would be very pleased to enjoy the current status of Promise Keepers.

Promise Keepers now faces perhaps its most difficult challenge. In 2003, McCartney, who had been the most prominent public figure in the movement, stepped down as president and CEO to spend more time with his ailing wife and was replaced by Thomas Fortson. This transition came at a time when many have concluded that Promise Keepers has run its course. Fortson's response to such conclusions is illustrative of the past and future identity of Promise Keepers. "A movement certainly has a beginning and an end to it. . . . I think we've found this is more than a movement. We're dealing with men, and the needs of men have not disappeared. We, as men, are needier than we were 13 years ago."[8] In this brief statement Fortson captures much of the ethos of Promise Keepers—it is a movement and "more than a movement"; it relies on a linear sense of time that moves from beginning to end, and this linearity is informed by a narrative of decline because men need Promise Keepers "now more than ever;" and finally, Promise Keepers is both by and for men and (yet) speaks in the language of therapeutic "neediness." The development of a men's only, therapeutic, Christian social movement that seeks to transform the world by ministering to men's spiritual needs is a stunning innovation in American culture—and it poses a distinct challenge to democratic politics.[9]

Unlike most social movements that respond to social and cultural challenges with an emphatic commitment to engage in the difficult work of politics, Promise Keepers' response to the culture wars has been a concerted effort to help men create a stable, self-contained space protected from the corrupting influences of the world. If democratic politics requires the recognition of the value of pluralism, the enhancement of *sensus communis,* the expansion of the "in-between," and a commitment to worldliness, Promise Keepers instead encourages men not to pursue social transformation through political engagement, but personal transformation through private commitments of faith. Promise Keepers does not want men to become conscious pariahs who recognize their marginal status and seek to disrupt the arrogant comforts of those too "at home in the world." Rather, Promise Keepers encourages men to seek out the margins of a debased society and in this marginal space develop joyful and intense—but unworldly—relationships with other believers on the margins. Promise Keepers speaks in the language of sports and war, but situates the playing field and battleground not in the public realm of politics but in the private space of an individual man's body and soul. Promise Keepers may be creating godly warriors, but the battles they fight are largely private and personal rather than public and collective. To illustrate the anti-political prophetic politics of Promise Keepers, I focus on the jeremiads and "wisdom literature" of this Christian social movement, highlighting the innovative retellings of the Exodus narrative that help communicate its resonant and influential political theology.

## Promise Keepers and the Question of Politics

I want to briefly clarify a crucial and contentious point concerning the "political" character of Promise Keepers, since throughout my analysis, I refer to the *political* theology of the organization. The contentious element of speaking of the political vision of Promise Keepers is that the social movement explicitly and repeatedly declares that it is *not* a political organization, that it has no political agenda, that "politics simply can't touch issues of the heart."[10] As Promise Keepers asserts at its website, "Promise Keepers is politically neutral and is not politically motivated in any way. Promise Keepers has no candidate to endorse, no legislation to advance, and no partisan political agenda."[11]

To illustrate the "politics" of Promise Keepers, I can simply recount the social movement's often repeated stands on such pivotal social issues as abortion and homosexuality. For example, the Promise Keepers website has a page on the "abortion/pro-life issue," where it explains that one of the truths "men of action and conviction" must recognize is to "respect the sanctity of life and defend the defenseless [and] those in the womb are some of the most defenseless of all human beings." However, in the effort to maintain its pretense of being apolitical, Promise Keepers refrains "with regard to the pro-life movement" from "prescrib[ing] specifically how men should influence their world."[12] At its conferences some Promise Keepers speakers have been more passionate in their anti-abortion rhetoric. In Indianapolis in 1999, for example, Steve Farrar complained that the Supreme Court contradicted God and the Bible in a recent ruling holding that the "fetus" is not a "baby." "I want to tell you something else," Farrar continued,

> any political leader that supports partial birth abortion, where you take a full termed baby, jam scissors in the back of their head, put a catheter in there and suck their brains out, don't you tell me you're a Christian. That's a stench in the nostrils of a Holy God.[13]

With regard to homosexuality, Promise Keepers also has a page at its website where it makes its official "Homosexuality Statement" that tries to portray its position in purely theological terms.

> We believe that the Bible clearly teaches that homosexuality violates God's creative design for a husband and a wife and that it is a sin (Leviticus 18:22, Romans 1:24–27, 1 Corinthians 6:9–10) . . . [and yet] we invite homosexuals to be recipients of God's mercy, grace and forgiveness, available to everyone through a personal relationship with Jesus Christ. We therefore support their being included and welcomed in all our events.[14]

This sense of welcome should be understood in the context of Bill McCartney's outspoken support for Amendment 2 in Colorado, a 1992 state ballot measure prohibiting the granting of "special rights" to homosexual citizens. At a news conference to support the ballot measure and clarify his own position, McCartney referred to homosexuality as "an abomination against almighty God" (quoted in Abraham, 25). While McCartney maintains that his involvement in the campaign for Amendment 2 was "independent" of Promise Keepers, such maneuvering is more artful than credible, especially since two organizations—Exodus International[15] and Harvest USA—seeking to "cure" homosexuals by ending their "sexual disorders" through Jesus, regularly participate in Promise Keepers' stadium events as ministries "affiliated" with the social movement. In addition, in response to the efforts to have same-sex marriages legally recognized in the United States, the new president Tom Fortson proclaimed:

> I am not surprised at the confusion in America over this issue. While some courts and governmental agencies are attempting to change our laws regarding marriage, the struggle goes deeper than our legal codes. The morality of our law has its basis in the historic teaching of Scripture. Although Promise Keepers does not advocate for or against any legislation, political candidate or party, many of the issues of the day have a moral dimension. Promise Keepers stands strongly in support of the institution of marriage between a man and a woman as central to our civilization.[16]

As with the issue of abortion, these statements and positions can only be construed as "not political" in the narrowest of senses.[17] As an organization, Promise Keepers does not endorse candidates or legislation. However, as an organization, Promise Keepers does take stands on social issues, *and* its leaders can and do support specific positions and even candidates.[18] Thus, despite its emphatic claims to the contrary, it is clear that Promise Keepers is indeed a "political" organization.

Much like Billy Sunday, Promise Keepers preaches an anti-political prophetic politics. Promise Keepers has a *political* vision, and proclaims a *political* theology, but teaches that democratic political participation is, at best, a waste of time and energy or, at worst, a tainted activity that threatens to pollute the purity of God's chosen soldiers. Promise Keepers is thus a paradoxical, but political, social movement. It seeks to move its members away from the public sphere and toward the private sphere. It takes politically contested issues, such as questions regarding abortion and homosexuality, out of the public sphere of debate and discussion and moves them into the private realm of "issues of the heart."

As opposed to the feminist movement against which Promise Keepers commonly defines itself,[19] this Christian social movement argues not that "the personal is political" but rather that "the political is personal." This appropriation and reversal of the feminist ethic responds to social issues with therapeutic answers. Promise Keepers tells a story in which the terrifying and complex social "crisis" in the United States can be resolved only by taking that which is political and moving it back into the realm of the moral, the religious, the personal. The portrayal of the "social problems" threatening America, as personal and not political issues is, of course, a crucial feature of the jeremiads of Promise Keepers. Much of the way Promise Keepers delineates its identity and establishes the narrative context within which it acts hinges on the jeremiadic stories the social movement tells. It often relies on the innovative use of the resonant tropes drawn from the Exodus narrative.

## Promise Keepers' Jeremiads

Promise Keepers is clear about its desire to be the latest in the grand tradition of revivalist movements in the United States. In fact, Promise Keepers often explains its presence and mission in contemporary America by citing the capacity of revivalist social movements to change the political order of the nation. In his contribution to the central work of Promise Keepers philosophy, Bishop Wellington Boone writes:

> America's First Great Awakening . . . gave the colonists a unified biblical view of the principles of freedom and helped pave the way for the American Revolution. The Second Great Awakening, which preceded the Civil War, brought a conviction from God that slavery was a sin. . . . [T]oday . . . America needs revival. . . . And as men are transformed, the course of a nation can be changed. (1994, 26)

To appreciate Promise Keepers' vision for altering the course of the nation, we must examine both how Promise Keepers depicts the current state of America and the men whom they foresee leading the changes.

Virtually every sermon and essay in the Promise Keepers literature includes a depiction of the "crisis" in America. Of all these declarations, perhaps the most vivid portrayals of the sinfulness of the United States come from Bill Bright. In his Promise Keepers endorsed book, *The Coming Revival: America's Call to Fast, Pray, and "Seek God's Face,"* Bright, the founder and president of the Campus Crusade for Christ, writes,

> When reading the many portions of the Scripture, including the major and minor prophets, we are reminded again and again that if we—as a nation and as individuals—obey God, He will bless us. But when we disobey Him, He disciplines us. Tragically, we as a nation have disobeyed and

grieved God. . . . As a result, an avalanche of evil, crime, immorality, abortion, and drug addiction has devastated our country and broken the heart of our Lord. This disintegration of America is not news to you because, like ancient Israel, our nation has for the most part forgotten God and failed to obey his commands (Deuteronomy chapters 8 and 28).

Our nation has become like Sodom and Gomorrah, only worse, because we, as the most powerful nation on earth, export our pornographic filth and corruption to the rest of the world. We are not only destroying ourselves but are playing a major role in helping to destroy the moral and spiritual values of the rest of the world as well. (Bright, 22–23).

Bright later continues:

Crime and violence among our youth, race riots, rape, divorce, sexual promiscuity, teen pregnancy, abortion, AIDS, and drug and alcohol addiction have become epidemics. Like a cresting tidal wave they threaten to sweep away every decent vestige left in our society. As a result, Americans are experiencing a deepening sense of powerlessness and pessimism over the future of the country. (Bright, 51–52)

In these remarkable passages, Bright invokes the story of Exodus and the subsequent prophetic legacy to both describe and produce a state of crisis in the United States today. Bright defines the magnitude of the predicament (God's favor versus God's judgment), names the cause of God's displeasure, declares the social and political effects of this grievous sin of disobedience, and concludes with the suggestion that redemption lies waiting if Americans—the modern equivalent of "ancient Israel"—renew their covenant with God. While Bright is surely depicting what he conceives of as the nature of the troubles facing the nation today, he is, in telling this narrative, also generating a particular social, theological, and political vision of crisis and solace. Bright's vision of the causes or signs of the crisis are predominantly "social" or "personal": lack of prayer in school, abortion, drug addiction, divorce, teen pregnancy, pornography. Disaster in the form of God's judgment looms for the United States. Indeed, Bright uses the language of natural disaster—an "avalanche of evil" and "cresting tidal wave"—and this natural disaster has a super-natural origin: the response of an angry and broken-hearted God punishing a disobedient people. Solace is not immediately available (it is difficult to stop the momentum of an avalanche) in the pre-millennial vision of Bright. Order can be found only after the final judgment. The only hope for the nation is for a revival to sweep the land.

For Promise Keepers, the once proud nation is now living on borrowed time. Although an "avalanche of evil" has devastated the country,

God has still not shown the full measure of the wrath that is in his broken heart. As McCartney explained in an interview in the *Washington Post,*

> We are a nation whose morality has been on a downward spiral for an extended period of time now, and as men of God that professed Jesus Christ in this nation, we realize that we have dropped the ball. . . . Almighty God has chosen to hold back judgment and extend mercy, and we are trusting that the Lord is going to revive our sense of Christian responsibility, and it will be a great awakening to our land.[20]

Like many on the religious right, Promise Keepers is concerned with the "breakdown of the traditional family." Echoing Billy Sunday, for example, Dr. Howard Hendricks, in his contribution to *Seven Promises of a Promise Keeper,* proclaims that "No nation has ever survived the disintegration of its home life. Once the home goes, it's just a matter of time before it all goes" (Hendricks, 49). The compelling feature of the way Promise Keepers frames the "breakdown of the American family" and the moral gap it entails, is that this hazardous condition is primarily the result of a "crisis in masculinity." Writing on the eve of the Stand in the Gap gathering, McCartney asserted:

> The absence of responsible men from the home is now widely regarded as the most important cause of America's social decline. . . . What America desperately needs today is men who take responsibility for their actions, who are faithful to their families, who keep their word, even when it is difficult or costly.[21]

For all their nostalgic talk about the return to some golden age of the American family, where "father knows best," Promise Keepers is well aware that in the United States today fathers too often know very little and often are not even present to provide any answer whatsoever.

What is the essential cause of this crisis in masculinity and the resulting "breakdown of the American family" that Promise Keepers is so determined to resolve? Promise Keepers is centrally concerned with the confusing of "divinely ordained" categories of sex, sexuality, and gender. Promise Keepers is in large part responding to a world indelibly shaped by thirty years of feminist "gender trouble" in which the norms and boundaries of categories of sex and gender have been challenged, crossed, and substantially destabilized. Central to Promise Keepers' prophetic political vision is the belief that this confusion of categories is a fundamental deviation from the divinely ordained social order. For example, Stu Weber asserts, "Feminists insist . . . that men and women are the same, with no appreciable differences other than the obvious plumbing designs. Of course, nothing could be further from the truth" (50).

If the crisis in America today is the result of the breakdown of the normative conceptions of sex and gender, the path to solace requires the reassertion of these traditional categories of identity. Promise Keepers portrays this endeavor as divinely sanctioned but nevertheless difficult to realize in the United States today. Weber sympathizes with the men struggling to understand themselves in this rapidly changing world. "Life gets heavy sometimes. . . . It isn't easy being a man today. It isn't easy being the husband and the dad God calls us to be in this rapidly unraveling culture. . . . Masculinity is no small assignment" (15). The promotional brochure for Promise Keepers' 2000 stadium events conveys this message in bold terms:

> ARE YOU MAN ENOUGH? Men Wanted for Hazardous Journey. Expect resistance, worldly criticism, and possible persecution. Constant risk, with periods of darkness and isolation. Personal safety and financial security uncertain. Eternal rewards at journey's end. . . . Take a look around you. . . . The journey is real, and it is not for wimps. Your wife, your kids, and your friends daily face a gauntlet of lies, worldly filth, and temptations. It is a man's job to stand in the gap with integrity, as protector and leader. And it is time for you to step up to the plate.[22]

Challenging the masculinity of the men it hopes to train as leaders, daring them to follow Christ against the world, Promise Keepers has a mission to retake the nation once blessed by God as the "newly promised land." For Promise Keepers, this mission to re-create Christian masculinity represents the "errand" into the wilderness. On this errand, the men will be armed with the Scripture. As Weber puts it, "Think of the Bible as the owner's manual for your masculinity" (quoted in Kintz, 121). The journey is fraught with danger—"it is not for wimps"—but promises the ultimate reward of eternal salvation.

## Moses Is a "Man's Man"

As we saw with Billy Sunday and Martin Luther King Jr., much can be learned about a religious social movement's prophetic politics from examining its portrayal of Moses. If for Billy Sunday, Moses was the leader who learned courage and determination at his mother's breast, and for Martin Luther King Jr., Moses was the mature man who learned to lead through experience, for Promise Keepers, Moses is a "man's man

[who] was God's man" (*Men's Study Bible,* 73). Moses was the courageous leader who "had to confront Pharaoh . . . in his own house. . . .
The guy who had to take the heat from Pharaoh when God, true to his
word, sent those ten terrible plagues."[23]

To be this kind of brave and resolute leader—the kind of leader
Promise Keepers is encouraging its men to become—Moses must humble himself in worship of God—"being a man's man begins by being
secure in the fact that you are God's man" (*Men's Study Bible,* 73). For-
tunately, for Promise Keepers any man can become "God's man" and
thus every man can be a leader. Moses is a model, but Promise Keepers
teaches that all men can become Moses if they dedicate themselves to
God. The nation—and the revival that might save the nation—desperately needs men willing to answer God's call. And God, of course, is
always calling, a point that Promise Keepers commonly emphasizes
through retellings of the story of the prodigal son. The men who attend
Promise Keepers events may be struggling with sin—addictions to alcohol, drugs, pornography, adultery, or racial prejudice—but if they turn
to Jesus, these men can become leaders like Moses. As Luis Palau told
the men gathered at Shea Stadium for the 1996 Promise Keepers event,
"God is good and he is waiting for his boys to come home."[24] Once
these men come home to God, they can become leaders in their own
homes, accepting their "unique God-given responsibility for the spiritual health of their families."[25]

The aim of this portrayal of Moses, especially when coupled with the
retelling of the parable of the prodigal son, is to create an accessible
model of leadership. In his largely autobiographical book, *Breaking
Through,* Bishop Wellington Boone illustrates this conviction that men
can become like Moses: "There are times when I feel like . . . Moses, in
his intensity from God, pleading 'Let my people go.' Go where? Right
straight to the heart of God, nonstop into the face of Jesus, breaking
through into Christ's likeness" (1996, 175). Boone's depiction of Moses
here is fascinating not simply because he portrays himself like Moses,
but because of the direction of the mission of his Moses. In his invocation of the narrative scaffolding of Exodus, Boone (as Moses) is focused
on personal salvation, not societal liberation. His aim is not to go into
the world to transform the social order, but into himself to pursue
"Christ's likeness."

Perhaps the best illustration of Promise Keepers' depiction of Moses
as an accessible model of leadership comes from Jack Hayford in his
contribution to *Seven Promises of a Promise Keeper.* Consistent with

the sentiment of Boone, Hayford instructs his readers that they are just like Moses.

> For Moses, the call was to lead a nation, whereas your call and mine will likely be less visible. But make no mistake, we *are* leaders! And there is no avoiding the fact that people around us will be affected by whether or not we accept our call to God's purpose in our lives. (Hayford, 20–21)

As a means of illustrating how Promise Keepers are like Moses, Hayford tells a story about two men who heard the call of God. Notable here is less the description of how these men began to worship God, but rather the description of the men themselves: "Chuck was a hard-nosed guy, a tough hard-hat type to whom worship seemed more suited for women and children. Sam was a business executive—in many ways the precise opposite of Chuck except for his conclusions about worship" (Hayford, 21). Chuck and Sam—the tough guy and the executive—are leaders like Moses, because they (just like the men for whom Chuck and Sam are archetypes) are able to recognize that however "hard" and "successful" they might be, they still need to humble themselves before God. The Moses-like leadership exhibited by Chuck and Sam is manifested in the pursuit of personal private accountability.

Moses, Hayford explains, provides a model of "delivering worship . . . which frees a man from bondage, liberates his family to its greatest possibilities, and opens the way to the future without the entanglements of the past" (20). Much as Boone's Moses reflects a distinct break from the biblical Moses concerned with social liberation, Hayford's Moses reflects a curious innovation in the Exodus narrative. First, Hayford portrays Moses' work of liberation as an act of freeing his family—an act, in other words, of private and personal, rather than societal, concern. Secondly, this act of liberation delivers one into the future *"without the entanglements of the past."* How, we might ask, are we to understand Hayford's Moses in light of the Moses who repeatedly teaches lessons about the importance of memory—especially memory of the "entanglements" of being a sojourner in Egypt? Indeed, the ethic of Moses and the prophets is based upon remembering such entanglements and in turn learning to act justly to those who are the sojourners in Israel's midst. Liberated from memory, the story of Exodus becomes a triumphalist narrative in which the chosen people can stride forward into the future God has destined without being tied to the temporal world or the sojourners who inhabit the land. Promise Keepers distinctly portrays Moses as a leader, a warrior, a *man* whom Christian men can emulate if they are willing to act as God intended and lead. And where will these men lead? "Straight into the face of Jesus," directly toward a future liberated from history.

## Promised Land: An Orderly and Predictable Playing Field

The liberation from the entanglements of the past is illustrative of the temporal context established by Promise Keepers. To be sure, Promise Keepers is not arguing that the past does not matter; the organization's jeremiads tell a woeful story about the debilitating moral decay that has devastated the United States over the last forty years. Promise Keepers' argument is that this era of moral decadence need not doom the future of the nation—or at least the chosen men of God living within its borders. As the opening epigraph to this chapter suggests, one of the lessons of the Exodus story is the need for the nation, in the spirit of revival, to "seize the moment" and rededicate itself to the fulfillment of God's promise to the newly chosen people.

If the meaning of the past is simply a matter of God's promise, humanity's capacity to live up to the covenant, and God's judgment, the meaning of the future is also singular. God is coming to judge humanity once again. The apocalyptic end is coming, and woe unto the person who has not been saved by the blood of Jesus. Wellington Boone captures this element in Promise Keepers' political theology: "I believe we are in the end times. I believe I was born in this dark hour to declare the coming of God's Kingdom. God has given me faith and I possess great confidence that God is coming soon" (1996, 7). And when God comes, there will be a judgment. As McCartney told the men at the Meadowlands in 1999, "the unbelievers . . . [will be cast] into the fire of everlasting judgment. That's the reality for every unbeliever who has never been made alive." The believers, the chosen remnant, will be taken into God's kingdom. All of history is a direct path toward this day of judgment. God promises, humans act, God judges—for Promise Keepers that is the biblical truth of the relation between past, present, and future. With judgment impending, Promise Keepers' advice is clear and forceful—submit to Jesus and save yourself in the blood of the Lamb. Ultimately, human actions in this temporal order, in this gap, are meaningless—political participation especially. All that matters is accepting Jesus in your heart and leading your family to live within the protecting arms of the Father.[26]

This understanding of the temporal context in which they live is complemented by their vision of the spatial context of the United States, a nation Promise Keepers depicts in terms of a (once) promised land. Much like the ancient Hebrews in the desert, Promise Keepers speaks of the pilgrims who founded America as bringing order to the wilderness. For example, holding up a Bible, Steve Farrar explained to the Promise Keepers gathered in Indianapolis in 1999:

> [The] pilgrims took the principles of this book and they began to pour a foundation for a great nation. America has been blessed by God because of the foundation that America was built on. The most influential book in the minds of the pilgrims was not the Koran, the most influential book in the minds of the pilgrims was the not writings of Buddha or Laozi [sic]. The most influential book was the Word of God.[27] . . . Why did God bless this country? For several hundred years the majority of Americans, whether they were Christians or not, believed in the principles of this book. They believed in something called Moral Absolutes. They believed that God had given the law to Moses, Moses had brought that law down, that law became the basis for morality.[28]

In this history of the nation, Exodus tropes and the figure of Moses are employed to describe the America of the past as a land of order. Unlike the heathen nations, America is blessed by God because it is founded upon the "Truth" of "His Word." Tragically, for Farrar and Promise Keepers, the promised land of America once guided by the law of Moses now has fallen from its status as the new Israel; indeed, America is coming to represent the old Israel that forgot its covenant with God.

The order and predictability of the American promised land have given way to "moral relativism." Gary Oliver lays a big part of the blame on the teachings of American universities over the last thirty years, particularly the often cited work by Joseph Fletcher, *Situation Ethics*.[29]

> Thirty-five years ago, our country followed the Judeo-Christian ethic. Few people questioned that chastity was a good thing, that hard work was the duty of every responsible man, that homosexual conduct was wrong, that it was never right to lie, cheat, steal, or commit adultery. But today, our ethics and morals are no longer based on Jerusalem; they're based on Sodom and Gomorrah. If you take situation ethics to its logical conclusion, you end up with Auschwitz, Dachau and Buchenwald.[30]

Given the state of "moral free fall" in America, in the apocalyptic political theology of Promise Keepers, Buchenwald often appears to be right around the corner.[31] Luis Palau states the matter simply: "America needs

Promise Keepers committed to evangelism like never before. Billy Graham once said, 'It's either back to the Bible or back to the jungle.' The jungle truly is creeping up on the United States" (Palau, 199).

The only hope of restoring the United States as promised land is a revival saving the nation. In a fascinating piece of historical and theological reasoning, Bill Bright declares:

> I believe God has given ancient Israel as an example of what will happen to the United States if we do not experience revival. He will continue to discipline us with all kinds of problems until we repent or until we are destroyed as was ancient Israel because of her sin of disobedience. (47)

The destruction of the first promised land is intended as a lesson for the second promised land; the judgment of God is coming unless the prophetic vision of returning to God's word changes the face of the nation. This vision of ecclesiastical history is a consistent component of the creation of narrative context vital to the worldview preached by Promise Keepers.

Promise Keepers is doing its part to create this revival to transform the context of the nation and the identity of the citizens in the United States. Each gathering at a sports stadium can be understood as an effort to take back, or re-create, the order of the promised land yard by yard. Holding its regional events at sports stadiums—and actively utilizing the athletic atmosphere of these spaces—is one of the prominent innovations of Promise Keepers.[32] The use of sports stadiums works perfectly with Promise Keepers' mission to inspire men to return order to America. As Randy Balmer notes,

> The world of athletics offers an orderly universe, a refuge from the larger world. What all major sports have in common since the age of industrialism are clear boundaries and precise delineations. The rules may be complex, but they are also precise, with every situation and contingency provided for. Something is either in bounds or out of bounds, fair or foul. (89)

The rules of sports, like the law of Moses, are authoritative absolutes. Success, Promise Keepers preaches, is a result of dedication, teamwork, and following the right game plan. Coach McCartney (and he is generally called Coach in Promise Keepers circles) expressed this perspective at the Stand in the Gap event: "We need a precise plan. Can't be a guy leave here without knowing exactly what we're going to be doing. So that the right hand will know what the left hand is doing, we have a plan." However, unlike in sports, there is little room for spontaneity at Promise Keepers stadium events. Men are taught not just what, but how, to pray.[33] And unlike at sporting events, total unity replaces support for different teams. Denominational, ethnic, racial, socio-economic differences are transcended as everyone roots for Jesus; and the men do cheer, rousing one another with shouts of "We love Jesus, yes we do, we love Jesus, how about you?" The finest expression of this total unity I have seen was a T-shirt sold by Promise Keepers at the 1996 event at Shea Stadium. In big block letters, the shirt proclaimed simply that "Yes, We All Agree!"

As with Billy Sunday, the figurative language of athletics (and the military) is the common rhetorical coin for Promise Keepers. "Coach Mac's" sermons, in particular, are noted for their tone akin to a locker-room, pre-game pep talk. Typical of this mode of speech is the statement McCartney made in a 1993 *Men of Action Newsletter.* "God is recruiting players for His dream team, and nobody is to be left on the bench. He is calling all of us to sacrifice our ambitions for personal glory to the well-being of the team."[34] Designating God as the coach and other Christian men as teammates goes a long way toward making religion and piety seem less effeminate and more accessible to Promise Keepers' target audience. For Promise Keepers, the events it sponsors at sports stadiums are designed to re-create order, to figuratively re-create the promised land—and do it in a manner in which men can be challenged in a comfortable, familiar space.

In the post-9/11 era, Promise Keepers has begun reemphasizing its use of military language that had waned in the late 1990s.[35] Speaking to a nation at war, and to citizens longing for the type of stability and leadership presumably to be found through militarism, Promise Keepers' newest campaign, the "Platoon Challenge" to reach "A Million Men at the Cross" uses persistently militaristic language to describe and define the endeavor. Promise Keepers challenges men to join a "mission," to be part of God's "fighting force" empowered to "enlist . . . interested soldiers . . . [to] recruit a neighbor, or a few guys at church." These "small fighting forces" should designate a "headquarters" and establish a "standard operating procedure." Each individual "platoon must develop acute radar awareness of its surroundings" so that the "team [is] properly positioned for its course of action." Every soldier in the platoon needs a "wing man" who will "care enough to speak up when [he] sees [his] buddy drifting from the Mission: God's glory." The soldiers in these platoons are charged with "identifying targets" and working through prayer and outreach projects to bring men from their local communities and "the world" to meet Jesus at the cross.[36] Accountability prayer groups are thus essentially masculinized by the language and logic of war. The emphasis Promise Keepers places on re-establishing orderly boundaries in the promised land is also a central feature of its reconstruction of the chosen people who might play on this great ball field, or march across this glorious battlefield.

## "The Mighty Men of God" and the Politics of Chosen-ness

Despite Promise Keepers' best efforts to generate a revival in the United States that will enable the nation to once again live up to its status as a promised land, the great expectation is that rather than God's blessing, America will receive God's harsh judgment. If, as a nation, America is not able to regain its status as "God's new Israel" inhabited by a chosen people, Promise Keepers does hold out great hope for the future of the "remnant of believers."[37] Promise Keepers, in other words, still employs the trope of chosen-ness derived from the sacred story of Exodus, but it is very particular in delineating who this chosen remnant will be. Farrar invokes the Exodus story of Passover to illustrate this theme of chosen-ness in these last days before God's judgment:

> God won't put up with this nation much longer. He will intervene. . . . At some point judgment will come. . . . If judgment is coming put the blood over the doorpost of your house and get under the blood. Now let me make something clear to you, God has promised to take care of his people. But you have to decide . . . choose you this day whom you will serve. You give it all to Him with your whole heart—if judgment is coming you get under the blood. . . . What I'm saying guys is—either follow Christ or don't follow Him but make up your minds what you're gonna do.[38]

In responding to what it perceives as this current era of "cultural distortion," Promise Keepers asserts that boundaries of identity and order must be reestablished; the holy must be separated from the corrupt, the chosen from the disobedient. This political and theological vision of separating the believers from the unbelievers is a recurrent theme in the books, resources, and public sermons of Promise Keepers. For example, in his video seminar series *Personal Holiness in Times of Temptation*, Dr. Bruce Wilkerson asserts:

When God forgives you for your sins, He also separates you from the world and those who have rejected Him, and separates you to Himself. He adopts you as His son, and places you supernaturally within the Family of God. He transfers you from the Kingdom of Darkness to the Kingdom of Light. He saves you from eternal damnation and gives you eternal salvation." (9–10)

The stakes of this process of exclusion and separation are as high as possible. On the individual level it is the difference between heaven and hell; on the societal level it is the very future of the nation and the fulfillment or the demise of the God's promise to the "newly chosen people."

Most prominently, the emphasis on separation and the reconfiguration of the chosen community is sharply evident in the prophetic passage from Ezekiel, which Promise Keepers used as the organizing theme of the Stand in the Gap event in Washington, DC. Although Promise Keepers used only part of this passage in its publicity (the section I have italicized below), it is instructive to read it in context to help illustrate their emphasis on chosen-ness and exclusion. In a time of crisis and social disorder, Ezekiel speaks to the people the "word of the Lord" proclaiming:

Son of man, say to the land . . . there is a conspiracy of her princes within her like a roaring lion tearing its prey; they devour people . . . her priests do violence to my law and profane my holy things; they do not distinguish between the holy and the common; they teach there is no difference between the unclean and the clean; and they shut their eyes to the keeping of my Sabbaths, so that I am profaned among them. . . . The people of the land practice extortion and commit robbery; they oppress the poor and needy and mistreat the alien, denying them justice. *I looked for a man among them who would build up the wall and stand in the gap on behalf of the land so I would not have to destroy it but I found none.* So I will pour out my wrath on them and consume them with my fiery anger, bringing down on their own heads all they have done, declares the Sovereign Lord. (Ez. 22:23–26, 29–31)

Ezekiel decries the pollution of that which is holy and warns that if the boundaries that separate the sacred from the profane are not re-established, if the principles of social order and justice instituted at Mount Sinai are not obeyed, God's wrath will come down on the wayward chosen people. In the United States today, Promise Keepers asserts, a comparable national perversion is shaking the divinely ordained social order, and it is necessary to reassert the boundaries between the clean and the unclean, to reconfigure the community of the chosen. As McCartney says,

In Ezekiel's day the people of Israel had wandered far from God, their first love. The result for Israel was national disaster: military defeat from without, moral rot from within. Ezekiel despairs that no one is willing to come forward to climb the literal breach in Jerusalem's walls and act as a human rampart against the evils of his day. . . . We believe that God is again looking for a few good men who desire to honor Him in every area of their lives.[39]

Proclaiming that men should follow the example of Ezekiel, Promise Keepers is calling out its audience of men, asking them if they are willing to be the rare individual—the "one in a hundred" as Coach McCartney put it at the 1996 Promise Keepers event at Shea Stadium—who is willing to stand tall in the face of disorder and follow the word of God. As McCartney said to those men gathered at Shea Stadium, "God is looking for obedient men who are not ashamed of the gospel of Jesus and who are willing to go to great extremes."

This creation of a separate context to house an exclusivist identity seems to run counter to one of Promise Keepers' most notable goals— the call for racial and denominational reconciliation and the creation of "unity" among men of God. In *The Power of a Promise Kept*, Greg Lewis tells a story of Pastor Van Roland, a Promise Keeper who led his church into an "AIDS ministry" in his local community. Explaining the lessons he learned from Promise Keepers and their application to this ministry, Roland asserts, "If we as a church (universal and in our local congregations) truly want to be the living body that Jesus wants us to be, then the denominational walls, the racial walls, and all the other walls we've erected to separate us from each other have to come down" (quoted in Lewis, 154). There is in this vision a sentiment of democratic politics, particularly of visiting, of enhancing the *sensus communis*. Promise Keepers' efforts to pursue reconciliation has contributed to the increase in ecumenicalism and pluralism that has emerged among American religious bodies over the last fifteen years.

And yet, it is crucial to recognize that the goal of the racial reconciliation pursued by Promise Keepers is not justice but "unity." As McCartney asserts:

We *are going to reconcile* with our Christian brothers of different races, cultures, and denominations. We're going to break down the walls that separate us . . . [to] demonstrate the power of biblical unity based on what we have in common: our love for Jesus and our connectedness through Him. (1994, 164)

This focus on unity is telling, for Promise Keepers' approach to race is to attempt to transcend racial boundaries; that is, rather than focusing on historical racial difference, Promise Keepers stresses the essential same-ness of all men. Just as in the New Testament Jesus sought to transcend a history of cultural difference between Greeks and Jews, Promise Keepers seeks to liberate men from the entanglements of racial history in the United States so that individuals can be united as believers rather than divided by historically informed differences.

However, this "inclusive" conception of racial reconciliation among men—a conception of unity rooted in the essential sameness of all men—is only made possible through the exclusion of women. For all its preaching about transcending boundaries that divide men, Promise Keepers is emphatic about re-inscribing those boundaries that divide men and women.

Promise Keepers' approach to reasserting the boundaries between men and women takes many forms, but all aim toward the same goal. Stu Weber, for instance, confronts the issue in a characteristically blunt fash-ion, proclaiming:

> If we're going to be healthy again, men are going to have to become healthy men again (and women healthy women). It's time for men to stand up, get a grip on biblical manhood, and quit apologizing for being men. What this culture desperately needs are men who are confident in their God-given masculinity and His intentions for it. . . . Remember when men were men? And women women and the differences were obvious? Remember when you didn't have to wonder? And you weren't criticized for being a man? . . . But now, in a culture that wants to elevate a higher standard of so-called diversity, we're destroying diversity in its most beau-tiful and elemental form. (44)

In this striking passage, Weber argues that both individual and social health are predicated on clearly defined categories of gender identity. The desire for separation along "God-given" lines of gender will be real-ized after the elements that pollute—or "infect" (to use Weber's metaphor of health)—those categories are abjected. Arresting this cul-tural distortion, which has led to the masculinization of women and the feminization of men, is central to the identity of Promise Keepers as the "mighty men of God" and to its political vision.

Pursuing the "proper masculinity" appropriate for the "men of God" is predicated on excluding forces that challenge or destabilize their vision of manhood. Principally this means taking a stand against gay and bi-sexual men and against the challenges to "biblical" gender identity often at least implicitly attributed to feminists. The more explicit compo-nent of Promise Keepers' effort to re-assert clear definitions of "God-given" masculinity is its emphasis on the essential differences between

men and women. Feminist critics of Promise Keepers have often challenged the organization's assertions of divinely ordained gender identity.
Promise Keepers has responded to feminist critiques with the suggestion
that they (and the media) should speak to the wives of Promise Keepers.
One of the few women to ever officially speak at a Promise Keepers
event is Holly Phillips, wife of former Promise Keepers President Randy
Phillips. Her 1995 speech to the "promise-keeping men of God" is quite
instructive on the demarcation of gender difference and the crisis in
masculinity.

> On behalf of the women you men represent—sisters, moms, wives and
> daughters—I ask your forgiveness for not showing you the respect you
> deserve. I ask your forgiveness for the demeaning and belittling words we
> have uttered. I apologize for the ways we have coddled and smothered you
> with our protectiveness, thereby emasculating you. It has been done in
> ignorance. Understand that "mothering" comes naturally to us. It is our
> God-designed makeup. We simply misappropriated our calling.[40]

Women, therefore, are framed as responsible for the feminization of men
and the corruption of the "God-given" categories of gender. Moreover, if
women do not repent of their sins of emasculation and recognize their
"calling," they could continue to interfere in the "promise keeping" of
men. In each of these cases, then, not only are women at some level
responsible for the "crisis in masculinity," but also this crisis cannot be
solved and men cannot become "Godly men of integrity" unless clear
lines of difference are "re-established" between men and women.

The capstone of Promise Keepers' political vision of gender identity is
its controversial concept of male headship. As McCartney explained in
an interview on National Public Radio shortly after the Stand in the Gap
event, "Almighty God has mandated that the man take the spiritual lead
in the home. Isaiah 38:19 says 'A father to the children shall make
known the truth.'"[41] Promise Keepers' most well known assertion of
male headship is that of Tony Evans. In the central book of Promise
Keepers' political theology, *The Seven Promises of a Promise Keeper*,
Evans challenges the "sissified" men of America to:

> . . . sit down with your wife and say something like this: "Honey, I have
> made a terrible mistake. I've given you my role. I gave up leading this fam-
> ily and I forced you to take my place. Now I must reclaim that role."
> Don't misunderstand what I am saying here. I am not suggesting that
> you *ask* for your role back, I'm urging you to *take it back*. . . . [T]here can
> be no compromise here. If you're going to lead, you must lead. Be sensi-
> tive. Listen. Treat the lady gently and lovingly. But *lead*. (Evans, 79–80)

The political implications of this delineation of proper gender roles are profound. If men are divinely ordained as the "leaders" of the family, the question of power outside the household is, of course, closely related. Promise Keepers has been careful to make public statements that this notion of male headship does not mean that these men are calling for women to give up the equality they have won in the public sphere. However, the sincerity of these public comments is belied by the sentiments often expressed in their books. As Gary Smalley and John Trent succinctly proclaim in their book, *The Hidden Value of a Man: The Incredible Impact of a Man on His Family:* "There's no doubt that men, by God-given design, are leaders in science, industry, research and religion" (32). Ultimately, the "chosen men of God" who—like Ezekiel—will strive to lead the nation back to "God's vision" of moral order by reasserting the boundaries between holy and corrupt, clean and unclean, will begin their "holy war" by re-establishing the proper gender roles and appropriate authority God has "given" to men.

## Covenants of the Brotherhood of Believers

Exodus tropes of chosen-ness and mission were pervasive at Promise Keepers' Stand in the Gap event in Washington, D.C. The "sacred assembly" began with the blowing of the shofar by a group of Messianic Jews and the proclamation of the chairman of the board of Promise Keepers, Bishop Phillip Porter: "We are as Moses was, standing on holy ground." At the conclusion of the day, the men gathered by Promise Keepers swore to a "D.C. Covenant" with God. This covenant of Promise Keepers purposefully evokes the covenant made by the forlorn ancient Hebrews at the foot of Mount Sinai. Beginning with the admission of being "broken and humbled," Promise Keepers' covenant included oaths to "serve no other Gods beside You," "resist moral, ethical, and sexual temptations," "honor all women" and "intentionally love the brotherhood of believers."[42] By now, this pronouncement to "love the brotherhood of believers" should not be a surprise; while inclusive in its desire for ecumenical and multiracial unity in Jesus, Promise Keepers is also exclusivist in its intention to build walls around the community of the chosen, the pure remnant whom God will protect in the end-times.[43]

More subtly, the D.C. Covenant reaffirms Promise Keepers' commitment to the principle of male headship. To illustrate this point it is worthwhile to return to the biblical model of the covenant and compare it to the covenant sworn to by members of Promise Keepers. In the initial biblical formulation of the covenant, the agreement between the ancient Israelites and God is individual and inclusive. In Exodus, the text reads "The people all responded together . . ."(Ex. 19:8), and when the narrative of the making of this first covenant is retold in Deuteronomy, the text is even more vivid: "All of you are standing in the presence of the Lord your God—your leaders and chief men, your elders and officials, and all the other men of Israel, together with your children and your wives, and the aliens living in your camps . . ." (Dt. 29:10–11). Each member of the community makes an individual covenant with God. However, in the later reaffirmation of the covenant in the Book of Joshua, the commitment is made by the head of the household on behalf of the entire household. In its articulation of the covenant, Promise Keepers follows the model of Joshua, proclaiming "Today, each of us declares, 'As for me and my household, we will serve the Lord' (Josh. 24:15)." Thus, rather than employing the template of the inclusive covenant found in Exodus and Deuteronomy, in its covenant Promise Keepers pointedly chooses to emphasize this sense of "headship." In fact, this verse from Joshua was chosen by Promise Keepers to serve as the guiding biblical passage for its 1999 stadium conference series.

Indeed, much of Promise Keepers' 1999 conferences were dedicated to teaching men how to purify themselves in order to become God's chosen, take humble leadership in their homes, and thereby attain the promised land. The tropes of their retelling of the Exodus narrative permeated both the jeremiadic and wisdom portions of the conferences, but all centered on fulfilling the covenant of Joshua, and reaffirming the commitment of the brotherhood of believers to enter the appointed place. Perhaps the best example of this phenomenon comes from George Morrison, who is both McCartney's own pastor and a member of Promise Keepers' Board of Directors. At the Meadowlands in New Jersey, McCartney invited Morrison to join him on the stage to offer his "Understanding [of] the Times" in America today. Morrison spoke of the "battle we are about to face," linking Promise Keepers to the biblical chosen people of Israel:

> When the children of Israel were to face their greatest challenge and battle after coming out of the wilderness, God set them aside and said, "This is the land I am going to give to you." And Gentlemen, there is an area of this planet earth that God has set aside for you as believers in Jesus Christ. "That's your land, [God says] . . . and I want you to take it."

But God, Morrison continued, first commanded that Joshua take out the knife and circumcise his men to indicate that "they are set aside" as

God's people. Likewise, "God has set us apart. The knife has come and cut some things out of our lives. . . . God has set us free."[44] Promise Keepers is aiming to circumcise men, to mark them as chosen and set them aside, so that free and pure they can inhabit the promised land God has given them.

## The Wisdom of Promise Keepers

Thus far I have focused on how Promise Keepers generates its identity and political vision by utilizing the sacred stories of the Exodus narrative and the jeremiadic tradition. Although both are essential to the success of Promise Keepers and both illustrate Promise Keepers' place within the American tradition of Great Awakenings, together they still do not fully explain the use of the scriptural models by Promise Keepers. To gain a fuller understanding of Promise Keepers, it is crucial to also look at the "mundane stories" that lie within the context established by these "sacred narratives."

While these jeremiads represent some of the more striking elements of Promise Keepers' canon, the bulk of the books, resources, and sermons of Promise Keepers offer practical advice on how to strengthen marriages, achieve racial reconciliation, attain fiscal responsibility, avoid "sexual impurities," and improve one's efforts as fathers, friends, and members of the church community. These texts represent the "wisdom literature" of Promise Keepers. In keeping with the inter-relationship of the two modes of biblical literature, Promise Keepers uses the jeremiads to delineate the vision of the organization and mundane texts to provide pragmatic recommendations on how to live in the contingent and troubled world. The sense of crisis expressed in the prophetic narratives is maintained in the "books of wisdom." But rather than focus on the moment of salvation, Promise Keepers' wisdom literature (as is the case of the books of Proverbs, Ecclesiastes, James, Lamentations, and Job) offers considerations of how to live in the everyday world where there are still significant obstacles and fears blocking one's access to the promised land. Much of Promise Keepers' literature reflects the influence of the ever-expanding self-help movement in the United States. In basing its wisdom literature on this relatively new development in American culture, Promise Keepers illustrates the dynamic and innovative potential enabled by the use of sacred stories. The wisdom literature is designed to give counsel to these men, to enable them to triumph in the daily struggles to meet this standard of "holiness." As we should expect, given the emphasis placed on clear definitions of gender identity in its framing and employment of the sacred trope of chosen-ness, a central theme of the wisdom literature of Promise Keepers is advice on how to achieve and maintain a state of "proper Christian masculinity."

The predominant features of the mundane stories told by Promise Keepers are the symbols and metaphors of athletics. Their vision of athletic masculinity is buttressed by the shirts, banners, and other athletic accoutrements that permeate the atmosphere at Promise Keepers' rallies in sports stadiums around the country. There is no more vivid symbol of the integration between the sacred stories of chosen Christian masculine identity and the mundane stories of athletic masculinity than the specially produced "Man of His Word" versions of the New Testament given to each Promise Keeper after he dedicates his life to Jesus. For an organization that stresses the importance of obedience to the literal and infallible word of God as one of the fundamental markers of belonging to the chosen community of Christian brothers, it is a phenomenon of striking rhetorical significance that scattered between the canonical works of the New Testament are full-page color photos and biographies of prominent Christian athletes. So, for example, nestled within the Gospel of John are the biographies and inspiring words of Reggie White, Orel Hersheiser, and Michael Chang. Perceiving these athletes and the other "promise keeping brothers" as common members of "God's dream team" is part of the "game plan" that Promise Keepers' leadership has, namely, of creating a brotherhood of men who are willing to "act as bulwarks against [society's] ill-informed and destructive choices, like offensive linemen protecting the quarterback."[45]

Having built the implicit challenge of holy Christian masculinity ("Are you man enough to be a member of God's team?") into their valorization of the strength and toughness associated with normative athletic masculinity, Promise Keepers' books and resources give the men models and practical advice about how to become a "mighty man of God." This wisdom literature utilizes a combination of two modes of expression: (1) narratives about men whose lives serve as models for the readers, and (2) clearly written "how-to" manuals with diagnostic devices, "discussion points," and didactic pieces of advice.[46] Promise Keepers readily admits that Christian men in America have failed to fulfill their mission. As McCartney said on *Meet the Press* in 1997, "The men of God in this nation have not stood in the gap for the gospel of Jesus Christ. We look just like society. We were never intended to do this. The guys that Almighty God has placed His spirit in should be living a life that offers an alternative to a world that is lost." The aim of

Promise Keepers' wisdom literature is to direct men on a path so that the chosen brotherhood has an identity distinct from the mainstream of society; Promise Keepers wants to inhabit the margins of America rather than be corrupted by the ungodly morass in the center of secular culture in the United States.

To reach men with this message, Promise Keepers relies on the art of storytelling; many of the books in the Promise Keepers wisdom literature are essentially collections of anecdotes designed to illuminate the path of living out the social movement's seven promises. For instance, a strongly recommended resource book, *The Power of a Promise Kept*, begins with this introductory proclamation by former Promise Keepers President Randy Phillips.

> This may be the most unusual book you've ever read. . . . [T]hese stories are about men like you. . . . [T]hey all know that their lives aren't perfect, though most have never told anyone their secret fears. They desire a deep friendship with another man, but they don't know how to start the process. They try to balance their priorities, but they feel trapped by circumstances they can't change. They want deeper relationships with their fathers and children, but they don't know how to break negative patterns of communication. They face tough decisions of conscience and they feel they have no one with whom they can confide. They muddle through marriage knowing their wives are unhappy, but they don't know what to do about it. They think about the bigger questions of life, like "Why am I here?" but are too busy to search for answers. Now, you probably don't fit all of those generalizations, but we'd guess you identify with one or more and could no doubt expand the list. That's why this book was written for you—to help real men, who are living life in the trenches, raise the standard. (1995, 1–2)

One of the striking aspects of this passage is the great weight placed on the private fears and concerns of men: longing for friendship, concerns about marriage and parenting, constraints in the workplace. The answers to such concerns are found in mundane stories of how "real men" just like them made difficult decisions to honor Jesus in their personal lives. These stories are designed to encourage men to strive to "put up big numbers" in the tests of their marriages and friendships, because God, McCartney explains, "is pleased with men who score high."[47]

As is the case here with McCartney's story of his own marriage, the wisdom literature of Promise Keepers often consists of autobiographical narratives coupled with instructions on how to follow these examples. While clearly demarcated boundaries of gender roles and identity and the pivotal tenet of male headship are central to Promise Keepers' political theology, the organization recognizes that establishing such a vision in one's daily life is more complex than simply reading Ephesians 5:23 to one's wife. In *The Hidden Value of a Man,* authors Gary Smalley and John Trent seek to provide clear models, lessons, and recommendations for practicing what Promise Keepers preaches. Beginning with an example of a man who struggles to learn how to properly (rather than selfishly) lead his family, Smalley and Trent proceed to explicate the call for headship they derive from Ephesians by comparing it to the type of military chain of command that enabled George H. W. Bush, General Colin Powell, General Norman Schwarzkopf and all the troops down to the individuals on the frontlines to "drive [Saddam Hussein] out of Kuwait."

> You didn't sense feelings of inferiority when pictures came in of General Schwarzkopf walking among his troops, shaking their hands, and praying with them before they went into battle. You sensed only loyalty, clarity of purpose and a mutual willingness to serve. And you sensed something else between he and his men—a genuine love. But someone still had to take the lead. They knew it. They needed it. And it brought them the quickest and most decisive victory in American military history. (44)

What is the lesson to be learned from this model of masculine leadership and "family" unity? Smalley and Trent conclude, "Loving leadership and voluntary submission. The message of Ephesians 5 is that husbands and wives need to get their plans clearly established. What hill are you going to take with your family? What plateau do you want to reach with your children?" (Smalley and Trent, 44). Even this contemporary model of masculinity is not enough to provide a clear path to fulfilling the mandate for headship they derive from Ephesians. Smalley and Trent next offer a mundane story of how Smalley and his wife, Norma, personally created a "family constitution" with Smalley "taking the lead in accomplishing that goal, and Norma submitting to that plan and supporting me" (Smalley and Trent, 45). But even this personal example is not precise enough about how to follow and fulfill Promise Keepers' vision of proper masculine headship; at the end of the book, Smalley and Trent provide specific models of "family constitutions." As this example illustrates, the "mundane stories" and didactic advice presented by Promise Keepers in its wisdom literature serve as practical personal guidelines for meeting the political theology disseminated in the organization's jeremiads. The detailed political strategies contained in the organization's books and resources function as the necessary complement to Promise Keepers' vision of prophetic politics.

Taking the self-help movement as a model does not just provide "divinely inspired" critical witness of the social ills plaguing the United States today, but also offers a programmatic conception of solutions. Videotapes of "seminars" led by experts encourage viewers to grapple with sexual addiction, failing marriages, male-male friendships, and racial reconciliation. Often the videotapes are part of a recommended package that includes workbooks, lists of weekly topics and exercises, and daily devotional prayers to assist in the journey. For example, the package *Personal Holiness in Times of Temptation* consists of a video-tape of a four-part lecture-seminar with a "Course Workbook" that follows each session. The workbook consists of daily devotionals and "video class notes" comprising fill-in-the-blank sections. Bruce Wilkerson, the author and leader of the seminar sessions, duly provides the exact words with which the men are supposed to fill in the blanks. This video series begins with the two-part somewhat paradoxical claim that men are responsible for changing their lives and that the first step in that process is submitting one's life to God and one's will to God's will. Herein lies the Christian male appropriation of the basic self-help message that recovery begins when the individual relinquishes the "impossible to realize" desire for self-control.[48] As Wendy Kaminer notes in her wonderful study of the self-help phenomenon in the United States, "codependency books" are replete with

> exercises, quizzes and sentence completions [designed to] assist you in self-evaluation. . . . The trouble is that for codependency consumers, someone else is always writing the script. . . . They are encouraged to believe in the impossibility of individual autonomy.[49]

Indeed, Promise Keepers stresses that a man cannot travel the journey to holiness on his own. He needs "brothers" who will keep him from being too willful, who will encourage him in submission to God. In his address at the Stand in the Gap event, McCartney brought this point home: "Can't no guy leave out of here as a Lone Ranger. Many guys have been traveling on their own, but we are going out of here with the same vision."

This commitment to "supportive teamwork" as essential to resolving the "crisis in America" is one of the basic tenets of Promise Keepers' theology. In all of their sermons, books, and resources, Promise Keepers stresses the importance of these small support groups of "committed brothers." Following the summer stadium events, Promise Keepers are encouraged to buy "The Next Step" video and workbook series that is designed to help individuals move "from the stadium to the small group."[50] As McCartney explains at the outset of the video, the vision for these accountability groups is based on a "military principle" or as Stu Weber told the gathering of men at a Portland Promise Keepers conference: "A little bit of advice from an old soldier: Never go into combat alone."[51]

For Promise Keepers this model of brotherhood is largely about surveillance. Yes, a man needs someone he can talk to, but, intriguingly, the way the movement talks about these relationships is largely framed in terms of living under the watchful gaze of another one of the chosen brethren. Coach McCartney, for example, has said in his stadium sermons that before big games he would encourage each member of his football team to play for someone they knew would be watching their performance.[52] Watching over your brothers and living as if you are being watched is a governing feature of the type of community Promise Keepers envisions creating, a vision often presented under the notion of "being your brother's keeper." One of the more recent tools Promise Keepers provides men in their battles with sin illustrates this point acutely. Promise Keepers now offers *Eye Promise*—"Internet accountability software" that uses an eye as a logo to make clear the message that men should imagine they are being watched by their brothers. "Like iron sharpens iron," Weber and other Promise Keepers leaders are fond of saying, so too can men hone one another's Christian masculinity.

Of course, lest any of this male-male bonding be perceived as homoerotic, Promise Keepers is quick to clarify that it does not encourage *that* type of relationship. Stu Weber often cites the relationship between David and Jonathan as the biblical model for his "tender warriors." Citing David's words to Jonathan, Weber pronounces,

> "*Your love to me was more wonderful than the love of women.*" What words are these? Perverted words? Twisted words? The words of some pathetic sexual deviate? No. A war-hardened veteran penned these words after his best buddy fell in battle. They were written by a warrior.[53]

The warriors Promise Keepers is training are marching together on their own battlefield, trying to live as "Godly men in an ungodly culture"[54]—and this ungodliness is largely defined by "sexual sins" of homosexuality, adultery, and pornography.

As an illustration, Steve Gallagher, founder of Pure Life Ministries, provides a fascinating retelling of the Exodus story to help men address the "prison of pornography." In an article titled, "Be Strong and Very

Courageous," which was posted on the Promise Keepers website, Gallagher begins with a passage from the Book of Joshua:

> "Only be strong and very courageous; be careful to do according to all the law which Moses my servant commanded you" (Jos. 1:7). As Joshua contemplated the task before him—destroying and driving out the wicked Canaanites from the Promised Land—he must have been overwhelmed. The enemy seemed so strong. Not only that, but they were deeply entrenched in fortified cities and would not be displaced without a tremendous battle.
>
> It is much the same for the believer who is bound up in habits of sexual sin. The enemy is powerful and deeply rooted within his soul. The man's adversaries in this battle are his own flesh and the agents of the enemy that keep him ensnared. Moreover, the pact the flesh and the devil have between them seems to make them invincible.
>
> If this describes you, the Lord has a word for you: be strong and very courageous! In other words, don't wimp out. . . . A few weeks previously, Moses had explained to Joshua and his men how the Lord would help them. . . ."And the LORD your God will clear away these nations before you little by little. . . ." (Dt. 7:20)
>
> This is a picture of how the Lord will drive out your enemies, as well.[55]

In this innovative version of the Exodus narrative, Gallagher depicts the identity of the promise-keeping men in his audience as akin to Joshua leading the chosen people into the promised land. This use of tropes drawn from Exodus should be no surprise. What is striking is the manner in which Gallagher depicts the context of the battle. The enemies inhabiting Canaan have in this retelling shifted from other "nations" to personal afflictions and temptations of the flesh. The spatial context is no longer a public space where a nation may flourish, but the individual soul of the man ensnared in sexual impurity. Rather than strength, courage, and faith leading to the fulfillment of the collective conditional covenant between God and the chosen people, men are now instructed to be strong to win the battle of their own flesh. Indeed, in this retelling of the Exodus story, rather than a collective promised land of the kingdom of God, every man has his own personal promised land of salvation.

## Therapy or Democracy, Piety or Politics

Beyond the structural and pedagogical models it has learned from the self-help phenomenon in America, Promise Keepers has also—more significantly—adopted a pattern in which social issues are reduced to personal problems. Shaped by the culture wars, Promise Keepers tells a story of crisis in America, a cultural confusion largely concerning issues of identity related to sex, gender, race, and the family. For Promise Keepers, such questions are personal, private matters caused by the forgetting of biblical truths—and resolvable only through revival. Thus, social issues are moved out of the public, political realm and conceived of as simply individual moral challenges. "Social problems are moral problems," McCartney argues, "[and they] ultimately have a spiritual cause."[56] Their Great Awakening is designed, they claim, to revitalize the spirit and create moral reform. This emphasis on personal, moral reform rather than social reform has profound political stakes.

If McCartney is correct and "social problems" *are* merely moral rather than political or historical problems, then politics is not a valid path for addressing these issues. Only faith and submission to "God's will" can lead to solutions. With regard to the goal of racial reconciliation, in its resources and public sermons Promise Keepers constantly stresses the importance of overcoming "racial barriers." However, Promise Keepers approaches the question of race in America as a matter of "personal prejudice." As a result, rather than confronting the historical and institutional problems of racism, or the relation between racial inequality and economic inequality, Promise Keepers suggests that racism can be overcome if only all God's children see that they are all alike and realize their "unity in Christ." McCartney proclaims that racial reconciliation can be achieved if an individual man is willing to take two steps: "Pray . . . [and] pursue genuine relationships with Christian men of different races . . ." (McCartney 1994, 165). Thus, in their approach to the social problem of racism, Promise Keepers is not concerned with questions of social justice, but merely personal reform, especially in one's behavior toward other Christians. This same pattern holds for all the "social problems" facing the nation, including matters of gender roles and relations. And herein lies the real difficulty. If racism is not a political problem and gender relations are not political problems and the challenges to normative masculinity are not political problems, then the only solutions or means of addressing these issues are personal and private; there is consequently no encouragement of political discourse and debate. Such an attitude, of course, leads to the decline of *sensus communis* and the shrinking of the public realm. It represents a rejection of the inclusive ethic of democratic visiting, of an embrace of pluralism that expands the world of possibility and creates space for an enrichment of understanding.

Let me offer a final example of Promise Keepers' disinclination to engage in visiting, in case the organization's exclusivist conception of the brotherhood of believers, belief in divinely authorized male headship, and commitment to pietistic rather than political approaches to resolving social ills have not sufficiently illustrated this point. One of the basic premises of visiting is willingness to appreciate and respect different perspectives, even if after learning about their conception of the common world, one holds these other perspectives to be wrong. For a pluralist democratic politics, visiting is invaluable, because it enables conversation—particularly conversations that compel one to defamiliarize one's own beliefs to more readily appreciate others (and inevitably learn more about one's own beliefs in the process). For all its talk about reconciliation, this appreciation of pluralism is dismissed by Promise Keepers. Promise Keepers board member James Ryle frankly expressed this sentiment at the 1997 Promise Keepers event in Pittsburgh. Speaking of potential different religious paths, Ryle explained to the thousands of men gathered at Three Rivers Stadium that there is only one, true road to God's glory, and that is through Christ. In itself, this expression of a religious conviction—especially at a revival aimed at bringing men to Jesus—is hardly surprising or problematic. What is troubling is how Ryle speaks of others who walk along different paths. In a manner that might even make Billy Sunday blush, Ryle proclaimed: "Let's say there are four ways to get to heaven. . . . Heaven's Gate [in which one] commits suicide, betrays family, shocks community and shames the nation." Or one could be a "Moslem [who] blows up himself and others in the name of Allah." Or one could be a "Hindu [who] gave milk and mooed for ten generations." Or one could be a Christian who gets to heaven simply "by belief in Jesus. . . . The only way to salvation is through Christ."[57] To put it mildly, Ryle's lesson on cultural chauvinism is not exactly a teaching on pluralist communication, representative thinking, or visiting; it is a chauvinism fundamentally at odds with pluralist democratic politics.

Indeed, according to Promise Keepers, in these days before God's judgment, there is no reason for democratic politics. Engaging with others who are different—be they worshippers of holy cows, radical feminists, or any other unbelievers—is a risk to one's own purity. And what is the point of such democratic participation anyway? Politics cannot solve issues of the heart—and all the social ills facing the nation, be they drug use, racism, divorce, or teen pregnancy—are fundamentally issues of the heart. The only reason to engage in conversation with unbelievers is not to listen and learn from them, nor to engage in representative thinking, but to spread the Gospel, to follow the Great Commission and convey the Truth. As expressed in its vivid jeremiads, Promise Keepers conceives of the contemporary United States as largely a threatening realm of unchristian disorder replete with pornography, drug use, abortion, homosexuality, and radical feminism. And, typical of prophetic social movements, Promise Keepers crafts its identity as not at home in the world.

However, rather than seeking to engage in the public realm of politics to seek social transformation, Promise Keepers generally prefers to create a safe and comfortable space on the margins. Like Billy Sunday, Promise Keepers trades homelessness for worldlessness. For a movement with a political theology that focuses on personal salvation and the coming days of divine judgment, this contained and guarded private realm is an essential goal. The promised land has become less a shared cooperative space and more a privatized and exclusive realm for believers. The challenge Promise Keepers poses to democratic politics is not simply a disinclination to countenance others in the public realm, listening to the many stories and engaging in the imaginative reflection that is the vital characteristic of representative thinking. These typically liberal concerns about religion's being the end of political conversation are only part of the challenge.

The other crucial element is a matter not just of *how* religious individuals and groups participate in the public realm, but *whether* they participate in this realm at all. The anti-political prophetic politics of Promise Keepers that encourages withdrawal from the public realm is perhaps a greater threat to democratic politics in the United States. The diminishing of worldliness, and the demeaning of its importance, is a hallmark of "dark times" for democracy. The greater impact of Promise Keepers on American political culture will be the result of this social movement's efforts to encourage privatizing, therapeutic responses to the challenges facing the polity. Denigrating the importance of democratic participation, dismissing structural analysis of social conditions, and discounting the legitimacy of political solutions presents a serious threat to American democratic politics. In its endeavor to move men and social issues to the private sphere, Promise Keepers challenges the validity of politics and thus weakens the capacity of politics to resolve social ills. When Promise Keepers pulls citizens from the public sphere, political dialogue loses not only their voices, but also their ears. Participatory democracy depends on both speaking and listening. If citizens are not willing to engage in political dialogue, indeed, if citizens are taught that political discussions are essentially insignificant, then organizations such as Promise Keepers will help create at best non-compliance, and at worst open hostility to decisions that emerge from the realm of politics. Hollowing out American democracy in this manner is potentially the greatest and most devastating element of this contemporary Christian social movement.

As Promise Keepers looks forward, there are some questions about its capacity to prosper in the 21st century. As Thomas Fortson says, social movements do often have a beginning and an end. For an anti-political religious social movement such as Promise Keepers, the problem is acute. Sustaining a social movement over time requires maintaining the active participation of members. Engendering such lasting engagement commonly requires definitive markers of success or failure that produce either the hope or fear necessary to motivate participation. For an anti-political organization like Promise Keepers, however, the markers are often hard to demonstrate. As Promise Keepers gained prominence throughout the 1990s, the indices of hope could be found in the growing number of men who participated in the stadium and arena events. The largest gathering of men organized by Promise Keepers, the 1997 Stand in the Gap event in Washington, D.C., marked the peak of Promise Keepers' success.

It has also become a day marking the movement's decline. In the ensuing years, Promise Keepers has never been able to match the numbers of 1997, and for a movement that gauged its success on such statistics, the shrinking participation has been palpable and dispiriting. Promise Keepers' problem, in the face of such a decline in participation, is that it had no other publicly accessible way to measure its success or failure. Because Promise Keepers' political theology diminished worldliness, pulling people out of the public realm and into the private sphere, the indices of hope or fear that sustain a movement were obscured from public assessment. It is hard to quantify how many souls Promise Keepers saved, or how many men became better husbands, or how many overcame personal prejudices, but since these were the "goals" Promise Keepers created, its own contextual framework made sustaining the social movement more difficult.

It is for this reason that religious movements often become more "political" over time. Revivals develop into efforts for political reform or action—witness Sunday's engagement in the issues of prohibition and America's role in World War I—so that the movement can continue to generate public interest and involvement. Thus far, Promise Keepers has not explicitly headed in this more obviously political direction—but there are signs that such engagement in the public realm might be more common in the future of Promise Keepers. (Fortson's press release on marriage amid the debates about same-sex marriage in America is one example.) To date, Promise Keepers has preferred to respond to social issues rather than take a more active approach. For example, Promise Keepers was invited by Mel Gibson to a private screening of *The Passion of the Christ* and has enthusiastically championed the film. Joe White, Promise Keepers honorary chairperson, proclaimed in his March 2004 online newsletter:

> God only knows how many billion will see Mel Gibson's "Passion of the Christ." To watch that movie and not be transformed is to have a heart filled with concrete. I don't believe the world will ever be the same. The intense criticism and scrutiny that Mel has received over the greatest work of his lifetime bears evidence of the anger of Satan and the hatred of the majority of Hollywood and our media over such a realistic, life-changing presentation of the passion of our Savior.[58]

Seeking to generate interest in the organization and renewed enthusiasm among members in response to social and political developments was perhaps most obvious in the aftermath of the attacks of 9/11. McCartney issued a public letter after the attacks that declared: "Americans have been deeply shocked and saddened. Many are in need of comfort. Many have been gripped by fear. . . . Men in our nation are looking for answers. I believe God in his Providence has uniquely positioned Promise Keepers to respond to these needs, speaking to men with real answers to their questions and doubts."[59] Such reactive measures have thus far failed to put Promise Keepers back in the center of public attention. Promise Keepers may yet rise to its peak level of cultural influence again. If not, it would be a failure of our own imagination to consider Promise Keepers an ineffective social movement. The diminishment of the public realm of politics, the pervasiveness of language of sinfulness and evil in American culture, the revitalization of muscular Christianity—coupled with the acceptance of therapeutic Christianity for men—are all indications that Promise Keepers has changed the nation.

# Chapter Five
## Call to Renewal: Demanding Democracy from Exile

The Hebrew prophets say that we find our own good in seeking the common good. The prophet Isaiah says that when we feed the hungry, take in the homeless, and "break the yoke" of oppression, then we will find our own healing. He also says the act of compassion requires that you "not hide yourself from your own flesh." In other words, compassion means to recognize the kindred spirit we all share together. And the Bible insists that the best test of a nation's righteousness is how it treats the poorest and most vulnerable in its midst.
—Reverend Jim Wallis, *Who Speaks for God?*

In the culture wars of the 1990s, not only were conservative religious forces re-invigorated in America, but progressive religious voices also joined the debates in significant ways. Providing an alternative vision of morality in America, groups such as Evangelicals for Social Action (led by Ron Sider) and the Politics of Meaning (led by Michael Lerner) made clear that religious groups were concerned not only with "sex and the family," but also with poverty, environmental degradation, and racial injustice. Call to Renewal, a group convened and led by the Reverend Jim Wallis, has been the most prominent and sustained of these progressive religious social forces.

Although it also relies on the American sacred story of Exodus, Call to Renewal provides an example of prophetic politics that is starkly different from that of Promise Keepers. Rather than emphasizing chosen-ness and promised land, Call to Renewal adopts the themes of "sojourners," wilderness and exile to define its prophetic politics. In its jeremiads, wisdom literature, and other documents—especially the writings of Call to Renewal founder and convener Rev. Jim Wallis—Call to Renewal seeks to develop a prophetic politics that is congenial to democratic politics.[1]

## Crying Out for Renewal

From its inception, Call to Renewal has explicitly framed itself as a political organization.[2] Following the 1994 mid-term national elections, in which the Republican Party won control of the Congress and the religious right rose to the peak of its influence in the decade of the 1990s, religious leaders outside of this ideological sphere began to organize as an alternative religious voice in American politics. Call to Renewal emerged as a voice of protest. In 1995, in response to what they considered draconian efforts for welfare reform, Wallis and a group of 55 other "inner-city pastors" gathered in the Rotunda of the United States Capitol and proceeded to read from the Book of Isaiah. "Woe to the legislators of infamous laws, to those who issue tyrannical decrees, who refuse justice to the unfortunate, who cheat the poor among my people of their rights, who make widows their prey and rob the orphan" (Is. 10:1–2, quoted in Wallis, 1996, 42). After being arrested in front of a group of eighth-graders who happened to be visiting the Capitol that day for a civics lesson, the religious leaders spent the day singing, talking, and planning in a D.C. jail. "Call to Renewal was born in that jail cell," Wallis has declared.[3]

The protest of this nascent organization actually followed the publication of a joint statement titled "Cry for Renewal," signed by almost one hundred Christian leaders representing an array of denominations and traditions; this statement in turn served as a founding document for the organization Call to Renewal.[4] Articulating the two initial goals of the organization, the "Cry for Renewal" announced the presence of a Christian voice that was an alternative to that of the "religious right" and offered a "new political vision." After a successful year of meetings and actions, including a "National Forum on Faith and Politics" and a series of speeches throughout the nation by Wallis (many of which received significant media attention), Call to Renewal decided that its first goal of offering an alternative to the religious right had been met. Accordingly, shifting away from a reactive, defensive position, Call to Renewal began to focus more emphatically on advocating its "new political vision." In 1997–98, Call to Renewal developed a "four-point agenda" representing the organization's primary political goals: a commitment to (1) "overcoming poverty," (2) "dismantling racism-white supremacy," (3) "affirming a consistent ethic of life," and (4) "rebuilding family and community."[5] In 1999–2000, Call to Renewal further honed its political agenda. While still pursuing each of these political goals—and in so doing, asserting the inter-relatedness of these aims—Call to Renewal committed itself to a ten-year campaign to overcome poverty. As an early public step in this endeavor, Call to Renewal emerged from its 2000 conference with a "Covenant to Overcome Poverty."[6]

Since that time, addressing the issue of poverty and wealth in the United States has become the definitive priority of the movement. While this shift has led to further re-articulations of Call to Renewal's goals and mission, the attention to this agenda has been complicated, unsurprisingly, by the attacks of 9/11 and the subsequent war on terrorism and war in Iraq. Along with other citizens and activists in the United States, Wallis focused a great deal of energy on the public debates leading up to the war in Iraq. Emerging as a central figure organizing other religious leaders to articulate a position holding the United States military invasion of Iraq as a breach of "just war" principles, Wallis swept across the country, and back and forth to England, proposing alternatives to war.[7] Since the onset of the war, Wallis has been a fierce critic of the Bush foreign policy. This engagement with the most pressing issue of the day has since become clearly linked to Call to Renewal's focus on poverty. Wallis and others in Call to Renewal have echoed Martin Luther King Jr.'s criticism of the war in Vietnam, in part arguing that the financial cost of war drains resources desperately needed to address the issue of poverty at home. As Wallis proclaimed in his Call to Renewal Pentecost 2003 sermon:

> Paying for war by cutting needed spending for the poor while giving unneeded tax cuts to the rich is morally unconscionable. The federal budget's priorities are a disaster for the poor, a windfall for the wealthiest, and thus directly conflict with biblical priorities. Budgets are moral documents. . . . Let me say this in my clearest evangelical language, this federal budget is unbiblical.
>
> A modern prophet like Micah once said: A nation that continues year after year to spend more money on military defense than on programs of social uplift is a nation approaching spiritual death. So said the Rev. Martin Luther King Jr.[8]

As it pursues its political agenda, Call to Renewal has structured itself as an umbrella organization or "federation," for faith-based groups across the country endeavoring to create a "new faith based network and voice for justice" (Wallis 1999, 2). At the center of the umbrella is the Sojourners community that publishes the bi-monthly magazine *Sojourners,* which Wallis edits. The Sojourners community also runs the Sojourners' neighborhood center in the Columbia Heights area of Washington, D.C., which offers food for the hungry, day care, and other services. The foundation of the organization among those most in need, coupled with the national voice generated by the magazine (whose editorial board and regular contributors include Walter Brueggemann, James H. Cone, James Forbes, Vincent Harding, Rosemary Radford Ruether, Cornel West, and Garry Wills) serves as a crucial framework for Call to Renewal. This combination allows Call to Renewal to listen and act in the streets while preaching to and leading a national audience. Every issue of *Sojourners* contains an update on the activities of Call to Renewal and much of the organization's "wisdom literature" first appears in the pages of the magazine. Wallis contributes at least one editorial of his own to each issue,[9] and there is considerable overlap among members of Call to Renewal's coordinating committee, the initial endorsers of the 1995 "Cry for Renewal," and the contributing editors of *Sojourners*.[10] The federation model enables Call to Renewal's coordinating committee to serve as a national voice on public policy based on the information it gathers from a diverse collection of affiliated local and national groups within the umbrella.[11]

With the Sojourners community at the center of the organization, the spokes of the Call to Renewal umbrella reach out across the nation, encompassing an array of denominational, racial, ethnic, gender, political and issue-based differences. At the 1999 Call to Renewal National conference on Churches and Welfare Reform, for instance, 800 people from 37 states and 29 denominations were in attendance.[12] Founding participants in Call to Renewal's Campaign to Overcome Poverty include representatives from across the theological and political spectrums of the Christian community in the United States.[13] As Wallis has written regarding bridging the conventional gap between liberal and evangelical Christians:

> The conventional wisdom still says that liberal Christians have a social conscience and evangelicals do not, preferring instead to focus only on the personal morality of issues such as abortion and homosexuality. The media in particular keep that perception alive. But the big story that most of the press (including the religious press) continue to miss is how much that reality is changing. On at least three key social issues—poverty, race, and the environment—evangelicals are exhibiting a growing conviction and conscience. In local congregations, poor neighborhoods, and legislative halls, a new evangelical activism and advocacy is emerging.[14]

In its efforts to develop a "new politics of hope," Call to Renewal speaks in the language of social movements—or at least in language derived in large part from the civil rights movement of the 1950s and 1960s (Wallis

1996, xv). While optimistic about its chances to meet such an aim, Call to Renewal is quite aware of the forces it is taking on: the complacency in churches, the predominance of consumerism in the United States ("materialism has become culture in America"[15]), forces on the "religious right" (including in the Bush administration) who are perceived as more inclined toward polemic than dialogue, and a skeptical political left suspiciously viewing any religious overtones as a source of divisiveness. Nevertheless, Call to Renewal is committed to realizing the delicate integration of prophetic religion and democratic politics. Its founding document, "The Cry for Renewal," begins with this claim and warning:

> We believe that the language of morality and faith can make a critical contribution to political discourse. . . . We are Evangelical voices who seek a biblical approach to politics, not an ideological agenda. . . . We challenge any political litmus test that distorts the independent moral conscience that faith can bring to politics. We are dismayed by those who would undermine the integrity of religious conviction that does not conform to a narrow ideological agenda. (Quoted in Wallis 1996, 201–3)

In its effort to carefully distinguish itself from the moralizing voices that have often been the predominant representatives of religion in the public sphere over the last twenty-five years, Call to Renewal explicitly marks the difference between such expressions of ideological faith and its own "biblical faith."

> True *biblical faith* focuses on the moral values that must be recovered to heal the torn political fabric; *ideological faith* would rend the fabric further in the pursuit of power. *Biblical faith* tries to find common ground between warring factions by taking the public discourse to higher ground; *ideological faith* fuels the rhetoric of "us and them" and breeds a climate for hate and even violence. *Biblical faith* holds up the virtues of compassion and community; *ideological faith* appeals to personal and group self-interest. *Biblical faith* understands our identity as the children of God as a call to humility and reconciliation rather than as a basis for attacking those who are less righteous. (Quoted in Wallis 1996, 203–4, my italics)

The "Cry for Renewal" contains the hallmarks that have continued to define the organization. The polity in the United States is perceived as a human-made "fabric," and it is the responsibility of citizens to consciously seek to mend, rather than further rend, this tapestry. This type of social and political engagement requires an inclusive search for "common ground" rather than an exacerbation of divisions—it calls for expanding what Arendt refers to as the "in-between." In acknowledging and explicitly addressing pluralism and difference in the United States, Call to Renewal does not stress the exclusive righteousness of the chosen of God, but rather the humble and common status of the "children of God." In principle, at least, the prophetic politics of Call to Renewal in its espousal of public-minded and politically oriented inclusive citizenship is quite distinct from the individualizing, privatizing prophetic politics of Promise Keepers and Billy Sunday. Of course, claiming to be committed to enriching democratic participation is a common step for social movements in America; the dedication to pluralist political discourse, to enhancing *sensus communis,* present in this founding document, should also be evident throughout the works of Call to Renewal.

## Carving Out New Political Space

An intriguing place to begin this exploration of Call to Renewal is with its emphatic efforts to distinguish itself from the religious right. As we have already seen in the "Cry for Renewal," this endeavor bears rhetorical significance as an act of self-identity. The manner in which Call to Renewal distances itself from the religious right also illuminates Call to Renewal's approach to politics, theology, history, and interpretation—considerations vitally important to this analysis of the organization's prophetic politics.

Call to Renewal's criticism of the religious right is especially poignant because of the nature of the complaint. First of all, the very need to define itself against the religious right is a powerful indication of the political context and significance of the culture wars into which Call to Renewal was born. In a polity in which "the nation is looking to faith communities as never before" in order to fill the gaps created by the federal government's decreasing role in providing social services, the predominant religious voices in America have been conservative and pietistic (Wallis, CTR 1997). Thinking primarily of the Christian Coalition, which along with the Family Research Council stood as the most powerful of the forces of the religious right during the mid-1990s, Call to Renewal felt compelled to remap the terrain of American political history in order to reclaim space for other religious voices. In his *Who Speaks for God?* Wallis writes:

> It is important to recognize what an historical aberration the Religious Right represents. For biblical religion to be put at the service of the rich instead of the poor, the powerful instead of the oppressed, of war instead

of peace, turns Christian teaching upside down. For evangelical religion to be used to fuel the engines of racial and class division, to block the progress of women, to undermine care for the creation, to fight the banning of assault weapons, to end public legal services to those who can't afford them, and actually encourage a public policy that abandons our poorest children runs counter to Christian Scripture, tradition and history. (1996, 17–18)

Call to Renewal's critique of the religious right is essentially three-pronged. The religious right is guilty of bad theology, bad history, and, as a result, bad politics. By briefly assessing the three components of this critique, a clearer picture of the principles espoused by Call to Renewal begins to emerge.

The theological challenge of the religious right offered by Call to Renewal is leveled on both the method and content of interpretation. In a direct attack on "biblical literalism," for example, Judith Gundry-Wolf criticizes the Southern Baptist Convention's official statement that a wife should "graciously submit to the servant leadership of her husband." Challenging this denomination's derivation of proper biblical social hierarchies on the "ancient household code" found in Ephesians 5:22–23, Gundry-Wolf emphasizes the broader egalitarianism found in the Gospels and in Galatians 3:28 and 1 Corinthians chapter 7.[16] In these theological responses to the religious right, Call to Renewal seeks to contextualize the teachings of the Bible and stress the broader lessons rather than isolated passages. As Ched Myers explains:

> Theological conservatives tend to have a high degree of confidence that the Bible itself can adjudicate all doctrinal and ethical disputes—when "properly" interpreted. Unfortunately, the correct interpretation is usually equated with the conservatives' own positions, such that its commitment to "biblical authority" too often ends up looking more like a kind of biblical authoritarianism. (35)

The point is not that there are no answers "in the book" (Wallis 1995, 260). Rather, Myers suggests approaching the text through "the popular education techniques pioneered by Paulo Freire . . . starting with what we know, drawing from our experience of the world, questioning and being questioned by texts we are studying" (Myers, 34–35). In other words, the Bible offers an invitation to inquiry and dialogue rather than a declarative monologue. Myers recommends acknowledging that

> The Bible is our foundational story and that the Bible will be read differently within the community of faith. . . . Each positional group must be

willing to articulate and to examine honestly the interests and values that underlie its reading of scripture. . . . No matter how passionate our viewpoint, we should always remain open to others, because scripture itself is multifaceted and further reflection may yield a more compelling reading. After all, our contexts as readers change through time and space.

Rather than insisting on "one true reading," Myers advocates an "embracing pluralism" and is careful to note that this step "does not preclude critical engagement with other positions. There are matters of integrity and justice at stake, and not all readings are benign or respectful" (Myers, 35, 51). This commitment to "theological pluralism" has helped enable Call to Renewal to attract support of conservative Christians sympathetic to the social movement's concerns with poverty in the United States.

Indeed, one of the questions that Call to Renewal is determined to raise in this dialogic exploration of the lessons of the Bible is why so little is said by the religious right about poverty and the gross disparities of wealth in the United States, despite the innumerable scriptural references to these concerns. Members of Call to Renewal argue that to listen to the concern over the immorality of homosexuality among the religious right, one would think that the Bible was far more concerned with such matters than issues of greed and materialism. And yet, as Wallis is fond of recounting,

> One of my seminary colleagues . . . [took] a pair of scissors to an old Bible, and proceeded to cut out every single reference to riches or the poor . . . by the time he was finished the Prophets were decimated, the Psalms destroyed, the Gospels ripped to shreds and the Epistles turned to tattered rags. . . . I used to take it out with me to preach. I'd hold it high above church congregations and say, "Brothers and sisters, this is our American Bible! It's full of holes!"[17]

The selective readings of the Bible proposed to justify a vision of the truth that supports only one's own position—an interpretation that raises no questions about one's own beliefs and well-being—is a form of what Call to Renewal would term "idolatry."[18] Members of Call to Renewal further assert that such a troubling theological interpretation is also indicative of much of the religious right's approach to history. In *Recovering the Evangel,* one of the Sojourners-produced study guides used by Call to Renewal, Mark Cerone critically analyzes the "selective reading of history" employed by the religious right. Cerone argues that this approach fuel[s] a sense of urgency to rescue the United States, restoring it to a place of moral authority and military supremacy. . . . This "godly heritage" . . . an idealized perception of U.S. history, and nostalgia for the "good old days" (the America of the late 1940s and '50s) are blended together to create a picture of where we came from and how to return there. (12)

Returning to this faith in America's mission to become a shining "City upon a Hill" leads one to an alarmingly idolatrous conception of the history of the United States. Most disconcerting for Call to Renewal, such a vision of the chosen status of the United States elides the history of racism that has permeated the nation from its founding. Arguing that racism is "America's Original Sin," Wallis concludes quite simply, "The brutal founding facts of our nation cannot be erased" (1995, 101).[19]

The narrow approach to biblical and historical interpretation on the part of the religious right inevitably leads, Call to Renewal argues, to troubling political conclusions. The reliance on interpretive approaches that never raise questions about their own status before God or in the polity leads toward a sense of hubris and self-certainty. "The religious right neglects the kind of spiritual values that might bring [the people of the United States] together, or heal the nation's wounds. . . . Instead, they tell us who to be afraid of" (1996, 4).[20] Indeed, Wallis concludes, the religious right is so convinced of the singular truth of its understandings of scripture and history that it is "guilty of one of the worst sins of politics: the denigration of 'the other'" (1996, 162). Such denigration, from Call to Renewal's perspective, is anathema to the biblical teachings the religious right purports to value so highly and the ideals of American democracy it proclaims to hold so dear.

This critique of the religious right suggests the modes of theological and historical analysis and political principles to which Call to Renewal ascribes. In differentiating itself so emphatically from the most pervasive religious voices in American politics today, Wallis and Call to Renewal have sought to develop a distinct form of contemporary prophetic politics. Examining more closely the stories Call to Renewal tells within the narrative scaffolding of the American sacred story of Exodus enables a further assessment of the movement's commitment to democratic politics.

## Call to Renewal as a Storytelling Movement

In a manner similar to Promise Keepers, Call to Renewal is emphatically a storytelling Christian social movement.[21] Utilizing jeremiads and wisdom stories replete with themes drawn from the Exodus narrative, Call to Renewal offers its own vision of the crisis in America and the path to not merely solace, but justice. This narrative path is marked by an understanding of conversion, a sense of identity evident in its depiction of Moses and of citizens as sojourners, of the spatial and temporal context shaped by the tropes of wilderness and exile, and finally by a dedication to accepting responsibility to expand the shared public world and seek justice within it.

Consistent with both its proclaimed prophetic political vision and the American sacred story of Exodus, Call to Renewal readily employs the pattern of the jeremiad in its exhortations. Three of Wallis' most recent books open with declarations of "crisis" in America. To take only one example, which may serve to illustrate the manner in which Call to Renewal conceives of—and defines—the crisis in contemporary America, Wallis begins *The Soul of Politics* with the following proclamation:

> The world isn't working. Things are unraveling, and most of us know it. Tonight, the urban children of the world's only remaining superpower will go to bed to the sound of gunfire. Bonds of family and community are fraying. Our most basic virtues of civility, responsibility, justice, and integrity seem to be collapsing. We appear to be losing the ethics derived from personal commitment, social purpose, and spiritual meaning. The triumph of materialism is hardly questioned now, in any part of our society. Both domestically and globally, we are divided along the lines of race, ethnicity, class, gender, religion, culture, and tribe, and threaten to explode our divisions into a world of perpetual conflict. (Wallis 1995, xiii)

There are a number of noteworthy elements of this story of crisis. First, Wallis refers to the obvious awareness on the part of his readers that there is indeed a crisis in the nation. There is a sense here of preaching to those who should be in the choir; these declarations reflect not so much missionary work as efforts to tell people what they already know in such a manner as to excite their passions.[22] Second, while there is something particularly American about the crisis—he suggests that divisions of identity have fractured "our most basic virtues of civility"—the crisis works on individual, community, national, and global levels. Strikingly, as is the case in the "Cry for Renewal," Wallis employs the metaphor of a "fraying" and "unraveling" tapestry, suggesting that the current state of crisis is caused by a neglectful people who have forfeited the responsibility of maintaining the social fabric. This human-centered metaphor indicates the possibility of solace found through nurturing or mending the tears in this tapestry. With regard to the content of the crisis, we should note that Wallis focuses on the ills caused by a "triumphant materialism" and divisions of identity. Typical of jeremiads, this is a bleak analysis of present conditions expressed in a tone of shame and judgment, but as Bercovitch reminds us, this gloomy judgment of present circumstances is but the first step in the jeremiadic pattern. The goal of prophetic politics—and of the jeremiadic proclamation—is to push us toward the future fulfillment of the apparently forgotten promise.[23] Despite the desperation and devastation in this articulation of crisis, the optimism of Call to Renewal's jeremiad is evident in the subheadings of this opening chapter of *The Soul of Politics:* Wallis takes his reader from "Signs of Crisis" to "Signs of Hope."[24]

Like the jeremiads of Promise Keepers, the stories Call to Renewal tells to legitimate its depiction of the crisis are a combination of narratives based on the author's personal experiences and the struggles of a multicultural and ecumenical gallery of American citizens. (The final 125-page section of Wallis' *The Soul of Politics* is essentially a collection of such stories.) In his most recent book, *Faith Works,* Wallis introduces the volume by saying,

> This is a book of stories about people who have acted on [a] positive vision of faith. . . . All through this book, I share my own life experiences and other stories from around the world that inform the lessons and give them a very human reality. . . . I hope readers will make another connection—between reading a book and joining a movement. (Wallis 2000, xxvii, xxviii–xxxix)

The crucial difference between the stories told by Promise Keepers and Call to Renewal is that the former's stories of crisis and solace are almost exclusively concerned with individual sin and salvation, while the latter's narratives emphasize structural injustices and social change. Rather than narratives about troubled marriages, Call to Renewal tells jeremiads of "sexual labor," "sexual violence," "sexism and advertising," and other illustrations of the "structure of sexism."[25] Rather than tales of individual problems with financial burdens, Call to Renewal offers illustrations of the "invisible poor" struggling in a "two-tiered economy."[26] Rather than presenting anecdotes about acts of individual prejudice, Call to Renewal recounts stories of "the system of racism."[27]

The difference between these two forms of storytelling is particularly clear in matters of race. The stories of Promise Keepers' efforts to engender racial reconciliation have been the source of much of the positive media coverage the organization has received. Call to Renewal also speaks of "racial reconciliation" as a vital goal in a nation torn by "America's original sin." However, Call to Renewal emphatically asserts that racial reconciliation that takes no account of broader matters of racial justice is a shallow veneer covering a deeper social wound. As Wallis has written:

> Sitting around the campfire together singing "Kumbaya" and holding hands will not suffice. Outside the church meeting rooms and stadium rallies where white and black Christians are hugging one another is a nation where racial polarization is on the rise, where the legacy of discrimination is still present, and where the majority white population is signaling its tiredness with the "issue" of race by voting down long-standing affirmative action policies. (2000, 130)

In short, the story of crisis in America described in the jeremiads of Call to Renewal is not—or not simply—a matter of misguided personal beliefs and behaviors. While revivalist politics always address individual behavior, Wallis argues such a limited focus is consistent with neither the message of Jesus nor the history of progressive religious engagement in the well-being of the American polity, and it will do little to end systemic racial injustice in the United States.[28] Indeed, he suggests in the introduction to *Faith Works,* "perhaps the greatest heresy of the twentieth-century American religion was to make faith into a purely personal matter and a private affair."[29]

Accordingly, the vision of hope in Call to Renewal's jeremiads is consistently a matter of social, rather than merely personal, transformation. As Wallis declares:

> There are periods in history when social crisis threatens to unravel society. But such times are often also eras of transition, invitation and opportunity. . . . At these historical junctures, ideological analysis and solutions are inadequate. . . . We see a crisis, we feel a hope, we discern a word, and we hear a call. It is a renewal of the heart to which we are now summoned. The crisis calls out for conversion . . . rooted in old traditions but radically applied to our present circumstances." (1995, 27)

This depiction of the current moment between past and future introduces two crucial concepts into Call to Renewal's efforts: the idea of the "summoned subject" and its understanding of conversion.

The notion of the "summoned subject" is, as Paul Ricoeur reminds us, of central importance in the prophetic tradition. The biblical prophets are depicted as being "summoned" by God to speak to the wayward people. These summoned subjects will be mediators between the caller and the society in which the subjects live. In the case of the biblical prophets, they stand at the margins of the community between God and the people of Israel, and are called to be conscious pariahs, addressing the troubled society from liminal positions.[30]

Wallis and Call to Renewal recognize that those beholden to the wayward society tell their own persuasive, if destructive, narratives—stories of the value of material possessions, stories about racial identity, stories about the poor deserving their fate, stories of American triumphalism and complacency, stories about rugged individualism and the diminishing importance of community. Standing on the boundary of the community, summoned subjects can always be seduced back into the comforts of a decaying culture. Much as the Hebrews liberated from Egypt longed for the fleshpots of their house of bondage, so too will these contemporary pariahs be seduced away from the call.[31]

In response, Call to Renewal urges people to accept the challenge and responsibility of "not being at home in the world" defined by materialism, racism, and self-satisfaction. To cultivate and support conscious pariahs—and to contest the seductive, if destructive, stories told by proponents of the society in crisis—Call to Renewal responds with stories of its own; stories that invariably involve both individual and social transformation. These stories of hope are portrayed as narratives of conversion; they are a call back to the center of America, an effort to re-engage. Stories sensitize listeners and hopefully, in Arendtian terms, re-animate the organs needed for engagement in the shared world. This revitalization of the organs of democratic sensibility is central to Call to Renewal's vision of conversion.

For Call to Renewal, conversion is both political and religious—or, rather, it is a religious conversion that must also be political. The rhetorical significance of conversion is, of course, quite powerful in evangelical Christian circles in the United States where the understanding of conversion as a personal "coming to Christ" has extraordinary discursive resonance.[32] Call to Renewal challenges this personal and privatized notion of conversion, arguing that the process involves not just personal but also social and political transformation. Indeed it is often through the language of conversion that Call to Renewal links not just the personal and political but also the categories of religion, politics and history. As Wallis explains:

> Conversion in the Bible is always firmly grounded in history; it is always addressed to the actual situation in which people find themselves. In other words, biblical conversion is historically specific. People are never called

to conversion in a historical vacuum. They turn to God in the midst of concrete historical events, dilemmas and choices. That turning is always deeply personal, but it is never private. It is never an abstract or theoretical concern; conversion is always a practical issue. Any idea of conversion that is removed from the social and political realities of the day is simply not biblical. (1992, 5)

As a matter of both personal and social transformation, conversion involves not withdrawal, but re-engagement with the world.

Fulfilling this role of the summoned subject (or summoned social movement) requires the development of what Call to Renewal calls a "prophetic politics."[33] Wallis argues, "The prophetic tradition insists that religion that does not manifest itself in *action for justice* is false religion. The Hebrew prophets boldly proclaimed that God rejected the worship and prayers that ignored social justice" (1995, 230, my italics). The visionary hope of Call to Renewal is that

A *prophetic politics* rooted in moral principles could again spark people's imagination and involvement. We need a personal ethic of moral responsibility, a commitment to justice with the capacity also for reconciliation, an economic approach governed by the ethics of community and sustainability, a restored sense of our *covenant* with the abandoned poor and damaged earth, a *reminder* of shared values that calls forth the very best in us, and a *renewal* of citizen politics to *fashion a new political future*. (1995, xxii, my italics).

Conversion in this sense leads to a regeneration of the very tools Arendt would argue are vital for democratic politics: the capacity for imagination, a broad sense of responsibility for the world in which one lives, a commitment to justice and the maintenance of a sustainable public realm, a capacity to remember and make promises, a concern for memory and stories of the past, and the hopeful potential for a new future. This conception of prophetic politics, carefully crafted through Exodus themes of covenant and memory—and committed to a democratic ethos—is at the heart of Call to Renewal's mission and is amply evident in the themes it utilizes from the Exodus narrative.

## Moses Is Just Like Us

Billy Sunday depicted Moses as a warrior who learned discipline and faith as an infant at his mother's breast. Martin Luther King Jr. spoke of Moses as a leader schooled by the arduous experience of being a stranger in a strange land. Promise Keepers portrays Moses as struggling against private weaknesses as he pursues personal transformation.

Call to Renewal has an equally particular vision of Moses as a very human figure rather than a "super-hero" (Wallis 2000, 259). For Call to Renewal, Moses is "just a simple goat herder . . . out in the desert, with a family and without great ambitions." Highlighting the extensive argument between Moses and God in chapters 3 and 4 of Exodus, Wallis stresses, "Moses is . . . a reluctant leader right from the beginning." But he does hear the call, and, as a summoned subject, goes and does the work of liberation. The lesson to be learned, Wallis concludes, is that Moses is "like us. He didn't feel up to the job, he didn't feel self-confident, he didn't want to be a hero. . . . Moses is not a good super-hero role model. Moses is a better example of how extraordinary things can be accomplished through ordinary people—like us." Indeed, Wallis continues:

> Most of the people I know who made a difference were not super-heroes either. . . . They just felt a sense of calling and commitment that enabled them to do important things . . . the call may not always be as clear as a voice from a burning bush, but most of us have a pretty good idea about what we should do.[34]

This depiction of Moses as an ordinary human is, of course, aimed at inspiring his audience to join the work of "conversion" to decisively shape the "reconfiguration" of the polity. If Moses is a super-hero, Wallis fears, the populace will be passive at best and, more than likely, resistant murmurers—patterns of behavior which Call to Renewal perceives as all too common in contemporary America. Speaking, for instance, of the chains of poverty in black America, Eugene Rivers declared that "for many of the poor, it is not a question of them getting out of Egypt, it is a question of getting Egypt out of them." (Rivers, CTR 2000)

The quotidian qualities of Moses help make the story of Exodus accessible for people "looking for themselves" in the saga of the struggle for liberation. "Generations of people have taken courage, found strength, and discovered hope for their own liberation through the exodus of the Hebrews from their captivity," Wallis writes:

> This . . . is our own story. It is the story of . . . all those who have been afraid to do what they knew was right. Moses' excuses are much like our own. . . . Rosa Parks . . . Martin Luther King Jr. . . . the freedom ride[rs] . . . Desmond Tutu . . . were all afraid as were all the others who have stood up for justice, witnessed for peace, or given their lives for freedom.

But each one of them had heard a call. . . . Let the Pharaohs of our day be warned: New calls are being heard . . . and they are calls to a new vision for this world. New visions are made possible when people in all circumstances respond to the call. (1995, 238–39)

This portrayal of Moses as both accessible and an inspiration for political courage was at the heart of the plenary remarks by Marshall Ganz at the 2000 Call to Renewal Conference. Ganz situated his analysis squarely within the Exodus narrative by reminding his audience of the lesson of the Passover Seder that "Egypt was not then, but now, that slavery was not just then, but now, and that the work of liberation did not end then, but must be done now." Ganz went on to speak of "Moses, the organizer . . . was the Jew who was raised as an Egyptian. His identity was with the oppressed, but he understood the tools of the oppressor. And in fact, he had to spend a lot of time in the desert to figure out how to put these two pieces together before he could go back and do the work of liberation."[35] Ganz's portrayal of Moses is intriguing, for it carries the reminder that Moses understood—and to some extent benefited from—the unjust practices of Egypt. In this light it is crucial to note that Ganz is speaking to a largely middle-class audience, striving to sort out its own sense of culpability for what are framed as the injustices of American society. Ganz's vision of Moses tacitly acknowledges these questions of guilt and privilege but pushes his audience to move beyond any paralysis caused by such qualms and use their knowledge of the system to act and organize with the poor.

For Call to Renewal, the inspiration of Moses lies not with an image of God's warrior, steeled from birth for the work of liberation. Its model of Moses is intended to be accessibly human—with all of the doubts, flaws, and uncertainties any person might bring to the "struggle for justice." This Moses—humble, doubtful, but courageous—was neither simply born a leader nor turned into a leader through a transformative moment. Instead, he was someone who grew into a leader over time—a conversion process marked by struggles, failures, and frustrations, but also by learning, commitment, conviction, and partnership with God. This model of Moses is that of a summoned subject who pushes for the conversion of a people and strives for social transformation.

## Sojourners in the Wilderness, Citizens in Exile

This call for social transformation is also reflected in the metaphors of identity and context that Call to Renewal draws from the narrative scaffolding of Exodus. Quite unlike the exclusivist claims of chosen-ness and the veneration of America as God's shining city on a hill celebrated by Billy Sunday and Promise Keepers, Call to Renewal opts for the Exodus metaphors of sojourners and wilderness made familiar by Martin Luther King Jr. The identification of themselves—and, at a basic level, all people—as sojourners is made plain by the use of the term as the title of the magazine and the name of the community that serve as the voice and the grounding of this social movement. The trope of sojourners is also evident throughout the movement's stories and wisdom literature and while the characterization of the setting of the United States as a wilderness is less directly evident in the words of Call to Renewal, the qualities associated with wilderness are essential to Call to Renewal's portrayal of the nation. Moreover, and more controversially, Call to Renewal has been willing to frame the temporal and spatial context of the United States and its citizens as being in a condition of exile. This trope of exile provides a clear figurative link between the story of the liberation from Egypt and the stories of the biblical prophets upon which Call to Renewal bases so much of its political vision.

We have already seen that Call to Renewal is quite unwilling to romanticize American history in order to burnish the nation's image as a beacon to the world. Instead, Call to Renewal is characteristically blunt, for example, moving the history of slavery from the periphery back to the core foundation of the nation. As Calvin S. Morris writes in one of Call to Renewal's study guides on race in America:

> The Founders of this nation faced a dilemma posed by the conflict between freedom and slavery. A people proclaiming as the bedrock of their political existence the concept of human liberty as a natural endowment given by God nonetheless held others in chains. Thus, the United States was founded upon political and moral ambiguities so profound that its characterization of itself as a land of freedom and human liberty has to it the sound of hypocrisy. And after 200 years, the national conundrum is yet with us.[36]

And it is not just the idol of white supremacy that continues to haunt the United States; the historic legacy of the inequality of women also provides troubling links between past and present in the United States. "The persistence of sexism challenges men to have their own conversion and transformation. If relinquishing white privilege is required for racial justice, the relinquishing of male privilege will be necessary for gender justice" (Wallis 1995, 145).[37] The founding "political and moral ambiguities" continue to define the nation, leaving the United States in a place akin to the "shifting sands" of the wilderness.

And yet, despite the critical assessment of the history of the United States, Call to Renewal does not explicitly depict the nation as a "wilderness." Whereas for King, the metaphor of America as wilderness was a critical piece in his retelling of the Exodus story of liberation, Wallis and Call to Renewal rarely speak so directly in these terms. Instead, and quite interestingly, Wallis asserts,

> The biblical theme that perhaps best fits our present condition is the theme of *exile*. We do not live in the promised land. . . . Nor do those who have experienced the "sweltering heat of oppression," as Martin Luther King used to say, yet know a true exodus in America. Despite the invocation of other religious themes in our early American history, the theme of exile has been the experience for many in modern America. Malcolm X and radical Christians like Daniel Berrigan and William Stringfellow have even referred to America as Babylon. (1995, 262)

The relationship between the metaphors of wilderness and exile is complicated and weighty. The context of the wilderness does not presume the earlier habitation of a promised land. The Biblical setting of the wilderness is the temporal and spatial region between the Exodus from Egypt and the entry into the Promised Land in the book of Joshua. The prophets write from a temporal and spatial region that post-dates this entry into the Promised Land, a context best described as a state of exile. That is, some of the prophets (e.g., Ezekiel, Nehemiah, Second Isaiah) spoke during periods of physical exile in which the Hebrew people had either been evicted from the land or "political exile" in which they were living in the land but under "foreign" rule. Other prophets (Jeremiah, Hosea, Amos) wrote during periods in which Hebrew kings may have ruled the lands of Judah and Israel, but the polity might aptly be described as in exile from the principles established in the Torah. The vision of the prophets during such periods was to call the kings and people back to the forgotten covenant. The temporal context of exile is, thus, defined by prophets challenging the presumptions of present conditions by revitalizing a critical engagement with the past.

In the American context, the distinction between wilderness and exile bears great rhetorical significance. If one emphasizes wilderness, the sentiment is that the promised land lies as yet unsettled, still in the future. If one speaks of exile, the implicit message is that the nation can (at least in principle) be conceived as a promised land now tragically in a state of decline. This distinction is, admittedly, quite delicate and Wallis is not nearly as precise in his articulation of this distinction as King. While it is plainly evident from his numerous discussions of the history of the United States—particularly the racial history of the nation—that Wallis does not consider any American era as a time of the promised land, he nevertheless uses the metaphor of exile to describe the state of the nation.[38]

An alternative interpretation of the metaphors of wilderness and exile perhaps is helpful in mediating this tension. In considering the relation between wilderness and exile, Martin Buber emphasizes the significance of the "wings of eagles" passage from Exodus 19:3–6: "You yourselves have seen what I did in Egypt, I bore you on eagles' wings and brought you unto me. And now listen to my voice and keep my covenant, *then* you shall be to Me, out of all peoples a precious treasure" (cited in Buber 1967, 129). The point Buber makes is that the Hebrew people are not chosen or special before liberation, during liberation, and not even in the forming of the covenant, but rather in the keeping of the covenant—*if* you keep the covenant, *then* you shall be a precious treasure unto me. Accordingly, it can be argued that until the covenant is kept, all people are in a constant state of exile. The promised land remains not yet inhabited, and thus the wilderness and exile become virtually synonymous.

In large part, Wallis' willingness to speak of America as in a state of exile rather than wilderness is indicative of Call to Renewal's heavy reliance on the biblical prophets for its political theology.[39] Indeed, for Wallis one of the key biblical texts on the depiction of exile is the story of Nehemiah. As Wallis recounts the story in *The Soul of Politics*, Nehemiah was a prophet in a time of exile. Upon learning of the destruction of Jerusalem, Nehemiah goes to the ruling king of Babylon, Artaxerxes, and requests permission to rebuild the holy city. Upon receiving permission, Nehemiah returns to Jerusalem and "gathers the survivors still in and around the city. . . . 'Come, let us rebuild the wall of Jerusalem so that we may no longer suffer disgrace,'" says Nehemiah. "'Let us start building!' the people exclaimed. The Scripture says, 'so they committed themselves to the common good.'" Wallis concludes, "This is the prophetic call after the exile" (1995, 262). Prophetic leadership gathers people together, rebuilds the foundation of the polity, generates hope in the rebirth of civic space, and inspires commitment to the common good.

Isolated efforts of prophetic politics, however, are never in themselves enough to move a people out of the wilderness, or out of exile, and into the promised land. Neither Moses, Nehemiah, Isaiah nor any of the other prophets could establish the land of milk and honey as a fixed and stable place in even the best of times. The conditional covenant is never kept for long. The need for prophetic voices, reminding the people of what they inevitably will forget, resurfaces. Indeed, later in the book of Nehemiah is an equally compelling example of prophetic political action. Leading the Israelites out of "exile," the prophet Ezra gathers "all the people" in front of the Water Gate of Jerusalem and, along with other scribes, stands before the gathered children of Israel and reads to them "the book of the law of Moses. . . . And they read from the book, from the law of God, clearly; and they gave the sense so that the people understood the reading" (Neh. 8:1, 8). Nehemiah goes on to lead the gathered people in rituals, confession, and lessons in remembrance in the effort to renew the polity.

Like Nehemiah, Call to Renewal is striving to rebuild the foundation of the nation. Like Ezra, Call to Renewal strives to regenerate civic space and common understanding by returning to them their history, including a renewed appreciation of the role of revivalist social movements in the struggles for abolition, women's suffrage, the rights of workers and civil rights. Carving out space in contemporary political discourse for Christian voices that avoid the idolatrous theology and selective history of the religious right, Call to Renewal aims to rekindle the prophetic tradition in the United States from its place in exile.

## On a Journey

In identifying itself through the Exodus theme of sojourners, Call to Renewal is seeking to use the resonant scaffolding of Exodus to promote a vision of democratic politics that emphatically rejects the exclusionist ethos of chosen-ness. In making this rhetorical move, Call to Renewal claims the legacy of Martin Luther King Jr. and the civil rights movement and extends the implication of the metaphor of soujourners beyond King's efforts.

As the convener of Call to Renewal, Wallis recognizes that he has two fundamental organizational challenges. First, Call to Renewal faces the problem of bringing together Christians from an array of backgrounds, convincing believers that ecumenical good will can overcome denominational suspicion. Second, he faces the challenge of promoting a religious social movement in a political context often suspicious of religious engagement in political issues. To both of these challenges, Wallis responds initially with an explicit acknowledgement of the potential divisiveness of religiosity. Then, he creates an inclusive organizational ethos by inviting people to listen to one another under the common status as sojourners. We might think of this move as an Exodus two-step: rejecting the exclusivist political identity of chosen, while still crafting common political ground around the scaffolding of Exodus. In the introduction of *Faith Works,* for instance, Wallis sets the inviting tone for these lessons on faith and political involvement by acknowledging at the outset that

> Tragically, religion has too often been a sectarian and terribly divisive force. . . . Religion is often used as a sword to divide, rather than a balm to heal. And religious leaders can be guilty of the kind of power-politics tactics that tear people apart instead of bringing them together. Toward one another, the different religious communities sometimes behave no better than rival street gangs. (2000, xxv–xxvi)

By not just bemoaning the manner in which religious identity can take on exclusionist overtones, but rather by going so far as to compare religious groups to "street gangs," Wallis joins the forces of those who reject political claims in the name of any "brotherhood of believers." Pursuing a political and theological vision that welcomes rather than elides or minimizes difference, Wallis declares,

> Fordham University's Dr. Beatrice Bruteau asks the right question: "How big is your *we?*" Can we expand our vision of community beyond our own skin, family, race, tribe, culture, country and species? Spiritual life is more than what we believe, it also includes how we relate. Who is included in the *we* and who is not? That is both a spiritual and a political question. How we answer it will likely determine our future. (1996, 86)

Breaching these chasms is enabled by conceiving of all people as sojourners—particularly when coupled with the Exodus imperative of treating sojourners justly, "for you were sojourners in the land of Egypt" (Ex. 23:19). It is hard to overstate the weight Call to Renewal places on this question of inclusion. As Wallis says, the need for people to connect across boundaries is both "a spiritual and a political question." At stake in these "sojourners' relations" are both individual and social transformations.

Achieving such an inclusive pluralistic political ethos is no small task, Call to Renewal readily acknowledges, but it is vital to the movement's effort to enhance the *sensus communis* in American public life. The "crisis" in these terms is that in the United States today: "The walls and chasms between us seem to be growing every day. . . . A serious commitment to bring people together across the racial, cultural and economic divides doesn't seem to even be on the political agenda, much less near the top of it" (Wallis 1996, 87). Call to Renewal is striving to generate a prophetic politics that subjects "all projects, initiatives, decisions, and policies to new criteria: whether they make justice more possible for all of us and especially for those on the bottom, whether they allow us to live in more harmony on the earth, and whether they increase the participation of all people in decision making" (1995, xxi).

Call to Renewal does not merely leave this vision as a sweet-sounding fantasy. Guided by the principle that we should "be idealistic about where we are going and practical about how to get there," Call to Renewal espouses organizational beliefs that shape the practices of the movement.[40] In the wisdom literature of Call to Renewal, Wallis and the other organizational leaders have established movement principles that hew closely to my conception of democratic politics—a conception that depends on "visiting" and willingness to engage in redemptive history.

### The Wisdom of Call to Renewal: Visit, Redeem, Organize, and Discover Common Ground

The great emphasis of Call to Renewal's wisdom literature is the encouragement of analysis and action that begins with a willingness to explore perhaps familiar territory from a different perspective. The study guides push readers to question their assumptions, listen to others' stories, and then reconsider the pattern of one's behavior and underlying structures of society. The aim is to develop methods for overcoming what Wallis calls "civic poverty." Renewing American democracy, Call to Renewal suggests, will be the result of actively creating an environment that encourages appreciation for the array of perspectives that permeate this pluralist land. For Call to Renewal, the inspiration for such visiting comes not from Arendt and Kant but the biblical prophets and Jesus. The great deficiency in American political discourse, it argues, is the absence of the voices of those most in need. The consistent question posed by the prophets is: "How do we treat the poor, the stranger, the outcast, the weak, the vulnerable, the children? The Hebrew prophets saw this as the truest criterion of a nation's integrity" (Wallis 1996, 37). Hearing the cry of the oppressed,[41] listening to the stories of those rarely heard in the American public sphere, opening our eyes to the perspectives of other sojourners—this is the demand of the prophets, declares Call to Renewal. It is the ethic conveyed (as we saw with King's reading of the parable of the Good Samaritan) in the teachings of Jesus. As Wallis explains:

> In Matthew 25, Jesus challenges his disciples saying, "For I was hungry and you gave me no food, I was thirsty and you gave me nothing to drink, I was a stranger and you did not welcome me, naked and you did not clothe me, sick and in prison and you did not visit me" [ . . . ] Jesus is here asking, "How much do you love me? I'll know how much you love me by how you love those who are most vulnerable." He is putting himself in their place. The Son of Man, as Jesus is described in this scene, is taking the place of the poor, forgotten and lonely of the earth. (1995, 82–83)

For Wallis, Jesus here offers not just a lesson on, but a model of, visiting. Jesus puts himself in the place of others, sees the common world from their perspectives—but always remains the "Son of Man." In other words, Jesus is no tourist passing lightly through the place of the poor and forgotten, nor is he an assimilator who loses his own identity and "becomes" the "other." He remains Jesus but gains enriched understanding by seeing as himself from the perspective of another. This is the lesson Jesus teaches his disciples, and it is the path toward democratic understanding that Wallis and Call to Renewal encourage.[42]

The possibilities (born of visiting) for new perspectives and stories to enter into the public discourse is enhanced by the approach to history encouraged by Call to Renewal. In drawing links between past, present, and future, Call to Renewal's wisdom literature is fundamentally informed by a belief that by "study[ing] and challeng[ing] history . . . [we can] open our minds to fresh understandings" of present political issues (Brennan, 78). It is from such "fresh understandings"—understandings often generated by listening to new stories (or different voices telling the same stories)—that hope for the future is born. Wallis' often repeated (and self-described "best line") captures this sentiment quite clearly: "Hope is believing in spite of the evidence, then watching the evidence change" (2000, 324). In contrast, the evidence provided by what Dienstag calls "reconciliatory history" is singular and unchanging, thus allowing for little, if any, possibility of a different future. Wallis adamantly warns against such an approach to history.

> When history appears to be static, it is the oppressed who are shut out. History is [then] not only closed, it is closed against them. The past is forgotten, the future is foreclosed, and there is only the never-ending present to be endured. . . . What cannot be allowed to be believed or imagined is the possibility of hope for a new day. (1995, 280)

The political possibilities enabled by visiting and redemptive history—the hope for a renewed democratic polity—is a central theme in the wisdom literature of Call to Renewal.

If anything clearly illustrates the vast differences between Promise Keepers and Call to Renewal, it is a comparison of the wisdom literature from each organization. Promise Keepers adopts a therapeutic model aimed at saving marriages, improving personal finances, raising obedient Christian children, addressing personal prejudice, developing male friendships, and overcoming addictions to pornography, gambling, drugs, and alcohol—all in the effort to become a better Christian man. Call to Renewal, in sharp contrast, pursues not a therapeutic healing but rather, strategic political organizing. The aim is not individual health or personal salvation, but collective action for social justice. Consistent with its prophetic vision of developing a proactive and progressive social movement, "speaking truth to power," and reinvigorating the public sphere in America, the wisdom literature of Call to Renewal is a virtual "how-to" political manual. In its study guides, organizers' handbooks, and conference seminars, Call to Renewal espouses its political vision and paves the way for the journey. Each of the national conferences sponsored by Call to Renewal has included training sessions on how to lobby members of Congress—an activity to which the final day of the conferences are dedicated. Such strategy sessions include analysis of the bills currently before Congress, dissemination of both statistical and anecdotal data, and advice in the art of public advocacy with government offices.[43]

Such appeals to federal legislators are far from the only organizational training offered by Call to Renewal. Other features of Call to Renewal's wisdom literature include advice on building grassroots coalitions on the local level, organizing town meetings, starting community kitchens, managing the media, fundraising, and creating local "Call to Renewal Roundtables." The materials on organizing and advocacy provided by Call to Renewal are emphatically practical and quite detailed. In addition to the general counsel on the process of political mobilization, Call to Renewal addresses the content of political issues through its study guides.[44] The guiding aim of these collections is to combine insights into contemporary social questions in the United States with specific pathways for social transformation. And while these study guides can often be repetitive and didactic, they also maintain a significant methodological difference from the workbooks and study guides of Promise Keepers. Promise Keepers study guides, such as *Promise Builders, Strategies for a Successful Marriage,* and *Personal Holiness in Times of Temptation* are replete with fill-in-the-blank exercises, true-false "self-inventory tests" for evaluating personal strengths and weaknesses, and exercises in repetitive prayer. The essays in Call to Renewal's study guides, in contrast, lead to open-ended questions that call for interpretation and analysis of the readings and examination of how the lessons of the readings might be applicable to one's life.[45] These open-ended questions are an ingredient to the basic lessons in democratic politics that Call to Renewal strives to teach in its wisdom literature.

A fine example of this message is found in a Call to Renewal board member's essay in *Crossing the Racial Divide*. In this piece, Rev. Yvonne Delk begins from the declaration of Martin Luther King Jr.: "This is no time for romantic illusions and empty philosophical debates about freedom. This is a time for action . . ."[46] and then proceeds to offer a concise "five-part strategy to dismantle racism"—a strategy illustrative of Call to Renewal's approach to racism in the United States.

1. We must start from a historical perspective and not just an individual perspective . . .
2. The focus must be on systematic racism and not primarily on prejudice, bigotry or bias . . .
3. We must start from the perspective of truth-telling and stop the denial that racism exists . . .
4. We must be color-conscious and not color-blind . . .
5. We must recognize that the work for change begins in those systems that we are a part of, beginning with our churches. (68–69)

What is striking about her plan is its emphasis on history (and especially collective and institutional history), the stress on telling and listening to stories that illuminate, rather than "transcend" or elide, the reality of systematic racism in the United States, and finally the commitment to action that is immediate and enriched by the understanding produced by historical analysis and political dialogue.

Delk suggests, and Eugene Rivers makes clear, that a political strategy based on visiting with those whose perspectives are most often ignored will fundamentally change the conversation concerning issues of race and class in America. This shift holds true as much for those who consider themselves "good liberals" as it does for any other sector of the polity. At the Call to Renewal conference 2000, Rivers spoke of trying to employ some of the principles advised by Delk in his efforts to address the needs of poor black men in Boston. Bringing these men into dialogue with largely white middle-class folks was a struggle, Rivers found, because rather than striving to understand the "anger of the poor, black man," the middle-class folks wanted credit for even being willing to address questions of poverty at all. "These middle-class progressives [were] disappointed, wishing that these poor, black men would act a little more like Martin Luther King Jr., that they spoke more about the 'beloved community' rather than 'bringing the noise'" (Rivers, CTR 2000). In other words, the middle-class folks Rivers speaks of, for all their good intentions, were little more than "tourists"; true visiting only occurs when one is willing to engage with the perspective of another as it is, rather than as the tourist wishes it to be. Expanding the practice of such visiting and the representative thinking that ensues would "fundamentally change the power relations that currently govern the [political] dialogue" in the United States (Rivers, CTR 2000). Democratic politics informed by visiting can and should be threatening to entrenched power relations and patterns of political discourse. Ultimately, it is the work of conscious pariahs to "bring the noise," to unsettle people and make them less at home in the world. And from this demand to be countenanced, a step that expands the shared world, push forward to the hard work of democratic engagement.

Indicative of Call to Renewal's commitment to creating a renewed civil political discourse through visiting—or the enhancement of representative thinking through the welcoming of different perspectives—is the manner in which Call to Renewal has addressed the two most divisive social questions in Christian America today: abortion and homosexuality. In both cases, Call to Renewal has sought to initiate dialogue between those who hold divergent views. Rather than adopt the more typical model of "attack, defend, and retrench," the organization has sought not just to illuminate common ground but also to model how that common ground can be discovered.

The conversations on abortion developed by Call to Renewal illustrate this concern with both the content and process of dialogue quite clearly. For instance, at the 1997 Call to Renewal conference—the second national conference sponsored by this nascent organization—pro-life activist Frederica Mathewes-Green and pro-choice advocate Naomi Wolf were invited to conduct a plenary on Finding Common Ground on Abortion. Framed as a model of how to initiate a conversation among activists concerned with the contentious issues surrounding the question of abortion, this dialogue was notable not so much for any shocking breakthroughs on policy questions; the key message is the lesson taught about dialogue itself.[47] "Fundamental to common ground [is] to respect that people are going to disagree. Common ground is not about compromise or negotiation" (Wolf and Mathewes-Green, 33.) Rather than persuasion, simple understanding is the goal of such beginning common-ground dialogues. To that end, Wolf and Mathewes-Green suggest a model that ensures a degree of visiting that leads to the expansion of the "in-between." In their model each participant is asked to listen to the stories told by another and then repeat each story as accurately as possible. This process of "reflecting back" demands that each person is listened to and understood. While such dialogue can be unwieldy, it is, Wolf and Mathewes-Green argue, an important first step in discovering common ground. From these initial conversations, the participants in such dialogues are encouraged to find a position on social policy in which there is mutual agreement and take collective action to resolve these particular issues (without, it should be noted, falling into the trap of having these efforts become a testing ground for broader ideological areas of disagreement).

Call to Renewal is striving to develop just such common-ground efforts on questions surrounding homosexuality in the United States. Its approach is to begin by declaring that there are "honest differences between Christians about what the Bible says about homosexuality" (Wallis 1996, 129). However, recognizing the differences about homosexuality should be the beginning and not the end of the conversation. For instance, those who might disagree on Christian perspectives on homosexuality might be able to find common ground on the causes of the "breakdown of the heterosexual family" (which, Wallis asserts, "has very little to do with homosexuality") and the need for the "civil and human rights" of all citizens to be protected. "To be both pro-family and pro-gay civil rights could open up some common ground that might take us forward" (Wallis 1996, 130). Such a common ground dialogue on homosexuality has been modeled in the pages of *Sojourners* by Peggy Campolo and her husband, Call to Renewal board member Rev. Tony Campolo. Whereas Peggy Campolo reads the scriptural passages on homosexuality as "household codes" that ought to be read in their ancient context and not literally applied to contemporary society, Tony Campolo sees the biblical mandate as a clear call for homosexual celibacy. However, their disagreement does not keep them from either continuing to discuss the issue or from jointly pursuing social policies protecting the rights of gay and lesbian citizens.[48] Again, what is important for our purposes is not so much the content of their positions, but the principles of pluralist democracy modeled in their dialogue.

In both cases, the goal is not framed as total consensus or agreement on the "truth" or the essential Christianity of a position. Rather, the aim is to converse and learn, questioning yourself and the partner in the conversation. Difference is neither ignored nor entirely transcended. The aim is threefold: to strive to continue talking even when it is difficult, to discover what points of agreement do exist, and to take cooperative action toward common ends. In short these are lessons in coalition building.[49] These lessons are also akin to the value Arendt placed on using the exchange of stories to build and maintain relationships in the political process of wooing consent.

In its political dialogues, of which these discussions of abortion and homosexuality are examples, the aim is not the obliteration or denial of differences but a recognition that political discourse on divisive social issues need not be so dominated by antagonism that common aims cannot be discovered and acted upon. The process is governed by a commitment to relationships and a determination to act even in the absence of complete consensus or knowledge. Marshall Ganz addressed these themes in his discussion of Call to Renewal's potential as a social movement: "Relational work . . . is the foundational work of organizing." This relational work must not confine itself to the pursuit of "likeness," but must instead create space where differences can be expressed, discovered, and understood. According to Ganz, this space is created and enriched by stories. "We understand ourselves as individuals and communities as stories," and it is through sharing of stories that we can begin to understand one another and, as such, the world we share. The coalition building necessary for a pluralist social movement relies upon telling and listening to stories. For Call to Renewal, this narrative space is created within the scaffolding of Exodus. In particular, it is the innovative retelling of this sacred story that transforms the American story of Exodus from a tale of a chosen people in a promised land into an inclusive welcoming of sojourners in exile working together toward justice. Recasting the narrative as a story of a pluralist people organizing across chasms of difference to work together for social justice may enable a coalition between prophetic and democratic politics.

## A Covenant and a Call

In recent years, Call to Renewal has placed the issue of poverty and the "wealth chasm" in the United States squarely at the top of its political agenda.[50] Call to Renewal has not ignored its commitment to racial justice or attention to sex and gender issues (including what it conceives of as the breakdown of normative family structures in the United States).

Rather, it has resituated these concerns as components of its Covenant and Campaign to Overcome Poverty. By looking briefly at this innovative use of the Exodus trope of covenants, especially in comparison to Promise Keepers' "D.C. Covenant," Call to Renewal's commitment to develop a democratic prophetic politics is made even more clear.

The biblical covenant in Exodus—repeated in Deuteronomy, and Joshua and continually invoked in the books of the prophets—is an act of founding (and a call for refounding) the polity of the Hebrews. For Call to Renewal, however, the covenant tradition is less about refounding a promised land for God's chosen people than it is a matter of revitalizing the hope of the prophets that "the moral requirements of relationship and community serve to correct our human tendencies toward individual selfishness and exploitation of our neighbors and the earth" (Wallis 1995, 48). The intention is not that the covenant will lead the nation to be a light to the world, but that it should embrace the vast pluralism that defines American culture and speak with a prophetic voice about realizing social justice in the public realm.[51] Call to Renewal's Covenant to Overcome Poverty reads:

> The persistence of widespread poverty in our midst is morally unacceptable. Just as some of our religious forbears decided to no longer accept slavery or segregation, we decide to no longer accept poverty and its disproportionate impact on people of color. In the biblical tradition, we covenant together in a Call to Renewal. By entering this Covenant, we commit ourselves to:
>
> 1. Prioritize people who are poor—both in our personal, family, and vocational lives and in our congregational and organizational practices—through prayer and dedication of our time and resources.
>
> 2. Decide our financial choices in ways that promote economic opportunity and justice for those in poverty.
>
> 3. Evaluate public policies and political candidates by how they impact people who are poor.
>
> 4. Challenge racism, dismantle the structures of racial injustice and white privilege still present, and seek reconciliation among all groups in our society.
>
> 5. Nurture the bonds of family and community and protect the dignity of each person.
>
> 6. Organize across barriers of race, denomination, and social boundaries in common commitment and action to overcome poverty in our own communities, our nation, and our world.[52]

This Covenant, initially sworn to by seventy Christian leaders from across the theological and political spectrum, makes a declaration of individual and collective commitment to create bold social transformation. In so doing, it expresses a prophetic politics that utilizes a concept of covenant in a manner sharply different from Promise Keepers' "D.C. Covenant."

Recall that the "D.C. Covenant" sworn to at Promise Keepers' 1997 Stand in the Gap gathering was an extraordinary commitment to pietistic devotion to Jesus and God "the Father." Not particularly concerned with historical or political context, the "D.C. Covenant" is a commitment to become "men of integrity," who, as heads of their households and members of a "brotherhood of believers," might be worthy witnesses to Jesus.[53] Call to Renewal's Covenant is an emphatically outward-looking document that proclaims and adopts a legacy of progressive revivalist religion in the United States and is based on a political commitment to raise questions of poverty and racism in America. Whereas Promise Keepers' covenant is in keeping with biblical tradition in its repeated exhortations to worship God, Call to Renewal's covenant makes no explicit mention of God at all. Rather, it invokes a "biblical tradition" of promoting economic opportunity and justice for the poor. The Covenant, for Call to Renewal, is a political statement more than a spiritual proclamation—or better, it is, by virtue of the political commitments expressed, a spiritual statement.

In its accompanying document, "The Campaign to Overcome Poverty," Call to Renewal elaborates on its analytic framework for assessing the issue of poverty and the strategies for promoting and fulfilling its Covenant. This "Campaign" begins by acknowledging and identifying the complexity of the causes of poverty as well as past failures of both individuals and faith-based organizations to adequately address the growth and effects of poverty in the United States. Central to this endeavor is the building of a pluralist partnership between not just "members of churches and other faith-based organizations" but also with figures from government, business, labor, philanthropy, and the non-profit sector. The Campaign is cast as an "invitation to dialogue" rather than a "detailed blueprint for overcoming poverty." It sets seven "moral priorities" for the United States: "(1) full participation by people of all races; (2) a living family income for all who responsibly work; (3) affordable, quality health care for all, regardless of income; (4) schools that work for all our children; (5) safe, affordable housing; (6) safe and secure neighborhoods; and (7) family-friendly policies and programs in every sector of society." Call to Renewal then declares that "We are not committed to any particular ideological method or partisan agenda to achieve these goals, only that they be achieved. . . . Political disagreements can no longer be allowed to justify public inaction while those in poverty continue to be neglected."[54] To support this effort—and in particular to enhance political engagement at the grassroots level—Call to Renewal has launched Christian Anti-Poverty Online Resource (CAPOR), a website that provides detailed analysis of welfare and tax policy, calls to action and talking points, event coordination, contact information for other organizations working on similar issues, theological analysis of public policies, and a guide to political organizing.[55] Included in the section on political advocacy is the assertion:

> Advocacy has a special meaning for people of faith. It means speaking up for and with those who are poor and injured—disempowered people who are intentionally or unintentionally hurt by the actions of others. But advocacy also means speaking up for our values as people of faith. It is working to see those values realized in public policy—the policies and practices of corporations, institutions, government, and the church. Advocacy is an important way to respond to God's call to work for justice in society and creation. . . . It is based on democracy—the idea that people have a right to be involved in decisions made by governments.[56]

This conception of democratic engagement also includes crucial advice to "talk to people who disagree with you."[57]

Here again Call to Renewal's prophetic politics embodies principles of democratic politics. It begins from a commitment to strive to transform the world in a manner that seeks social justice. It pursues this social transformation by casting a critical eye on the past as a means of understanding both the causes and challenges of the present "crisis." It links the prophetic principles to practical calls to action. It is dedicated to pluralism, especially the need to expand the "in-between" so that neglected voices can be heard. It advocates with and for these neglected voices by speaking as conscious pariahs moving back and forth between the margins of society and the halls of power. It pursues the fulfillment of a covenant by visiting with others and through the exchange of stories and ideas building relationships and coalitions. As Wallis says, in a nation suffering from a "crisis" of social division, it is quite simply "time to listen to one another's stories, and try to reach a better understanding of each other" (1996, 62). By listening to and learning from this exchange of stories, Call to Renewal is challenging citizens to revitalize their commitment to and capacity to enhance a democratic public realm. The common ground shared by members of Call to Renewal appears in its prophetic ethos and is manifested in the actions one takes to expand the shared world to countenance the sojourner and pursue justice for the most vulnerable. In contrast to the ecumenical spirit of

Promise Keepers, for whom the source of unity is a commitment to Jesus as the source of personal salvation, the common ground for Call to Renewal is a shared political commitment based on the prophetic understanding of justice and the determination to evidence one's love of Jesus through acts with, and on behalf of, those suffering in poverty in this nation of wealth.

# Chapter Six
## Politics in the Wilderness

We Americans are the peculiar chosen people—the Israel of our time; we bear the ark of the Liberties of the world. Seventy years ago, we escaped from thrall, and besides our first birth-right—embracing one continent of earth—God has given us, for a future inheritance, the broad domains, of the political pagans, that shall yet come and lie down under the shade of our ark, without bloody hands being lifted. God has predestined, mankind expects, great things from our race; and great things we feel in our souls. . . . And let us always remember that with ourselves, almost for the first time in the history of earth, national selfishness is unbounded philanthropy, for we cannot do a good to America, but we give alms to the world.
—Herman Melville, *White-Jacket*

No philosophy, no analysis, no aphorism, be it ever so profound, can compete in intensity and richness of meaning with a properly narrated story.
—Hannah Arendt, *Men in Dark Times*

Melville's classic articulation of the American sacred story of Exodus still resonates in the United States, offering a narrative that frames the nation's foreign policy as a manifestation of political theology. Such triumphalism is present in assertions that the United States serves as a force for "civilization," bringing the good news of American culture and capitalism to primitive places—even such "backward lands" as what the Bush administration has referred to as "Old Europe." The 20th century was indeed an era of American triumphalism, and the current talk of the United States serving as a benevolent empire for much of the world carries more than a hint of the suggestion that "we cannot do a good to America, but we give alms to the world."

Yet, American citizens from across political and theological spectrums readily acknowledge the different ways the United States has failed to live up to "divine expectations." Prophetic social movements in the United States respond to perceptions of such failures by offering their own versions of the American sacred story—many of which explicitly challenge the triumphalist presumptions—to define the crisis in the nation and express a commitment to transform the world. Their success in large part depends on telling a "properly narrated story." For a story to be properly narrated in this sense, the storyteller must recognize the cultural context in which it will be heard—a properly narrated story must resonate with its listeners.

Each of the four expressions of prophetic politics discussed—Billy Sunday, Martin Luther King Jr., Promise Keepers, and Call to Renewal—sought, or seeks, profound change in the United States. Each has constructed its political identity and political vision from within the narrative scaffolding of the American sacred story of Exodus. Consistent with the basic jeremiadic pattern, there is a presumption of decline, of principles once held, and now forgotten. Even the progressive Call to Renewal, as its name implies, speaks in a language of *re*-newal, of revitalizing the forgotten principles of the polity—and of "the church."

Examining the history of prophetic voices in American politics, Sacvan Bercovitch concludes that the possibilities of profound change through prophetic politics are so limited that the American jeremiads are fundamentally conservative in their commitment to normative customs in America. Bercovitch writes:

> The American Jeremiahs . . . invested the symbol of America with the attributes of the sacred. . . . The revelation of America serves to blight, and ultimately to preclude, the possibility of fundamental social change. . . . To condemn "false Americans" as profane is to express one's faith in a national ideology. In effect, it is to transform what might have been a search for moral or social alternatives into a call for cultural revitalization. (1993, 179)

Bercovitch sees prophetic social movements as so determined to *renew* America that there is no room for the *new*. Rather than a radical introduction of a "revolutionary" political, ethical, or social vision, prophetic social movements are necessarily reformist, calling the nation back to a vision of its founding principles and narratives. Indeed, the prophetic politics of Billy Sunday, Martin Luther King Jr., Promise Keepers, and Call to Renewal all fit this description. Moreover, this assessment can also be applied to the biblical prophets. Neither Isaiah, Jeremiah, Ezekiel, Nehemiah, nor Micah sought to introduce a radically new social or political vision to the Hebrew people. Rather, they sought to "give people back their history," to follow the edict of the Exodus narrative to remember.

Such an argument about the conservative nature of prophetic politics has merit, but is ultimately limited in scope. First, decrying prophetic politics for being merely reformist is in part based on the mistaken notion that practitioners of prophetic politics claim to be something other than such forces of reform. Moreover, and more importantly, the critique of prophetic politics as conservative or reformist misses the crucial point about the relationship between narratives—and especially sacred stories—and politics. The sacred stories of a society provide a horizon within which citizens understand themselves and one another. In a nation as marked by pluralism as the United States, there are a number of narrative frameworks that enjoy this "sacred" status. For a social movement to create enough popular momentum to have its voice heard, it must speak in a language or express its political vision within a narrative framework that enjoys familiarity. The stories told by a social movement must resonate in order to achieve any modicum of success, even a step as basic as being recognized.

However, as the various uses of the American sacred story of Exodus by Billy Sunday, Martin Luther King Jr., Promise Keepers, and Call to Renewal illustrate, any given narrative is open to interpretation and retelling. This is not to say that a sacred story can be deployed in a manner that bears no relation to the "foundational story" itself or previous forms of interpretation. The stories carry some measure of what we might call "elective affinities" and bear a cultural legacy that is powerful, even if fragmentary. Moreover, for an interpretation of a sacred story to be persuasive, it too must resonate. In this way, all social movements (at least those that are "reformist") are "conservative," but they are not simply so. Paul Ricoeur's conception of the "dialectic of sedimentation and innovation" at work in the telling and re-telling of narratives suggests the necessary relation between the need for familiarity and the desire for change that social movements must consider when telling narratives.

As Sidney Tarrow observes, social movements and practitioners of "contentious politics" commonly have a significant impact on political culture, even when social movements seem to fail to meet their stated goals: "Their actions set in motion important political, cultural and international changes" that can succeed in shaping the political discourse for future generations (1998a, 2). Thus, Billy Sunday did not "save" the United States, but he did lay the foundation for future generations of conservative evangelism in American politics. Likewise, Martin Luther King Jr. and the civil rights movement of the 1960s did not achieve all of their political goals. Among their many accomplishments, however, they did popularize retellings of the Exodus narrative in which America was no longer the promised land but instead the wilderness. Successive social movements—including Call to Renewal—can now tell the story of America as wilderness with more resonance.

Tarrow's reminder of "success in failure" meshes with Ricoeur's narrative theory of innovation and sedimentation. What was an innovative retelling of the sacred story of Exodus can become the sedimentation that provides the ground for future story re-tellers. Whether or not Promise Keepers succeeds in its effort to "re-establish" the United States as a haven for the brotherhood of believers, the movement has retold the Exodus narrative in an innovative manner that has reframed conversations about religion, piety, and gender (especially masculinity), enhanced the popular relationship in the United States between athletics and religion, and has further engendered a connection between Christianity and the anti-political therapeutic impulse in America. Similarly, whether or not Call to Renewal ultimately succeeds in its efforts to "overcome poverty," its retelling of the Exodus narrative to teach inclusion and economic justice has helped build coalitions across ideological lines and even reinvigorated the religious left. Just as Call to Renewal has built its retelling of the American sacred story of Exodus on the sedimentation provided by Martin Luther King Jr., Promise Keepers' political theology of Christian masculinity has roots in the muscular Christianity of Billy Sunday. Future expressions of prophetic politics have the potential to benefit from the innovations of Promise Keepers and Call to Renewal. Indeed, both Promise Keepers and Call to Renewal have accomplished a reinterpretation and revitalizing of the Exodus narrative that is "innovative" now but potentially a stabilizing sediment in the future.

## Piety or Politics: The Challenge of Religion and Democracy

The great difference between the prophetic visions of Promise Keepers and Call to Renewal is that the former preaches an anti-political theology while the latter teaches that religious commitment should lead to political engagement. If participatory democratic politics requires open and pluralistic public discourse, then the anti-political prophetic politics of Promise Keepers presents a significant potential danger. By preaching an influential pietism, Promise Keepers represents a paradoxical social movement that draws energy away from the public sphere. Like Billy

Sunday sending men home to protect the heart of the nation, Promise Keepers instructs its men to become "offensive linemen" guarding the private sphere against "ill-informed and destructive choices."[1] Democratic politics rests on "visiting," on entering the public realm, encountering those with different beliefs and opinions, and seeing the common world from different perspectives. While Promise Keepers is ecumenical and multiracial, its emphasis is on transcending difference in the name of unity with Jesus. "Representative thinking" and democratic politics are based on recognizing, appreciating, and learning from differences, not transcending them. The danger to democracy of the anti-political prophetic politics of Promise Keepers is not simply that it does not encourage visiting; in drawing citizens away from the public realm, Promise Keepers removes not only their voices from public discourse, but also their ears. Without the participation of these citizens in public discourse, an enormous portion of the population remains at best indifferent and at worst hostile to the debates and decisions that occur in the realm of politics. Non-compliance and indifference without discussion are enervating forces in a democratic polity.

Promise Keepers compounds this problem by preaching a theology that encourages citizens to wait for God to transform society. Whether it is the "supernatural avalanche" wished for by Bill Bright, the "economic collapse" that Steve Farrar says will be a sign of God's wrath, or simply Bill McCartney's teaching men that "politics simply can't touch issues of the heart," the message taught to members of Promise Keepers is to get your own house in order and hope to become a part of the chosen remnant that will survive God's judgment. Promise Keepers, in short, represents the Arendtian nightmare—sapping the strength of democratic politics and preaching the futility of human engagement in the public realm.

In sharp contrast to the anti-political pietism preached by Promise Keepers, Call to Renewal espouses an emphatically democratic prophetic politics. Whereas Promise Keepers draws people out of the public sphere, Call to Renewal is committed to introducing the often absent voices of the poor into political discourse. Rather than seeking to transcend difference, Call to Renewal portrays pluralism as the source of its energy and success and even welcomes dissension among its leaders. Moreover, in its wisdom literature, Call to Renewal provides models and lessons of a democratic process that seeks to recognize and learn from differences, discover common ground (but not total consensus), and then take action toward addressing an "inclusive agenda" for social justice (Wallis 2000, 316). Wallis asserts:

> Bringing ethics into public debate should not entail "imposing religion"
> on policy decisions; rather, using the multiple religious and ethical tradi-
> tions and resources of our national life could help us achieve deeper under-
> standings of the issues at stake, and even yield some agreements and
> acceptable compromises. (2000, 288)

Not content to wait on God, Call to Renewal preaches the need to move
from religious commitments toward political activism; indeed, for Call
to Renewal, "the test of any authentic faith is action" (Wallis 2000,
xxvii). The vision of Call to Renewal is to create a social movement that
reconciles prophetic and democratic politics.

## Prophetic Politics Between Past and Future

If the history of retelling the Exodus narrative teaches us anything, it
teaches that *all stories are forgettable*. The trope of retelling stories of
foundations is central to the Exodus narrative. The commandment to
retell the story of liberation from Egypt, the covenant at Mount Sinai,
the journey to the Promised Land, is repeated throughout the books of
the Hebrew Bible. "You shall teach them diligently to your children, and
you shall talk of them when you sit in your house, and when you walk
by the way, when you lie down and when you rise. And you shall bind
them as a sign upon your hand; and they shall be as frontlets between
your eyes. And you shall write them on the doorposts of your house and
upon your gates" (Dt. 6:7–9). So central is this edict to retell the story of
the founding and so prominent is this tension between remembering and
forgetting that by the time the prophet Jeremiah speaks to a nation that
has not adequately "retold" its founding stories, his most hopeful promise is of a new, more indelible covenant.

> Behold, the days are coming, says the Lord, when I will make a new
> covenant with the house of Israel and the house of Judah, not like the
> covenant which I made with their fathers when I took them by the hand to
> bring them out of the land of Egypt, my covenant which they broke,
> though I was their husband, says the Lord. But this is the covenant which I
> will make with the house of Israel after those days, says the Lord: I will
> put my law within them, and I will write it upon their hearts; and I will be
> their God and they shall be my people. And no longer shall each man
> teach his neighbor and each his brother,[2] saying "Know the Lord," for
> they shall all know me, from the least of them to the greatest, says the
> Lord; for I will forgive their iniquity, and I will remember their sin no
> more. (Jer. 31:31–34)

Jeremiah here offers a vision of the future that some might call utopian. It is a future in which the assessment of Isaiah—"Therefore my people go into exile for want of knowledge" (Is. 5:13)—is no longer a threat because the knowledge of the law is present in every heart. Jeremiah's vision of a new covenant amounts to a vision of a new person, a new promised land, and with it come new standards. No longer is the commitment of Exodus to the memory of the liberation from Egypt the pivotal condition of the covenant, or the principal characteristic of the "Holy Nation." God's willingness to forget the sins of the people signals the abandonment of the requirement of remembrance; indeed, there is no longer a need to remember, for the law is indelibly present. It is a vision in which Moses and the prophets are superfluous—this new covenant requires no stories to be told. It is a "utopia" in which narratives are not needed. It is a vision in which the gap between past and future has been effaced. With the loss of the need to remember, with the loss of the need for stories, with the loss of the gap between past and future, it is also a place where freedom—or at least free will—is not present as a challenge to humanity.

By all accounts, however, Jeremiah's vision has not come to pass. Humans continue to negotiate the tension between remembering and forgetting. Humans continue to navigate the gap between past and future. Humans continue to need, to tell, to listen to stories. And "prophets" continue to emerge, to re-use the symbols and themes provided by the narrative horizon of the community and tell new, particular, and contextually informed stories that mine the past in order to understand the present and offer hope for the future. This is the prophetic mission, "to reactivate out of our historical past symbols that have always been vehicles for redemptive honesty" (Brueggemann, 49).

Prophets help us live in the uncertain gap definitive of the human condition. Explaining the role of the prophet as storyteller and mediator of this present gap between past and future, Abraham Heschel writes:

> The future is no simple continuation of the present. . . . [T]he situation here and now is but a stage in the drama of history. Whatever happens now affects the past; it either shapes or distorts events that are going on. By history we do not mean the "gone" or the dead past, but the present in which past and future are interlocked. (1969, 173–74)

It is significant that Heschel sees the prophets as envisioning history as a drama. A dramatic script provides plot and dialogue but leaves open the capacity for actors to interpret their lines, react in different ways to others on stage, and open up possibilities within the dramatic horizon for new interpretations and meanings. In other words, it allows for the dialectic of sedimentation and innovation. In contrast to Jeremiah's vision, our hope might be that prophetic drama, like political narratives, is never fixed or complete, but rather always open to re-telling as present conditions lead us to revisit the past and in so doing re-imagine the future.

## Prophets and Pariahs

The need to re-imagine the future is of particular importance in times of crisis. The capacity to express such imagination through stories is most necessary and also most dangerous in dark times for democracy. In such periods, the great tension that defines the relationship between narratives and politics is most palpable. When the threat of meaninglessness haunts our lives, we crave the clarity and inspiration of a well-told story. When the hunger for meaning is so acute, we are ill equipped to judge what we should eat.

In such times, the narratives of prophetic politics offer a particularly robust meal, but one that poses considerable challenges to democratic public life. In times of crisis, when the tenuous order of the world is fundamentally shaken, such narratives of tightly bound and often "divinely authorized" causality are all too attractive—but also all too dangerous. Practitioners of prophetic politics speak with a presumption of conscience informed by divine inspiration, by the call to tell a story of crisis and redemption. As Jean Calvin instructs in his lectures on Jeremiah:

> Why are prophets and teachers sent? That they may reduce the world to order: they are not to spare their hearers, but freely to reprove them wherever there may be need; they are also to use threatenings when they find men perverse . . . prophets and teachers may take courage and thus boldly set themselves against kings and nations, when armed with the power of celestial truth.[3]

There is a great longing for prophetic visions, for "celestial truth"— especially in times when the slow work of democracy is perceived as depleted, bereft, and incapable of addressing the "crisis" afflicting the world. Democracy is then often tragically misunderstood as a noble system of governing that is viable only in times of plenty and contentment—when patience can be rewarded and collaboration benignly tolerated. In such times, we are willing to step back and reasonably consider the contingency of our circumstances—what could have happened, what might occur. When the cries of crisis are in the air, democratic deliberation is often conceived as a luxury a people cannot afford. In such dark times, democracy can become merely a legitimating façade for the decisive leadership of a "saint" whose conscience dictates a definitive and uncompromising plan of action. In such times, the longing for meaning, solace, and hope makes listening to other stories more difficult and yet more vital. Attention to listening, to seeking alternative stories, brings narrative back from the brink of ideology and locates us in the realm of political dialogue.

How then can we learn to listen well? Ironically, perhaps, lessons on listening are often conveyed through the stories themselves. With regard to the Exodus narrative, the delineation of identity and context—chosen people in a promised land or sojourners in a wilderness—convey lessons about how a story should be heard, about the proper attitude of listeners. Social movements that seek to transform the world teach such lessons not just in their jeremiads, in their retellings of sacred stories, but in their wisdom literature as well.

Perhaps the chief lesson of democratic wisdom is the importance of recognizing proclamations made in the public realm as opinions rather than truths, or as stories about truth rather than "truth itself." This is the lesson Arendt derives from Lessing's assertion: "Let each man say what he deems truth, and let truth itself be commended unto God" (quoted in Arendt 1968, 31). As a lesson in democratic listening, the aphorism instructs us to enter into the exchange of stories in the public realm not in pursuit of truth, but in friendship, in pursuit of relationships with fellow humans above all else.[4] Accordingly, we as listeners should be keen to call claims of truth into question as we strive to cultivate the democratic space where a plurality of opinions can be shared. For Jim Wallis, this attitude is a hallmark of democratic prophetic politics, of the dedication to taking the stance of the critic challenging the easy assumptions and arrogant convictions so often expressed in the diminished public realm. "Like the prophets," he says simply, "we must call certainty into question" (1995, 53).

Calling certainty into question is vital to the work of the conscious pariah; not quite at home in the world themselves, conscious pariahs also unsettle the convictions and accepted norms of those all too comfortable in an unjust world. Such settled convictions and norms generally rest on uncritical perceptions of the past, the target of the withering backward glance of the prophet. Calling certainty into question is the prodding work of a listener who seeks not to destroy but rather nurture relationships. The hard work of democratic politics lies not just in hearing another's story, but in countenancing this story teller—in listening, striving to understand, and then responding. This type of democratic listening evidences what Arendt would call a "love of humanity" rather than a "love of truth."

However, there are great limitations on the capacity of the conscious pariah to transform the world. As the struggles of prophets—biblical and modern—attest, society is by no means readily transformed. Change, when it comes, is often gradual, incremental, halting—and reversible. Moreover, the life of the conscious pariah is often devastating; hope followed by despair, success (never assured in the temporal realm of politics) won at the price of suffering and sacrifice. King refers to the life of the prophet, or the conscious pariah, as a "vocation of agony."[5] In such conditions, the relative ease of "being at home in the world" is a seductive temptation to the pariah, because it entices with either the intense relationships of pariah people who stay on the margins in an initially "forced" but ultimately accepted state or with assimilation into the dominant culture.

Democratic prophetic politics is never simply an effort to assimilate, or even to gain legal rights, but rather it is an effort to transform the world: to create dramatic social change that may include, but is not fully manifested in, formal legal change. King, although called a "civil rights leader" sought not simply legal rights, but a "revolution of values." Likewise, Call to Renewal is seeking not simply a change in welfare policy, but a change in democracy in America, a transformation of religion and politics, and radical changes in the redistribution of wealth and the process of determining this distribution. The prophetic politics of Martin Luther King Jr. and Call to Renewal seek to question and transform the social and political context, the identity of the participants in public life, and the endeavors that such actors might take in this newly configured political realm.

In contrast, the prophetic politics of Billy Sunday and Promise Keepers seek not the dangerous place of the conscious pariah not quite at home in the world, but rather the powerful and protected status of chosen worldlessness. This direction leads to a form of withdrawal from political engagement and instead aims for the space of personal, rather than societal, transformation. The appeal of this path is one of detached innocence, or a return to the innocent and stable state of a context (the home) and identity (the chosen) that is beyond interrogation, that is beyond democracy. At all times, and especially in dark times, the comforts of home, a promised land of milk and honey, beckon like a mirage to which one can "return." This "home" represents an innocent world under God's protection, a second coming of Eden, a less fragile world, a world before politics. But we must resist this mirage, for in it the shared world is depleted, plurality is narrowed, and the hope recedes that something new, something innovative, will enter the world.

"The prophet is the figure of crisis," writes Paul Ricoeur, and in dark times prophets arise telling resonant stories.[6] They represent danger— and they represent hope—for a fragile public world. The democratic challenge for those who would be prophets is to become conscious pariahs to teach citizens how to tell and how to listen to stories, so that we might learn how to live not quite at home in the world—and indeed so that we do not seek to become at home in the world at all. The democratic lesson of such prophets is that the public realm of politics should not be a place of safety and security—a promised land—for anyone. Rather, the realm of democratic politics is an unsettled and unsettling place—a wilderness—for everyone.

# Notes

## 1. Prophetic Politics in the United States

1. The use of religious language of crisis is common not just during times of war or recession in America. Rather such themes and metaphors enjoy a consistent presence in American political culture seemingly independent of empirical reality. For my purposes, what is vital is the perception of a crisis rather than the "reality" of a crisis; indeed, as I discuss religion and democratic politics, the *perception* that a crisis exists is not necessarily any less meaningful than empirical data that "prove" a crisis exists.

2. The presence of such fervent belief lies in contrast to the "mindless tolerance" that Alan Wolfe in *One Nation After All* (1998) argues is predominant in American culture.

3. There is an irony of using Arendt's work on democratic politics and storytelling to help explore the role and status of religion in democratic life. Arendt herself did not assess religion through the analytic lens of storytelling, preferring instead to think of religion primarily in terms of faith and belief—and thus a threat to the world of politics, which is the realm of opinion.

4. In contrast to "secularism," Lincoln proceeds to distinguish between two broad ways of conceiving the role of religion in the world: maximalist and minimalist. For maximalists, "religion ought to permeate all aspects of social, indeed of human, existence." For minimalists, such as Kant and other champions of the secularist Enlightenment, religion should be restricted "to an important set of (chiefly metaphysical) concerns, [that] protects its privileges against state intrusion, but restricts its activity and influence to this specialized sphere" (B. Lincoln, 5).

5. The conflict between religious faith and secular, scientific progress is perhaps best captured for those proponents of the secularism thesis in the Scopes trial in which William Jennings Bryan and the "rubes" he represented won a Pyrrhic victory over Clarence Darrow and Darwinian theory. On the status of the Scopes trial in 20th-century American culture, see the wonderful history by Larson, *Summer of the Gods* (1997). For critiques of the notion of "secular America," see *Unsecular America*, ed. R. J. Neuhaus (1986).

6. On George W. Bush and the role of religious themes in his political response to September 11th, see B. Lincoln. On Bush's use of his "conversion narrative" in his 2000 election campaign, see Gutterman 2001.

7. These data are from "Faith-Based Funding Backed, but Church-State Doubts Abound." The Pew Research Center for the People and the Press, April 10, 2001.

http://people-press.org/reports/display.php3?ReportID=15. The Pew Forum on Religion & Public Life provides invaluable studies on the relationship between religion and politics in the United States.

8. The current popularity of the *Left Behind* series, which offers a fictionalized account of longtime Christian activist Tim LaHaye's pre-millennialist theology of the coming Armageddon, is but another indication of the significance of religion in American public life. The book series—the twelfth book was published in March 2004—has sold more than fifty million copies. In addition to the theological tracts, graphic novel versions of the story, companion series for kids, parallel series for the military, and new political thriller series, two feature films have already been made, and, of course, corresponding merchandise is available at http://www.leftbehind.com.

9. In his effort to diminish the role of government in providing social services to citizens and encourage "faith-based" institutions to step into the breach, President Bush is fond of explaining, "Government cannot put hope in people's hearts or a sense of purpose in their lives." "President Emphasizes Need for Welfare Reform" July 2, 2002. http://www.whitehouse.gov/news/releases/2002/ 07/20020702–2.html.

10. See Dobson and Thomas, *Blinded by Might: Why the Religious Right Can't Save America* (2000).

11. Paul Weyrich, "A Moral Minority? An Open Letter to Conservatives," February 16, 1999. To be sure, Weyrich did not heed his own advice for long. Galvanized by the election of George W. Bush, he has rushed back into the political fray.

12. Jackie Stevens, in her work on the politics of sex crimes, writes: "I find it rather bizarre that while the Louisiana state legislature's 1990 vote against abortion rights took place literally in the midst of people swaying while clutching Bibles, praying and clicking their rosary beads, an intellectually influential assortment of post-modern thinkers across disciplines actually pretends that God is dead" (125).

13. See Stephen Carter, *The Culture of Disbelief* (1993).

14. Abby Ellin, "Seeing Overeating as a Sin, and God as the Diet Coach," *New York Times,* May 29, 2004. http://www.nytimes.com/2004/05/29/national/ 29religion.html.

15. See Kramnick, xlvii.

16. See Tocqueville, 292. Most common secular and academic understandings of the role of religion in American politics emphasize its function as a form of social control and stability. For example, writing about the role of the Constitution in enabling the prominence of religion in the United States, Randall Balmer has argued: "[R]eligious disestablishment has helped to ensure political stability in the United States by siphoning social discontent into the religious sphere and away from the political arena. . . . Religion, then, has tended to protect government from the paroxysms of revolution in part because the First Amendment established a kind of free market of religion" (5).

17. Tocqueville, 290. The same can also be said for his analysis of Roman Catholicism. What is striking about Catholicism in America, Tocqueville writes, is that "nowhere else do [priests] care so much for the spirit and so little for the letter of the law" (Tocqueville, 449).

18. See Tocqueville 534f. where he speaks of "preachers hawking the word of God" and other illustrations of "religious madness."

19. For an explanation of "revival" from one of the most prominent American practitioners, see Charles Grandison Finney's *Revivals of Religion,* especially "What a Revival of Religion Is." For a recent exploration of the role of the jeremiad in contemporary American politics, see Murphy.

20. In doing so, I follow the work of Stephen Crites, which I discuss in greater detail in chapter 2.

21. On the creation of American identity around narratives of the Constitution, see Wolin, *The Presence of the Past* (1989).

22. Cf. Hartz, *The Liberal Tradition in America* (1955).

23. Scholars of the history of religion and politics in America have long noted the prominence of Exodus themes from colonial America on through the Revolution, Lincoln's Civil War speeches, the struggles for liberation by African Americans, and into the cultural fabric of contemporary America.

In one of the most influential works on religion and American political culture in this century, "Civil Religion in America," Robert Bellah illustrates the centrality of the Exodus story in the United States and the links between Exodus and the prophets. I do not address the question of "civil religion" per se. Nevertheless, there is significant overlap between my discussion of the American sacred story of Exodus and Bellah's assertion of the centrality of the symbols of Exodus in America's civil religion. Bellah concludes his essay with the declaration: "[America's civil religion] does not make any decision for us. It does not move us from moral ambiguity, from being in Lincoln's fine phrase, an 'almost chosen people.' But it is a heritage of moral and religious experience from which we still have much to learn as we formulate the decisions that lie ahead" (41). In a sense, my project begins from this point as I—thirty more complicated years later—examine how the American sacred story of Exodus has been and is still being used to help frame our understanding of social crises and political possibility.

24. Biblical retellings of the Exodus narrative in the books of the prophets also demonstrate such variation in emphasis and elision. On the differences among the prophets, their missions, and their stories, see Heschel; Blenkinsopp; and Brueggemann.

25. Buber 1965, 34. In the Exodus narrative, Buber writes: "[T]he ignominy [of bondage] has obviously been raised to the level of a folksong, as a prelude to the story of Exodus, ever enchanting the audience; the story which is constructed round the recurrent leitmotif that the God of Israel has liberated his people from the "servitude" of Egypt in order to take them into his own 'service.' This epic with its repeated transition into hymn must be grasped after its own fashion and according to its own impulses, in order to understand what this legend of tribulation has meant for the generations of the people from those who composed it down to those who, in our own later day, recount it at the Passover Evening, that most historical of all historical festivals of the human race" (1965, 34).

26. On sinfulness in the United States, see Gutterman 2005. See also Jim Morone's *Hellfire Nation: The Politics of Sin in American History* (2003).

27. See Stark and Christiano, "Support for the American Left" (1992).

28. An explanation of why I chose these four expressions of prophetic politics is in order. I do not claim that these four are comprehensively representative nor that they provide a definitive line of historical development. That is, Billy Sunday is a distinct and oddly under-appreciated figure in the development of popular Christian evangelism in 20th-century America, but a focus on his dynamic expression of prophetic politics is not meant to disregard the significance of such figures as William Jennings Bryan, Billy Graham, or Francis Schiller, to name but a few. In addition, this exploration of Martin Luther King Jr. is not intended to slight the Social Gospel movement nor diminish the influence of Reinhold Niebuhr. Nor, incidentally, am I suggesting that King's is the only major voice of the civil rights movement. Likewise, the choices of Promise Keepers and Call to Renewal are not intended to suggest that they are the only—or even the most important—sources of prophetic politics among contemporary Christian social movements. And while I do argue that Promise Keepers is beholden to the example of Billy Sunday and Call to Renewal is indebted to Martin Luther King Jr., this is not to assert that one can draw a straight causal line connecting each pair, nor that Billy Sunday and Martin Luther King Jr. serve as the most important, let alone only, foundation on which the two contemporary movements stand. These four expressions of prophetic politics illuminate the religious landscape of American religious culture, because they make distinct contributions to debates about race, class, sex, and gender, issues about which religious voices speak most potently in contempo-

rary American politics, and finally, because each of these practitioners of prophetic politics offers rich examples of storytelling.

29. Within the literature concerned with social movements, my work is most akin to examinations of "symbolic communication" and "collective action frames" exemplified by the work of Snow and Benford, "Master Frames and Cycles of Protest" (1992), and Tarrow. Tarrow's work in particular has helped shape this project—both because he has written provocatively about religious social movements (1998b) and because of his emphasis on the cultural impact social movements may have even when they fail to meet their goals (1998a).

30. The saying serves as an epigraph to the chapter on "Action" in *The Human Condition,* 175.

31. See Elk Grove Unified School District v. Newdow et al., No. 02–1624 (O'Connor, J., concurring).

## 2. Narratives and Politics

1. Much of Arendt's critical analysis of totalitarianism rests on her assessment of the ability of such regimes to respond to the hunger of people by force-feeding them a single narrative meal. See *The Origins of Totalitarianism* and her essay "On Violence" (1992).

2. On the question of "recognition," see Fraser and Taylor. See also Markell, *Bound by Recognition* (2003), for an insightful assessment of the limits of theories of recognition; Markell instead offers a nuanced understanding of "acknowledgement."

3. The significance of storytelling has increasingly been recognized as a central feature of Arendt's work. Seyla Benhabib, for example, writes, "The vocation of the theorist as storyteller is the unifying thread of Arendt's political and philosophical analysis" (Benhabib, 124). Melvyn Hill agrees, concluding, "For her, the stories that citizens tell are the source and remain the touchstone of political thinking" (Hill, 277).

4. For rich explorations of Arendt's writing on storytelling, see the work of Beiner; Curtis; Disch; and Calhoun.

5. See, for instance, Rorty, "Religion as Conversation-stopper" (1999).

6. For an influential illustration of this sentiment, see Neuhaus, *The Naked Public Square* (1984).

7. This position has been popularized by Carter in *The Culture of Disbelief.*

8. John Adams was not alone among the founders in conceiving America through the lens of Exodus. Adams wrote: "I always consider the settlement of America with reverence and wonder, as the opening of a grand scene and design in Providence for the illumination of the ignorant, and the emancipation of the slavish part of mankind all over the earth" (quoted in Tuveson, 25). Michael Walzer reminds us that "In 1776, Benjamin Franklin proposed that the Great Seal of the United States should show Moses with his rod lifted and the Egyptian army drowning in the sea; while Jefferson urged a more pacific design: the column of Israelites marching through the wilderness led by God's pillars of cloud and fire" (1985, 6). Even though these recommendations were not approved, the presence of these tropes illustrates the rhetorical resonance of the Exodus story and prophetic jeremiads in American political culture.

9. Quoted in Elazar, 18. It is worth noting that Johnson's retelling of the American story employs the language of the Gettysburg Address—"conceived in liberty and dedicated to the proposition that all men are created equal"—which itself is a "refounding" of the "American covenant" within the Exodus framework.

10. It is hard to find a politician whose common refrain "God Bless America" is not conveyed in harmony with the "Puritan" assumption often expressed that God already has, in fact, chosen America distinct from the nations of the world. Indeed,

George W. Bush has taken to saying, "May God continue to bless America" at the close of his speeches.

11. On the religious and political identity of early New England, see the work of P. Miller; Bercovitch.

12. On the "middle colonies," see Wertenbaker, *The Founding of American Civilization* (1963).

13. On the continuing influence of the jeremiad in the United States, see Murphy; Gutterman 2005.

14. In his provocative *Plurality and Ambiguity*, David Tracy writes: "Interpretation seems a minor matter, but it is not. Every time we act, deliberate, judge, understand, or even experience, we are interpreting. To understand at all is to interpret. To act well is to interpret a situation demanding some action and to interpret a correct strategy for that action. To experience in other than a purely passive sense (a sense less than human) is to interpret; and to be 'experienced' is to have become a good interpreter. Interpretation is thus a question as unavoidable, finally, as experience, understanding, deliberation, judgment, decision, and action. To be human is to act reflectively, to decide deliberately, to understand intelligently, to experience fully. Whether we know it or not, to be human is to be a skilled interpreter" (Tracy, 9).

15. On "ecclesiastical history" and the American polity, see Zakai, *Exile and Kingdom* (1992), especially his discussion of the metaphor of wilderness.

16. See Geertz, 5.

17. We are also, it bears considering, a part of stories of which we are unaware. Such obliviousness may have no discernible impact on our lives—or this basic lack of awareness of stories of which we are a part may shape our lives in unanticipated ways. Part of critical self-reflection then demands the ability to consider the stories that inform our identities in the world, understanding that self-discovery is in part the discovery of such narratives.

18. Narratives consist of a number of elements, including plot, tone, character, and setting. In this study of the Exodus narrative in the United States, I am particularly concerned with setting and character. For a fuller treatment of the political lessons conveyed by the plot of the Exodus story, see Walzer 1985.

19. In his influential discussion of the "chronotype" in *The Dialogic Imagination* (1981), M. M. Bakhtin explores the inter-relationship of time and space in narrative constructions.

20. The status of "promising" in modern Western political philosophy could not be of greater significance. The social contract tradition, for instance, rests on concepts of promising. Nietzsche, in the opening section of the second essay of *On the Genealogy of Morals*, goes so far as to declare: "To breed an animal *with the right to make promises*—is this not the paradoxical task that nature has set itself in the case of man? Is it not the real problem regarding man?" (Nietzsche, 57). Arendt celebrates "promising" (and "forgiving") as vital faculties for the practice of politics.

For a careful and provocative study of the notion of promising in modern political theory, see the recent work of Mark Button.

21. As Ricoeur states: "In this sense, it is true that life is lived and stories are told. An unbridgeable difference does remain, but this difference is partly abolished by our power of applying to ourselves the plots that we have received from our culture and of trying on the different roles assumed by the favorite characters of the stories most dear to us. It is therefore by means of the imaginative variations of our own ego that we attempt to obtain a narrative understanding of ourselves, the only kind that escapes the apparent choice between sheer change and absolute identity. Between the two lies narrative identity" (1991, 32–33).

22. Although this book focuses on one particular "sacred story"—the Exodus narrative in America—I by no means want to suggest that this is the only "sacred story" in the United States. In the plural society in which we live, there are, of course, competing

"sacred stories" that establish different horizons for a particular historical entity (be it nation, community, organization, or individual).

23. The concept of "interpretive communities" is thoughtfully developed in the work of Stanley Fish.

24. Nietzsche 1980, 10. Among the more striking elements of this passage is that even the philosopher who sought the "transvaluation of values" acknowledges the need for some "horizon."

25. Benhabib also uses the metaphor of sediment, but in a manner different from Ricoeur. For Benhabib, sediment is what covers and obscures. Her account of Arendtian "pearl diving" speaks of "excavat[ing] the original meaning of the phenomenon which lay covered by sedimented layers of historical interpretation" (Benhabib, 126). For Ricoeur and myself—and I think for Arendt as well—sediment is not what covers pearls but is rather the remainder that can itself be carefully used in retelling stories. A pearl, after all, begins as a grain of sediment and becomes a lustrous object.

26. Machiavelli's advice in bk. 3, chapt. 1 of the *Discourses on Livy* that a wise political leader must return his or her people back to their founding moment and principles is but one of many canonical illustrations.

27. This approach to history, according to Dienstag, is perhaps best exemplified by Hegel.

28. See also Benjamin who in his "Theses on the Philosophy of History" argues for the present to "seize memory" and "wrest tradition away from conformism"—that is, to pursue the fullness of historical memory. In this way, the past can be "redeemed" in the future. This capacity of the past to be redeemed, Benjamin says, is the "spark of hope" (Benjamin, 255).

29. Dienstag, 196. The Nietzsche quotation is from *The Gay Science*, 1:34.

30. The fears of those who would exclude religious voices from the realm of politics rest on this concern over the univocal telling and interpreting of stories. Ernst Bloch would disagree with this characterization of these retellings of the Exodus narrative as univocal. In *Atheism in Christianity*, Bloch engages in a biblical exegesis in which he excavates the "underground text" to find the expressions of dissent evident in the Scriptures (1972, 14). I find Bloch's reading a compelling reminder about the always present possibilities of (re-)interpretation.

31. This point is central, for example, to Walter Benjamin's essay "The Storyteller." Both Ricoeur and Arendt cite Benjamin's dire warnings about the loss of the capacity of storytelling in their own theories of narrative.

32. This analysis of MacIntyre rests on my reading of *After Virtue* (1984), especially his influential discussion in chapt. 15, "The Virtues, the Unity of a Human Life, and the Concept of a Tradition."

33. Bill Bishop, "The Schism in U.S. Politics Begins at Home." *Austin American-Statesman*, April 4, 2004, http://www.statesman.com/specialreports/content/specialreports/greatdivide/0404divide.html.

As Timothy Noah reports in *Slate*, a "landslide county" is defined by Bishop "as one in which the presidential nominee of one party receives at least 60 percent of the vote. In 1976, 26.8 percent of American voters lived in landslide counties. By 2000, that proportion had nearly doubled, to 45.3 percent." See Noah, "Mister Landslide's Neighborhood," *Slate*, April 7, 2004, http://slate.msn.com/id/2098387.

34. In the United States, the pluralism definitive of the social order has long offered the nation multiple "sacred stories," many of which offer competing ethics in their most common interpretation. Thus, though Louis Hartz may be correct in his assessment that the United States is predominantly a Lockean nation, the presence of a complete "Lockean consensus" is challenged by competing "sacred stories" that offer moral frameworks counter to possessive individualism. James Young's *Reconsidering American Liberalism* (1996) and Wilson Carey McWilliams' *The Idea of Fraternity in America* (1973) offer two distinctive alternatives to the predominant narrative of the Lockean consensus.

35. Such a scenario reflects the most excessive implications of Michel Foucault's notion of "micropower." However, Foucault, of course, also noted that all power meets resistance. A crucial element of resistance in this case is the power of memory, specifically, the memory of competing stories. This form of resistance is in part what Milan Kundera intends in his often noted assertion: "the struggle of man against power is the struggle of memory against forgetting." The power of memory is not just individual but social and historical. Walter Benjamin's sense of "brushing history against the grain," Foucault's "subjugated knowledges," Ernst Bloch's sense of "non-contemporaneity," each in their own way offer a sense of the traces of competing stories and interpretations "of which we are a part." In these concepts, we find visions that unsettle the unity of MacIntyre's vision and offer the capacity to resist the confines of tradition through new interpretations of governing narratives.

36. Arendt 1977, 14. The potency of even a fragmentary set of traditions should not be underestimated. Cultural residue remains, marking how we understand the world. As Seyla Benhabib states: "Even when the thread of tradition is broken, even when the past is no longer authoritative simply because it has been, it lives within us and we cannot avoid placing ourselves in relation to it" (Benhabib, 125).

37. Curtis' evocative essay on the democratic possibilities found in Arendt's aesthetics pursues the manner in which Arendt's theory allows for these fragile beings to engage in meaningful politics in their everyday lives.

38. A recent work that captures this sense of visiting quite powerfully is *The Best of Enemies: Race and Redemption in the New South* (1996) by Osha Gray Davidson. Davidson recounts the story of Ann Atwater and C. P. Ellis and their collective work on court-ordered school desegregation in Durham, N.C., in 1971. Davidson traces the life histories of Atwater, an African American civil rights activist, and Ellis, the Grand Cyclops of the Ku Klux Klan of Durham. Compelled to work together, the two eventually develop a respect based in large part on the mutual sharing of stories. This is a case, in other words, in which visiting enables democratic political participation. Curtis (2000) also discusses *The Best of Enemies*, see 137ff. See also Studs Terkel's interviews with Atwater and Ellis in *Race: How Blacks & Whites Think & Feel about the American Obsession* (1992).

39. In this sense, democratic communication allows for many different authors of stories and many different interpretations of these stories, whereas authoritarian communication allows only for a single author and a definitive interpretation.

40. Kim Curtis astutely notes, "this is one of Arendt's idiosyncratic departures from Kant, who actually conceives of representative thinking as 'abstracting from one's own contingent situation to think in the place of *any* other man.' Arendt, by contrast, is arguing for a more complex thinking that, as we shall see, is far more demanding of our imagination with respect to *particular* others than Kant's representative thinking" (1999, 177n30).

41. This is not to say that judgments, even as "invitations," are not decisive in the short term, nor that the consequences of such decisions can be undone. Representative thinking does not lead to paralysis. The effects of judgments become the source of further exchange of stories and the subject of both interpretation and judgment. In this discussion, I situate Arendt's notion of judging within my broader argument about narratives and politics. Beiner's interpretation of Arendt's account of judgment disputes their political import, preferring to leave judging as an aesthetic matter. However, I am more convinced by Curtis' strong thesis on the relation between aesthetics and politics in the work of Arendt. See also Disch 1996, 141ff. for an account of the political implications of Arendt's discussion of visiting, representative thinking, and judging in the *Lectures on Kant*.

42. For a similar argument about the disruptive impact of visiting and narrative identity, see Hammer, "Incommensurable Phrases and Narrative Discourse." Hammer argues, "Self-constancy, though, requires neither sameness nor closure since the narrative

that is constitutive of identity, the story of a life, is itself (by the nature of action) always in the process of being composed" (483).

43. Of course, it is of great (although not exclusive) importance that individuals from dominant or normative backgrounds learn to visit, since individuals occupying the "margins" are compelled to see the world from the perspective of those in the center all the time.

44. Disch discusses Arendt's post World War II correspondence with Karl Jaspers where she uses this phrase. See Disch 1996, 192ff.

45. This admiration is a recurring theme in *Men in Dark Times* (1968).

46. Not being quite at home in the world is not a position that Arendt glibly endorses—her consciousness of the despair of post-World War II German-Jewish identity is caution enough against such a conclusion. On Arendt's concerns about post-War Jewry, see her *The Jew as Pariah: Identity and Politics in the Modern Age* and *Rahel Varnhagen: The Life of a Jewish Woman*. See also Barnouw; Bernstein.

Ultimately, for Arendt, the world can never serve as an individual's "home" in the conventional sense of a safe and protected space. The public world is the source of much of value for Arendt, but it must and should fail to be a source of solace, comfort, safety.

47. For an illuminating discussion of the Arendt's categories of pariah, parvenu, and conscious pariah, see Disch 1996, 172ff. See also Ring, "The Pariah as Hero: Hannah Arendt's Political Actor," and Locke, "Unashamed Citizenship."

48. Disch 1996, 186–87. Disch concludes that the conscious pariah "is none the worse" for not identifying totally with any group or place (1996, 187). This assertion tends to minimize the struggles and sufferings of conscious pariahs. As I will address in my analysis of King and Call to Renewal, the life of a conscious pariah is rarely easy.

49. Paul Ricoeur speaks of the prophet as a "summoned subject . . . so radically decentered that it is at first uprooted from its initial setting. Amos is taken from his flock, as was Moses" (1995, 265). See also Bonnie Honig, *Democracy and the Foreigner* (2003).

50. Orlie concludes, "Imaginative reflection, guided by *sensus communis,* 'liberates' us from the private conditions that block the impartiality and generality judgment requires and exemplifies" (159).

51. Arendt (1977, 222) quotes Kant's *Critique of Judgment,* section 19. Although some readers of Arendt (e.g., Habermas and Benhabib) see in this phrase a decided inclination toward the building of consensus, Dana Villa persuasively argues that while "Arendt invokes Kant in order to reassert the dialogical or deliberative moment as a necessary boundary" to Nietzschean agonistic expression beyond good and evil, "Arendtian plurality exceeds the consensus model" (Villa, 276). Arendt's dialogical, pluralistic concept of *sensus communis* emphasizes a communicative politics of both speaking and listening that is foreign to Nietzsche. The limits of the Nietzschean Arendt can be seen in their quite different views of promising and forgiving. Whereas Arendt sees these political faculties as invaluable, Nietzsche is both suspicious of promising as a constraint on future possibilities and of forgiving as a sign of weakness commonly produced by *ressentiment.* See Nietzsche, *On the Genealogy of Morals,* second essay. For Arendt on forgiving and promising, see 1990, 175; 1974a, 236ff., and Pitkin 1972, 147ff.

52. This point marks a distinction between Arendt and Kant; Kant *is* more concerned about consent, Arendt is more focused on creating and sustaining relationships through "wooing."

53. Culturally resonant narratives like the story of Exodus in America are of particular importance for appreciating an Arendtian conception of the relationship between narratives and politics. Even in the fragmented and fragile conditions, the sediment of culturally resonant narratives provides a capacity for enhancing the *sensus communis*

that Arendt valued, while always still offering the capacity for innovation that was pivotal for her celebration of the natality that animates politics.

54. The closing phrase in this passage is from Arendt 1982, 43.

## 3. Twentieth-Century American Prophets

1. An argument could be made for Reinhold Niebuhr, Billy Graham, Pat Robertson or Jerry Falwell, but this title likely falls on King's shoulders.

2. Both Sunday and King repeated their sermons with only modest changes during their years of preaching. The sermons I am discussing were widely disseminated both during and after their lifetimes. Moreover, themes drawn from the story of Exodus and the books of the prophets were a constant presence in the sermons, speeches, and writings of both men—and were quite familiar to their audiences, given the resonant status of this American sacred story. Thus, not only is there a coherence with regard to the repetition of particular sermons throughout the ministries of Sunday and King, but also there is a consistency throughout each preacher's corpus of work.

3. Sunday was an early proponent of "fundamentalism" in America. While he admitted he was by no means a rigorous theologian, he did assert (though did not always practice) the need to read the Scriptures literally. King's father, the Rev. Martin Luther King, Sr., was also inclined to read the Scriptures in a literal fashion. In part as a result of his studies at Crozer Theological Seminary and his doctoral work at Boston University, the younger King broke with his father theologically on this method of approaching the Bible.

4. *The New Bill James Historical Abstract* names Billy Sunday as the fastest Major League Baseball player in the 1880s—and the best-looking player of the decade as well. See James, 41.

5. Compare, for example, the call of Ezekiel, Ez. 1:28ff.

6. These figures represent those who heard Sunday speak in person; toward the end of his career, Sunday began to explore the new medium of radio, anticipating the development of broadcast evangelism that now figures so prominently in American popular culture.

The statistics on Sunday's ministry are central to the reports of the success of his evangelism and his emphasis on statistics should be no surprise, given his prior career as a baseball player. Sunday measured himself—and was measured by others—by the size of the crowds, the amount of the "gift offering" he collected, and the number and percentage of his listeners who "hit the sawdust trail" at the beck of his altar calls. See Frank, 176ff., McLoughlin, 1955, 46–48, 81, and passim.

7. The innovations attributable to Sunday include the growth in scope and order of revivalist organizations, the use of popular music as a basis for hymns, the employment of common vernacular from the pulpit, and an ecumenical, minimalist theology. On Sunday's status in 20th-century conservative American revivalism and "men's movements," see Longinow.

8. D'Emilio and Freedman, 172. I cite this work on sexuality because the cultural changes the authors describe were a source of primary concern for Sunday. On the social upheaval to which Sunday was responding, see also McLoughlin 1955, 36ff.

9. The clash between evolution and Christian fundamentalism would, of course, reach its peak—but, witness the recent developments in Kansas and elsewhere, not its culmination—with the Scopes trial in 1925. On the Scopes trial, see Larson, *Summer for the Gods* (1997).

10. Elsewhere in his sermon "Nuts for Skeptics to Crack," Billy Sunday uses the framework of Exodus to compute the age of human history. He declares that because

there is one empty coffin in Egypt that was built for a Pharaoh, it must be because it was designed for the leader who died chasing Moses into the Red Sea. Accordingly, we can conclude that human history is, as the Bible teaches us, approximately six thousand years old. See Sunday 1965, 91ff.

11. Sunday's paeans to women and motherhood are part of a long line of evangelical idealization of "natural" gender roles. On the cult of domesticity, see Rudy; Balmer, 71ff.

12. Sunday 1965, 228. On its face, this is a fascinating claim for a "biblical literalist" especially in light of the themes of memory and forgetting that permeate not just Exodus, Leviticus, Numbers, and Deuteronomy, but also the retellings of the story in the books of the biblical prophets.

13. As he says later in the same sermon: "There wasn't a college professor in all Egypt that God would trust with that baby" (1965, 233). The idea that one could be both a college professor and a mother, was, of course, beyond his ken.

14. Implicit in this sermon—as in many of the sermons delivered by Sunday—is the middle-class status of his audience. Replete with remarks about how men treat their secretaries at the office and the frivolous leisure time activities of society women, Sunday is clearly not speaking to the secretaries or the women who were working in the homes of these leisurely society women. According to the United States Department of Labor, by 1910, 20 percent of workers outside the home were women. On Billy Sunday as a middle-class phenomenon, see also McLoughlin 1955, 217.

15. In this sermon, Sunday actually makes a great deal out of Moses' mother serving as his wet-nurse; for Sunday this is an illustration of God's just and good humor.

16. In his sermon, "Under the Sun," Sunday emphasizes the faithful patience of Moses in a striking way: "And then there was Moses. He had a vision that pierced the clouds and went far beyond the sun when he saw that 'the reproach of Christ' would bring him greater and more lasting riches than the treasures of Egypt . . ." http://www.biblebelievers.com/billy_sunday/sun13.html.

17. This latter image of Moses is clearly the figure celebrated by King. For an interesting comparison between Sunday and King on lessons a mother teaches her son, see footnote 75 below and the poem "Mother to Son" by Langston Hughes that serves as a centerpiece of King's speech in 1957 announcing victory in the Montgomery bus boycott. In that poem (and in King's speech) the central lesson is to keep moving forward, to not wait for anyone to hand you justice, but to go forth and assertively seize it—in other words, a decidedly non-premillennialist, political message.

18. Sunday was offered great sums of money to take his persona to the secular stage, but he always declined. George M. Cohan would eventually create a character based on Sunday, but received only mixed reviews as critics held the actor up to the performances of Sunday himself.

19. Probably Sunday's most artistic imitator, Aimee Semple McPherson (founder of the International Church of the Foursquare Gospel), took this technique to its logical conclusion, hiring actors to illustrate her sermons.

20. Sunday 1970, 63–64. Sunday apparently delivered this sermon year after year at almost every revival. People attending the events knew that the sermon was coming eventually and would call out requesting Sunday to "deliver the goods."

21. Many of Sunday's sermons are also filled with sympathetic stories about the rich who, despite their wealth, still suffered miserably by being far from Jesus.

22. "Show Thyself a Man," Sunday Papers, Reel 112, June 17, 1917.

McLoughlin notes a rare exception in which Sunday (in his sermon "Jekyll and Hyde") declared, "*Society must share the responsibility* of these people who become criminals, thieves, thugs, cut-throats, drunkards, and prostitutes." However, McLoughlin, points out, within the same sermon, Sunday moves from this assertion back to his more familiar refrain of "individual responsibility" (1955, 145–46).

23. Bruns recounts a time when Billy Sunday and Emma Goldman led concurrent campaigns in Paterson, New Jersey in 1915. Two years earlier, the I.W.W. had led a strike of silk-workers in Paterson that was ultimately defeated after violent reprisals. Labor forces nevertheless believed the experience of the strike left a lasting solidarity amongst the working class, whereas the local industrialists and political leaders sought to maintain the uneasy calm that developed in the wake of the 1913 strike. In 1915, Goldman led protests against the city, and industry responded by sponsoring Sunday's revival campaign. The contest between organized labor and Sunday resulted in the labor hall inexplicably burning to the ground, Goldman leaving Paterson in symbolic defeat, and Sunday delivering a month of sermons that ended on Pentecost Sunday with twelve thousand people in attendance and another five thousand turned away at the door of the tabernacle. See Bruns, 189ff.

24. See Sunday, "Under the Sun," http://www.biblebelievers.com/billy_sunday/sun13.html.

25. As "Sunday's director of men's work, the Rev. Isaac Ward explained . . . to a group of Boston ministers [in 1916]: 'We never touch labor troubles. . . . We teach only the old-time gospel of the cross. . . . It's the only solution to the problem of capital and labor. . . . Labor agitation disappears in some places because of [our] meetings in the plants and factories. That is its moral and economic value. In some places, strike agitation has been eliminated altogether'" (McLoughlin 1955, 237).

26. See, for instance, his sermon "Home, Sweet Home," in Sunday 1965, 212–25.

27. The sermon opens with Sunday abruptly declaring: "I say to you, young girl. Don't go with that godless, God-forsaken, sneering young man that walks the streets smoking cigarettes. He would not walk the streets with you if you smoked cigarettes. But you say you will marry him and reform him; he would not marry you to reform you. Don't go to that dance. Don't you know it is the most damnable, low-down institution on the face of God's earth. . . . Don't go with that young fellow for a joy ride at midnight" (1970, 107).

28. Sunday was not alone preaching a gospel of muscular Christianity. As Clifford Putney discusses in *Muscular Christianity: Manhood and Sports in Protestant America, 1880–1920* (2001), muscular Christianity enjoyed broad appeal, especially but not exclusively in white Protestant circles, during this era. From Theodore Roosevelt to the YMCA to Amos Alonzo Stagg's role in the development of college football at the University of Chicago, proponents of muscular Christianity had a broad impact on American culture.

For a fascinating history of the social construction of masculinity during this period of American history, see McLaren, *The Trials of Masculinity: Policing Sexual Boundaries, 1870–1930* (1997). McLaren examines the record of criminal trials and psychological and sexological testing during this period in order to explore the texture of "normal" and "aberrant" masculinity in the United States.

See also Prothero's discussion of the Men and Religion Forward Movement, 93–94.

29. I take this phrase from Bruns.

30. In the "Booze" sermon, Sunday illuminates the muscular vitality of the "Christian man" by contrasting this vision with a detailed description of the diseased and decaying body of the drinker of alcohol.

31. "Show Thyself a Man," Sunday Papers, Reel 12, June 17, 1917.

32. Bruns, 266. Bruns also notes that Sunday's attacks on various "liberal Protestants" and "higher critics" often focused on their "foreignness." See Bruns, 121.

33. Congressional Record, 65th Congress, 2nd Session, Washington DC, 1918, LVI, 761.

34. And in this light it is important to note that the claims Sunday makes about the Mayflower Compact are remarkably—though conventionally—overstated. While the compact does proclaim a commitment to create a "civil body politick" and to enact and

follow laws for "the general good of the colony," this agreement affirms the affiliation with King James. The compact does not say anything about rights and individual liberties, including the right to "worship according to the dictates of our conscience." The pilgrims restricted anyone who was not a member of the church from participating in politics. Given Sunday's beliefs about decency and responsibility being attributes only of Christians (see McLoughlin 1955, 137), it is not entirely unfair to see such religious tests for office as outside Sunday's ideal for America.

35. Sermon notes, Sunday Papers, Reel 9, May 1917.

36. Sermon notes, Sunday Papers, Reel 9, May 1917.

37. The most influential books written about King in the last twenty years convey this sentiment in their titles: David Garrow's *Bearing the Cross*, evoking King as a Jesus figure and the Taylor Branch trilogy, *Parting the Waters, Pillar of Fire*, and the forthcoming *At Canaan's Edge*, which of course evoke the connection between King and Moses. My discussion of King admittedly follows in this tradition.

For a rich and detailed study of prophetic religious tradition and the civil rights movement, see Chappell, *A Stone of Hope: Prophetic Religion and the Death of Jim Crow* (2004).

38. The iconography of Malcolm X over the last fifteen years in even "mainstream" African American circles contributes, of course, to the heightening of King's status in popular American culture. In *Making Malcolm* (1995) and *I May Not Get There with You: The True Martin Luther King, Jr.* (2000) Michael Eric Dyson carefully warns that while comparative analysis of Martin Luther King Jr. and Malcolm X can be of value, an approach that frames the two figures oppositionally is likely to flatten out the complexity of each figure and obscure more than it illuminates.

39. President Lyndon Johnson, who had spoken with King often early in his presidency and used King's language in winning passage of the Voting Rights Act and his Great Society programs, refused to meet with King over the last two years of King's life. Instead, Johnson presented A. Whitney Young as his administration's voice on race.

40. On "double-consciousness," see DuBois, 3ff.

41. One can think again of Moses who, after a riotous purge following the Hebrews dancing around the golden idol at the foot of Mount Sinai, moved himself and the tabernacle to the periphery of the wandering community.

42. King came to place greater emphasis on "global citizenship" after 1964, especially after having been awarded the Nobel Peace Prize.

43. Clearly, it is more than simply religious understanding that inclined each man toward these different modes of prophetic politics. However, we must be careful not to reduce their divergent political visions to differences in race, class, or region. Some of King's sharpest critics (and targets of his own criticism) were apolitical black ministers who kept their eyes so fixed on heaven that they ignored the world around them. See, for example, his final "I See the Promised Land" sermon in Memphis: "It's alright to talk about 'long white robes over yonder' in all of its symbolism. But ultimately people want some suits and dresses and shoes to wear down here. It's alright to talk about 'streets flowing with milk and honey,' but God has commanded us to be concerned about the slums down here, and his children who can't eat three square meals a day. It's alright to talk about the new Jerusalem, but one day, God's preacher must talk about the [new] New York, the new Atlanta, the new Philadelphia, the new Los Angeles, the new Memphis, Tennessee. This is what we have to do" (King 1986, 282). Aldon Morris in his wonderful work exploring the role of the black church in the civil rights movement, describes the mass meetings organized by the Southern Christian Leadership Conference as "resembling revivals" with King as the "charismatic minister" delivering a "new message" about the church pursuing social justice in this world, rather than preaching patience for deliverance in the next (Morris, 97ff.). On King's criticism of apolitical ministers, see also "Letter from Birmingham City Jail" (1986).

Likewise, some of Sunday's greatest opponents were the leaders of the Social Gospel movement whose ministry was aimed at resolving the very poverty Sunday himself faced as a child.

44. In their analyses of white Protestant American jeremiads, Miller and Bercovitch, for example, show little evidence of the presence of these tropes. However, the themes of sojourners and wilderness are far more common in the African American jeremiad tradition. See Howard-Pitney, *The Afro-American Jeremiad: Appeals for Justice in America* (1990).

45. Contrary to Niebuhr, King preached that a "beloved community" was possible in this world. See King's sermon, "The Death of Evil upon the Seashore."

46. Abraham Heschel, no minor authority on the prophetic tradition, spoke of King as a prophet, declaring quite simply, "The whole future of America will depend on the impact and influence of Dr. King" (quoted in King 1998, 23). King, of course, was quite aware and often explicit about his status in the tradition of the prophets and, aware, too, of the common theological and "practical" dualistic break between being a "prophet" and being a "priest." King ultimately leaned toward the latter—but not unequivocally. King was a more tempered "prophet" than was his predecessor at Dexter Avenue Baptist Church in Montgomery, Vernon Johns. King, in fact, sought to balance his responsibilities as a prophet with the duties of a priest he learned from his father Martin Luther King, Sr. At some level King succeeded in bridging this often either/or choice between priest or prophet, but ultimately he invested his energy more fully in the role of prophet—and certainly his reputation is as prophet not priest. When King spoke of other clergy, he—like Billy Sunday—often offered stinging rebukes of "priest-like" behavior. See, for example, "Guidelines for a Constructive Church" (1998) and "Letter from a Birmingham City Jail." On the distinction between prophet and priest see Ahad Ha-'Am, "Moses" (1981).

47. On the biblical prophets, see Heschel, *The Prophets*, vols. 1 and 2 (1969, 1975).

48. See Smith, *Conjuring Culture: Biblical Formations of Black America* (1994) and his discussion of Vincent Harding on the reversal of Exodus images, 72ff. This shift is also a recurring theme in David Howard-Pitney's *The Afro-American Jeremiad*.

49. This passage from Cone's *For My People: Black Theology and Black Church* is quoted in Smith, 71. In addition, Prothero explains, there is a long African American tradition of "merg[ing] Moses into Jesus and Jesus into Moses" (210). On this tradition, see also Eugene Genovese, *Roll, Jordan, Roll* (1976).

50. It is important to note that in his love for this "American Egypt," King also followed the pattern of the ancient Hebrews wandering in the wilderness, longing for the "fleshpots" of their old home across the Red Sea. In this regard, it is fair to ask whether this is a case of King being less like Moses (who presumably grew out of his love for Egypt) than like one of the "murmurers" Moses struggled to lead to the Promised Land.

51. Bercovitch (1993) makes such an argument about the ultimately conservative nature of the American jeremiad. I address this point in the concluding chapter.

52. Let me be clear here. I am by no means suggesting that the metaphors of the wilderness and soujourners had no place in the white Protestant jeremiadic tradition. The idea of the wilderness, in particular, was a prominent theme in early America (witness Samuel Dansforth's 1670 sermon, "A Brief Recognition of New England's Errand into the Wilderness," from which Perry Miller's study takes its name). However, as colonization and nationhood expanded, the conception of America as a *realized* promised land grew and the wilderness was pushed ever westward. Rather than a metaphor signifying the intractability of the wanderings of a people, the wilderness became simply those places that had not yet seen the light cast by the "city on a hill." America as wilderness gave way to America as promised land.

To illustrate this point one could look at the transformation and disappearance of the metaphor of wilderness in the sermons of prominent jeremiadic ministers since the founding of the nation in 1776. If nothing else, it should be apparent that the metaphor of wilderness was increasingly used to signify a personal realm of struggle, repentance and possibility for salvation rather than a social or geographic space. In social and geographic terms, the growth of the nation was a marker of dominion, of the taming of the wilderness into additional regions of the promised land.

53. It is worth noting that the sermon King had written and intended to deliver in Memphis on the Sunday following his assassination was titled, "Why America May Go to Hell." See Howard-Pitney, 182.

This production of King as an American conservative is aided by the postulate that Malcolm X is the "real" radical of the civil rights era.

54. Perhaps this is most marked in relation to issues of gender. Fairclough notes that King once wrote, "'The primary obligation of the woman is motherhood,'" and King never graced Septima Clark, Ella Baker, or Diane Nash (or other notable civil rights activists associated with SCLC) with the respect and recognition that was merited (Fairclough, 50). Nevertheless, King did not make maintaining conventional gender or sex roles a pivotal part of his vision. Indeed, King was often accused of preaching "unmanliness" because of his emphasis on nonviolent resistance and his own perceived passivity in the face of aggression during the mid-1960s. The contrast between King's expression of "black masculinity" and that of Malcolm X, Stokely Carmichael, and other figures in the black power movement became a significant issue in the popular imagination of the era. The crucial point here is that whereas King and Sunday may not have been too far apart in their respective understandings of gender, for Sunday the question of proper Christian masculinity was a central feature of his political theology, whereas for King the question stayed in the background and found only subtler and more indirect expression. Certainly, King often cited figures such as Sister Pollard ("My feets is tired but my soul is rested") and Rosa Parks as inspirations for his own courage in the civil rights struggle.

For further discussion on King and "unmanliness," see Howard-Pitney, 161.

55. Michael Walzer, for example, pursues this line of analysis in *Exodus and Revolution* (1985).

Even those whose analysis of identity is generally more critical and individual in focus return with fascination to this story. In this vein, perhaps no writer serves as a better example than Freud and his curious analysis of Exodus in *Moses and Monotheism*. That Freud reads the text in order to develop an argument about the vagaries of individual identity formation based on Moses' "true" lineage as an Egyptian is but one more example of the resonance of the Exodus story in the West with regard to questions of identity. Moreover, the political context in which Freud writes is indicated by his apparent intention to separate "Jewishness" from biology. For our purposes, Freud's account amply illustrates the many ways in which the text can be read—a theme central to my own analysis of prophetic politics in America.

56. What is intriguing about the onset of mass immigration is that the vision of America as a promised land is maintained, but the act of volition conveyed in the term chosen people begins to shift from that of God to that of the individual immigrant who has chosen to come to America. This shift fits well with Weber's thesis on the Protestant ethic in America. Weber explores the tension between a theology of grace and a socio-economy of individual will and volition. The increasing value placed on individual choice (such that today in the United States individual choice is all but seen as definitive of freedom), is coeval with the decline of theologies of grace. See M. Weber (1976).

57. Not that this should be a surprise: The political/ideological construction of racial and ethnic categories in America has long been recognized. Nevertheless, the elegance and stakes of this construction are high in light of the centrality of Exodus tropes in the United States.

58. It would make little theological sense to argue against segregation and for rigid and exclusive categories.

59. King, "The Birth of a New Nation," April 7, 1957, Montgomery, Alabama. http://www.stanford.edu/group/King/speeches/The_birth_of_a_new_nation_.html.

60. King expressed these words often; this passage is from a July 23, 1956 speech delivered at the American Baptist Assembly and American Home Mission Agencies Conference in Green Lake, Wisconsin. http://www.stanford.edu/group/King/papers/vol3/560 723.004–Non-Aggression_Procedures_to_Interracial_Harmony,_Address_at_the_American_Baptist_Assembly_on_American_Home_Mission_Agencies_Conference.htm.

61. I have found one exception. In a 1958 speech to the American Jewish Congress at its convention in Miami, King does offer an uncharacteristic use of the metaphor of "chosen-ness." There he states: "Our common fight is against these deadly enemies of democracy, and our glory is that *we are chosen to prove that courage is a characteristic of oppressed people,* however cynically and brutally they are denied full equality and freedom." King, May 14, 1958, Miami Beach, Florida. www.stanford.edu/group/King/papers/vol4/580514–009Full_AJC.htm (my italics) It is intriguing that such an assertion should come before a Jewish audience in a speech in which he is striving to draw close connections between Jewish and African American struggles for justice.

62. Quoted in Howard-Pitney, 146. In King's portrayal of the special status of suffering and its capacity to help illuminate God's design, he in a sense illustrates Heschel's belief that chosen-ness simply meant added responsibility.

63. See, for example, Benjamin Palmer, "National Responsibility Before God," especially 179–80.

On the subject of the "curse of Ham," it is worth noting that although Ham committed the fault, Noah (*not* God) curses Canaan, *one* of Ham's four sons and one who has no direct geographical connection to Africa. See Gen. 9:22, 24–25, 10:15–19.

64. Contrary to my argument, Cornel West in *Prophesy Deliverance! An Afro-American Revolutionary Christianity* (1982) argues that King *does* emphasize the peculiar exceptionalism of black people. West's assessment of King's exclusivist portrayal of African Americans is, I think, overstated. Given King's use of the Exodus narrative within an American cultural inclination toward exceptionalism, what is remarkable is how *little* weight King places on this line of interpretation. See, for example, King's sermon, "The Drum-Major Instinct," in which he explores the problem of exclusivity and the "need that some people have to feel superior" as the root of racism (1998, 177–78).

65. The exception here is King's common refrain that the rights of protest and religious freedom enjoyed by Americans should be an example for Communist nations.

66. See Walzer (1985) for illustrations of the many different people who have adopted the Exodus narrative.

67. These three passages are taken from King, "The Birth of a New Nation," April 7, 1957, Montgomery, Alabama. http://www.stanford.edu/group/King/speeches/The_birth_of_a_new_nation_.html.

68. Notice these are quintessentially "American ideals"; they are expressed in the words of Jefferson from the Declaration of Independence that King constantly referred to in his sermons as the "American dream" or "promise."

69. Critics will claim that my reading of King is overly generous in its celebration of his "inclusiveness"—after all, King's vision of the path to the promised land is distinctly Christian (and the language is masculinist). While this is quite true, it is important to note two intriguing aspects of this sermon. First, again King is discussing the lesson Americans can learn from Ghana; his aim is by no means to be an American missionary abroad. Second and relatedly, King nowhere here suggests that for Nkrumah and Ghana or Gandhi and India, the price of admission to the promised land of justice and freedom is conversion to Christianity. Contrast Billy Sunday: "I do not believe in this twentieth-century theory of the universal fatherhood of God and brotherhood of man. . . . You are not a child of God unless you are a Christian" (quoted in McLoughlin 1955, 137).

70. In this distinction we can see a crucial difference between the American jeremiad and the *African* American jeremiad.

71. King 1981, 83; italics in original. This passage continues: "And though the Kingdom of God may remain *not yet* as a universal reality in history, in the present it may exist in such isolated forms as in judgment, in personal devotion, and in some group life. 'The Kingdom of God is in the midst of you.'"

The theological underpinnings of this notion of the Kingdom of God are important to note. Most significantly, they reflect King's indebtedness to Augustine, an inheritance evident in King's overabundance of "light" and "dark" imagery. See Branch 1988, 76, 91. This idea of the "Kingdom of God" being "not yet" is also found in the theologies of two prominent continental figures that were contemporaries of King—Ernst Bloch and Jürgen Moltmann.

72. The incompleteness of this reading of the Exodus story—a reading with which I agree—is contrary to the interpretation offered by Michael Walzer in his *Exodus and Revolution*. Walzer argues that the manner in which the Exodus narrative conveys a linearity complete with beginning, middle, and end is a large part of the reason it has been embraced so successfully by revolutionary movements. His argument as to why such movements adopt the template of Exodus notwithstanding, I would maintain (along with King) that the end of the story—the presumed realization of the promised land—is at best temporary and fragile. While the ancient Hebrews are ultimately led by Joshua into Canaan, this land is, first, not long defined as a place of "milk and honey" and, second, not secured by the chosen people for long. The prophets who retell the Exodus story to remind the people of their covenant do so from either a nation in a state of decay or from a position of exile. Moreover, if, as King suggests, the promised land is a realm of the Kingdom of God on earth, such a place has enjoyed even less permanence than the promised land of the ancient Hebrews.

73. In this claim about the promised land, the model for King, of course, is Moses, who died rather than be allowed by God to enter the promised land.

74. The distinction between wilderness and exile is crucial for analysis of prophetic politics. For instance, the next chapter will illustrate that Promise Keepers (while occasionally using the metaphor of wilderness) is quite willing to speak in terms of exile in its depiction of Christians in America as victims of a secular humanism that has come to dominate this once religious/Christian nation. The subject of chapter 5, Call to Renewal, most often, like King, speaks in the metaphor of wilderness, but on occasion slips into the language of exile. A subtextual lesson is the near impossibility of finding rhetorical purity in prophetic politics; an analyst's standards are better attuned to degrees of emphasis rather than all-or-nothing dualisms.

75. The Hughes poem reads in part: "Well, Son, I'll tell you:/Life for me ain't been no crystal stair./It's had tacks in it,/Splinters/Boards torn up,/Places with no carpet on the floor—/Bare;/But all the time/I'se been a-climbin' on,/And reachin' landings,/And turnin' corners,/And sometimes goin' in the dark,/Where there ain't been no light./So, boy, don't you stop now" (quoted in King, "Mass Meeting at Holt Street Baptist Church," 1957, http://www.stanford.edu/group/King/papers/vol3/561114.013–address_to_MIA_Mass_ Meeting_at_Holt_Street_Baptist_Church.htm).

76. Ibid. Parenthetical comments are from the audience in the transcripts of voice recording. For another example, see King's March 25, 1965 sermon "Our God Is Marching On" delivered at the conclusion of the March on Selma, Alabama: "We are on the move now. The burning of our churches will not deter us. We are on the move now. The bombing of our homes will not dissuade us. We are on the move now. The beating and killing of our clergymen and young people will not divert us. We are on the move now. The arrest and release of known murderers will not discourage us. We are on the move now. Like an idea whose time has come, not even the marching of mighty armies can halt us. We are moving to the land of freedom" (1986, 229).

77. Michael Osborn makes a similar argument, observing: "more than just the counterpart of the Exodus narrative, the Good Samaritan story functions as its enabling condition. The Exodus myth will become reality, will carry listeners to the Promised Land, *if* they are willing to follow with full-hearted commitment the moral example of the Good Samaritan" (Osborn, 158).

78. This sermon is quoted in Good, 18ff.

79. With the cry, "My God, my God, why?" King links this retelling of the Exodus story with the cry of Jesus on the cross, "My God, my God, why hast Thou forsaken me?" (Mt. 27:46).

80. King 1986, 274, 277. As Arendt reminds us, "Memory, the mind's power of having present what is irrevocably past and thus absent from the sense, has always been the most plausible paradigmatic example of the mind's power to make invisibles present" (1978b, 2:11).

81. Consider here James Baldwin's letter to his nephew in *The Fire Next Time* (1962): They [white people] are, in effect, still trapped in a history which they do not understand; and until they understand it, they cannot be released from it . . . we, with love, shall force our [white] brothers to see themselves as they are, to cease fleeing from reality and begin to change it" (Baldwin, 8–9).

82. King 1986, 236–37. In a phenomenal statement of representative thinking, King concludes: "Somehow this madness must cease. We must stop now. I speak as a child of God and brother to the suffering poor of Vietnam. I speak for those whose land is being laid waste, whose homes are being destroyed, whose culture is being subverted. I speak for the poor of America who are paying the double price of smashed hopes at home and death and corruption in Vietnam. I speak as a citizen of the world, for the world as it stands aghast at the path we have taken. I speak as an American to the leaders of my own nation. The great initiative of the war is ours. The initiative to stop it must be ours" (King 1986, 238).

83. King, "Highlander Speech," September 2, 1957, Monteagle, Tennessee. http://www.stanford.edu/group/King/papers/vol4/570902–006–Highlander_Speech.htm.

## 4. Promise Keepers

1. These passages are from R. Phillips' introduction to *Seven Promises of a Promise Keeper* (1994), the central book explaining the mission of the Christian social movement. See 4–5, 9.

The Seven Promises of a Promise Keeper are:

1. A Promise Keeper is committed to honoring Jesus Christ through worship, prayer and obedience to God's Word in the power of the Holy Spirit.

2. A Promise Keeper is committed to pursuing vital relationships with a few other men, understanding that he needs brothers to help him keep his promises.

3. A Promise Keeper is committed to practicing spiritual, moral, ethical, and sexual purity.

4. A Promise Keeper is committed to building strong marriages and families through love, protection, and biblical values.

5. A Promise Keeper is committed to supporting the mission of his church by honoring and praying for his pastor, and by actively giving his time and resources.

6. A Promise Keeper is committed to reaching beyond any racial and denominational barriers to demonstrate the power of biblical unity.

7. A Promise Keeper is committed to influencing his world, being obedient to the Great Commandment (see Mark 12:30–31) and the Great Commission (see Matthew 28:19–20).

2. "Promise Keepers Affirms Marriage," March 11, 2004, http://www.promise-keepers.org/paff/news/paffnews276.htm.

3. "Promise Keepers Media Kit," http://www.promisekeepers.org/paff/mkit/paffmkit32. htm.

4. "Promise Keepers Affirms Marriage," March 11, 2004, http://www.promise-keepers.org/paff/news/paffnews276.htm.

5. McCartney, Promise Keepers letter, January 20, 1997.

6. In the wake of the Stand in the Gap event, comments such as the one made by Patrick McGuigan on the Jim Lehrer News Hour—Promise Keepers "are a force for the good. . . . I think it is fabulous"—represented the most common media analysis. In fact, far sharper criticism was reserved for any voices, particularly feminist voices, who offered analysis in opposition to Promise Keepers. At the same PBS roundtable discussion, Mike Barnicle bemoaned the "near-hysterical reaction among many in the media and many special-interest groups like NOW who give the public the impression that they are more afraid of people who pray in public than criminals who prey upon the public every single day. It is a weird thing that we are doing."

7. Trent Lott and Dick Armey are among the host of national government figures to attend Promise Keepers events. While fewer Democrats have made headlines attending Promise Keepers revivals, President Clinton did offer the group a warm welcome to Washington for its Stand in the Gap gathering.

Not all politicians are so enamored of Promise Keepers. Rep. Jesse Jackson Jr., for instance, was a rare national voice offering words of caution in the days surrounding Promise Keepers' 1997 Stand in the Gap gathering in Washington, D.C. Speaking of "liberation theology" and other Christian traditions that "advocate for human rights and equal protection under the law," Jackson asserted: "The Promise Keepers deny the legitimacy of most, if not all of these theological and biblical interpretations that have grown out of experiences of oppression, and resent our commitment to not go back—theologically, biblically, socially, politically, or culturally." Jackson, "Watch as Well as Pray," 1997, http://www.now.org/issues/right/promise/jackson/html.

8. Fortson is quoted in an article by Eric Gorski, "Promise Keepers to Shift Direction Under New Chief." *Denver Post*, October 6, 2003, B1.

9. The cultural influence of Promise Keepers is, while not easy to measure, quite palpable. From the proliferation of outspoken Christian athletes and men's only Bible study groups to the growth of Christian cultural markets in, among others, books, films, and music, Promise Keepers has contributed to marked changes in American culture. To offer one example, consider the central place George W. Bush gave his own participation in a men's only Bible study and accountability group during the 2000 campaign. Bush's experience featured prominently in his campaign autobiography, *A Charge to Keep* and in his stump speeches. While Bush's Bible study group took place in Midland, Texas, prior to the rise of Promise Keepers, the Christian social movement's influence in the 1990s surely increased the resonance of Bush's story in 2000. On Bush's use of religious narratives see Gutterman 2001.

10. Bill McCartney. "Promise Makers," September–October 1997, http://www.poli-cyreview.com/sept97/promise.html.

11. "Is PK a political organization?" http://www.promisekeepers.org/faqs/issu/faq-sissu27.htm.

12. "What is PK's position on the abortion/pro-life issue?" http://www.promise-keepers.org/faqs/issu/faqsissu25.htm.

13. Farrar, "Understanding the Times & Knowing What to Do About It: Lack of True Leaders Is Killing America." http://www.otherside.net/farrar/htm.

14. "Homosexuality Statement," http://www.promisekeepers.org/faqq/issu/faqsissu 214.htm.

15. Of course, Exodus International itself offers another striking retelling of the American sacred story. For this organization, the wilderness represents a life of homosexual

sinfulness, from which one must "exodus" in order to reach the promised land of heterosexuality.

16. "Promise Keepers Affirms Marriage," http://www.promisekeepers.org/paff/news/paffnews276.htm.

17. To further illustrate the "politics" of Promise Keepers, I could also address the explicit political activities of regular Promise Keepers speakers, such as James Dobson, Bill Bright, and Chuck Colson. Despite early financial support from Dobson's Focus on the Family, the endorsement of Gary Bauer and Family Resource Council, and regular appearances on Pat Robertson's Christian Broadcasting Network, Promise Keepers maintains that it has "no affiliation with the Christian Coalition or any other organization on the 'religious right.'" ("Is PK affiliated with the Christian Coalition or any other groups from the 'religious right?'" http://www.promisekeepers.org/faqs/issu/faqsissu28.htm.)

18. For example, The Reverend Joseph Garlington, who frequently serves as the master of ceremonies at Promise Keepers events, has been a prominent member of Senator Rick Santorum's (R-PA) campaign team.

19. The presence of feminists as the opposition runs throughout Promise Keepers literature and events. The explicit antipathy toward feminism was quite pronounced in the wake of the National Organization for Women's often broad-sided criticisms of Promise Keepers. One Promise Keepers leader of whom NOW has been most critical is Bishop Wellington Boone, who, as I discuss below, teaches that wives are called to submit to their husbands: "The degree to which a wife submits to her husband is the degree to which she is submitted to God" (Boone 1996, 21). During the 1997 Promise Keepers event in Pittsburgh, Boone explained his vision of the marriage contract to the men gathered: A father creates a daughter, guarantees her virginity, and gives her in marriage. "Your wife," Boone elaborated, "is at first what her father made her into, but she becomes what you her husband make her into." Following Boone's sermon, the Rev. Joseph Garlington praised Boone for his vision of gender equity and instructed the Promise Keepers in attendance at Three Rivers Stadium to "write a letter to NOW saying, 'You lied to me,'" about Boone and Promise Keepers.

Nearly all quotations from Promise Keepers conferences come from my notes. I attended Promise Keepers events in 1996 (Shea Stadium, New York City), 1997 (Three Rivers Stadium, Pittsburgh; Stand in the Gap in Washington, D.C.), and 1999 (Meadowlands, New Jersey). The quotations from Stand in the Gap and the 1999 Promise Keepers event at the Meadowlands are also from official Promise Keepers conference audio tapes. Steve Farrar's sermon "Understanding the Times & Knowing What to Do About It: Lack of True Leaders Is Killing America" was delivered at the Promise Keepers event in Indianapolis, July 10, 1999. The sermon is available at http://www.otherside.net/farrar/htm and a copy is also on file with the author.

20. "To Save the Nation," *Washington Post,* October 4, 1997, C7.

21. Bill McCartney, "Promise Makers," September–October 1997, http://www.policyreview.com/sept97/promise.html.

22. Promise Keepers' "Go the Distance" Promotional Brochure 2000, available at http://www.promisekeepers.org.

23. *Men's Study Bible,* 73. Of course, for Promise Keepers, Moses' gender is crucial—men, not women, are called to be leaders. As Weber puts it, leading "the infant nation of Israel out in the Sinai desert . . . [was] no Girl Scout picnic" (S. Weber, 99).

24. The other critical facet of the story of the prodigal son is, as Palau here illustrates, tapping into the yearning for men to develop better relationships with their fathers, father figures, and "God the Father." At the "Meet Jesus" page on its official website, Promise Keepers is forthright about this relationship with "Father God." Under the heading "Man to Man about being a son of God," Promise Keepers declares: "A man's relationship with his father is basic. The benefit of a strong affirming bond with 'Dad' is powerful" ("Personally Meet Jesus," http://www.promisekeepers.org/

meet/meet10.htm). In this vein, Promise Keepers is responding to a dynamic very similar to that which made Robert Bly and the mythopoetic men's movement so popular in the early 1990s. For an exploration of the mythopoetic men's movement see *The Politics of Manhood*.

25. Bill McCartney, "Promise Makers," September–October 1997, http://www.policyreview.com/sept97/promise.html.

26. The narrative of national redemption has been replaced by national degradation and God's reward for the few select believers left in Babylon. The popularization this prophecy story can be traced to the publication of the 1971 bestseller *The Late Great Planet Earth* by Hal Lindsey. Lindsey's attitude toward the nation is best summed up in his own epigrammatic claim: "God didn't send me to clean the fishbowl; he sent me to fish" (Quoted in Boyer, 299). In other words, the mission of the messianic Christian is not to contribute to the betterment of the world, the fishbowl, but rather to save a few worthy fish stuck swimming in murky waters. Lindsey's publication success led to a rapid expansion of prophetic remnant literature—churches providing prophetic visions of the coming Armageddon and ministers and lay people busily examining the signs of the times for evidence that the promises found in Daniel, Ezekiel, and Revelations were coming to fruition in these last days.

27. Farrar also peppers this historical analysis with an assessment of immigration and international relations in biblical terms:

> Why is it that people from all over the world have made extraordinary sacrifices to bring their families to this nation? . . . I submit to you that they've done that because . . . America was built upon biblical principles. I've got a question for you. How come nobody in your neighborhood is packing up their family and moving to Iraq? . . . How come nobody on your neighborhood is picking up their family and moving to Cuba? . . . Do you want to know why? Because we've got a different foundation than Cuba or Iraq. (Farrar, 1999.)

28. Ibid.

29. Much like Billy Sunday, a pronounced anti-intellectualism runs throughout the political theology of Promise Keepers. Beyond the common toss-away comments along the lines of "You don't have to be a Ph.D. to be an expert on the state of America . . ." and the general emphasis on the physical rather than mental qualities of men, more direct portrayals of the "conflict" between reason and Jesus are also part of the Promise Keeper canon. For example, at Shea Stadium in 1996, Luis Palau told the story of a "Nobel Prize-winning scientist" who once approached him after a sermon. The man said to Palau, "'My wife is going to heaven but I am going to hell. She is a good Christian woman, but I no longer believe the way I did when I was younger. The University stole my faith from me and I let them take it. . . . The University has made me unworthy to see God,' the man despaired."

30. Oliver, 84. Steve Farrar also addresses the devastating impact of teaching "moral relativism" at American universities in the 1960s:

> We had a bunch of university students in the 60s that were taught that moral relativism was right, you can do whatever you want to do. . . . Now here we are 30 years later. Where are those students that bought moral relativism hook line and sinker? . . . I'll tell you where they are. They are in the [Clinton] Oval Office of the White House of the United States of America. And I'll tell you where else they are. And you maybe saying, "Steve, you're getting political here." I'm not getting political, I'm getting biblical is what I'm getting. I'm not talking Democrat, I'm not talking Republican, I'm talking the word of God here. So where else are they, they are in our court system, they are in the Congress, they are in the House, they are in governorships all over America, and as a result we have a problem in this country because the foundations are being destroyed. You need to understand as a leader; I need to understand as a leader what we are up against. The foundations of this nation are being destroyed. (Farrar, 1999)

31. Ibid.

32. Of course, revivals have been held in sports stadiums before; in the United States such stadiums and arenas are the staple gathering places for masses of people. Promise Keepers' innovation lies in its use of the setting and language of athletics to promulgate its vision. Taking the "muscular Christianity" of Billy Sunday into the heart of sports-obsessed masculinity in America, Promise Keepers strives to march its revival down the American playing field.

33. At each of the stadium events I attended, men were asked to repeat exactly what a speaker had just said. Many times if the tone or pace of the response of the assembled masses was not deemed adequate, the speaker chastised this initial effort and redirected the men "No, say it like this. . . ." Such rote repetitions are clearly designed to aid in fixing the lessons of the sermons in the Promise Keepers' memories, in addition to creating a sense of transcendent teamwork. In a sense, the only spontaneity encouraged is for an individual man to decide to join the crowd answering one of the two or three altar calls typically held during the two-day stadium events.

34. McCartney, *Men of Action Newsletter,* Winter 1993.

35. Following the attacks, McCartney sent a letter to all Promise Keepers in which he encouraged the men to sign a "Pledge of Prayer and Support for President Bush." McCartney also instructed Promise Keepers to guard against "anger and bitterness" and instead reach out to "Arab Americans, Muslims, or anyone who appears foreign." See http://www.promisekeepers.org/devp/devp110.htm.

36. These passages and more information about the Platoon Challenge can be found at "The Platoon Challenge," http://www.promisekeepers.org/2003/2003130.htm.

37. The apocalyptic edge of Promise Keepers is largely consistent with the theology found in the extraordinarily popular *Left Behind* book series by Tim LaHaye and Jerry Jenkins. Promise Keepers sells the films based on the *Left Behind* series at its website—but includes the following disclaimer: "Promise Keepers understands that there are different interpretations of prophecy, and that Left Behind is a fictitious account of a 'pre-tribulation' scenario. Because no one knows for sure when prophesied events will occur, we view this as an evangelistically strong and entertaining movie that both believers and non-believers will enjoy and be challenged by" ("Left Behind: The Movie," http://www.promisekeepers.org/resc/resc116.htm).

38. Farrar, 1999.

39. McCartney, "Promise Makers," September–October 1997, http://www.policyreview.com/sept97/promise.html.

40. H. Phillips, "Costly Promises," 1999, http://www.strang.com/nm/stories/nm296s.htm.

41. Quoted in Van Leeuwen, 17.

42. "Covenant Transcript," http://www.promisekeepers.org/sitg/sitg13.htm.

43. Indeed, the D.C. Covenant in this vein recalls the Exodus theme of the purging the community of non-believers.

44. Passages from Morrison's sermon are from my notes taken at the Promise Keepers event at the Meadowlands in New Jersey, October 1–2, 1999.

45. McCartney. "Promise Makers," September-October 1997, http://www.policyreview.com/sept97/promise.html.

46. For example, in *Strategies for a Successful Marriage* (1994), by E. Glenn Wagner and Dietrich Gruen, and *We Stand Together: Reconciling Men of Different Color* (1995), by Rodney Cooper, the authors offer personal testimony and lists of "do's and don'ts" guiding men toward Promise Keepers' vision of divinely ordained families and racial unity.

47. This quotation is from McCartney's sermon at Shea Stadium, where he spoke of appraising his dedication to his marriage on a scale of 1–10, being humbled by scoring low numbers in the eyes of his wife, and in turn dedicating himself to scoring at least a 7.5 in the next six months.

48. The first song sung at the Stand in the Gap event sent this message, declaring simply and repeatedly, "I will surrender all to Thee my blessed savior."

49. Kaminer, 12–13. Kaminer notes that at least up to 1992 "most of the [codependency] books are written for women—interested in their husbands and fathers as well as themselves. According to one publisher, the codependency market is 85 percent female" (Kaminer, 15). I suspect that the growing popularity of Promise Keepers since 1992 and the development and expansions of its books and resource materials have (if one includes their products in the self-help category) substantially increased the percentage of self-help books designed for males.

50. John Bartkowski, in a thoughtful examination of Promise Keepers, raises the important point that accountability groups (while hierarchically structured by Promise Keepers as a national organization) are predicated on what he calls "democratic" language and use of space. Men meet in small groups, sit in circles, strive to push one another out of comfort zones, and seek to attract men representative of a diversity of race, class, and denominational backgrounds. The focus of these groups is on intimacy and personal challenge. This democratic impulse, however, is predicated upon—and ultimately diminished by—the anti-democratic exclusion of women and non-believers, and the use of private rather than public space. As Bartkowski concludes, "In the end, accountability groups provide for many of the men a sense of equality with their fellows even as they serve to reify particular types of social hierarchies. Indeed, it is only in preserving a sense of social order—God's order—that the men become liberated to explore the unfamiliar terrain of equality, social leveling, and solidarity during these encounters" (Bartkowski 2000).

51. Weber, quoted in *Promise Builders Study Series*, 73.

52. McCartney, Shea Stadium, 1996.

53. This passage from Weber's *Tender Warrior* is reprinted as Appendix A in Weber, 1995, 261, his italics.

54. *The Promise Keeper* 3, no. 1 (July–August 2000), 5.

55. Steve Gallagher, "Be Strong and Very Courageous: Emerging from the Prison of Pornography," http://www.promisekeepers.org/arti/arti118.htm.

56. Bill McCartney, "Promise Makers," September–October 1997, http://www.policyreview.com/sept97/promise.html.

57. Passages from Ryle's sermon are from my notes taken at the Promise Keepers event in Pittsburgh, Pennsylvania, July 25–26, 1997.

58. "Letter from Joe White, March 2004," http://www.promisekeepers.org/mmtc/mail/HTMLmail_MMTC_017W.htm

59. See letter from Bill McCartney on "Pledge of Prayer and Support for President Bush," http://www.promisekeepers.org/devp/devp110.htm.

## 5. Call to Renewal

1. Wallis plays a particularly important role in Call to Renewal—even more than McCartney's founding role in Promise Keepers. Wallis is not just the public voice of the movement; his essays and sermons express the heart of the theological and political vision of the movement, and his status and energy are vital to the success of Call to Renewal.

2. By political I do not mean partisan; Call to Renewal is explicit about its desire to engage in the political life of the nation, but it—like the other three examples of prophetic politics I have discussed—does not formally associate itself with a political party.

3. Wallis, Call to Renewal 2000 Conference Plenary. Hereafter citations from the proceedings of the three Call to Renewal conferences I attended will be indicated in the text by CTR 1997, CTR 1999, and CTR 2000, respectively.

4. For the full text of the "Cry for Renewal" as well as the list of endorsers of the document, see http://www.calltorenewal.org.

5. Information on Call to Renewal's "four-point agenda" is from the *Organizer's Handbook* distributed at the 1999 Call to Renewal Summit on Poverty.

6. For the full text of the Covenant and supporting documents, see http://www.calltorenewal.org.

7. See Wallis, "Prophetic Leadership," *Sojourners* 32, no. 1 (January–February 2003c): 7–8.

See also Anderson, "Not a Just or Moral War," on the broad opposition among church leaders to the preemptive war in Iraq.

8. Wallis, "Nothing Shall Make Them Afraid," Pentecost Sermon, June 9, 2003b. http://www.calltorenewal.org/resources/index.cfm/action/display_theological/item/Pentecost_2003_MR_Sermon.htm.

9. Many of Wallis' pieces in *Sojourners* find their way into his books, *The Soul of Politics* (1995), *Who Speaks for God?* (1996), and *Faith Works* (2000).

10. While the relationship between *Sojourners* and Call to Renewal is very strong, they do have distinct missions and points of emphasis. *Sojourners* is, for example, both more explicit in its commitment to theological exploration. And *Sojourners* also has a broader political scope, including attention to international affairs. Call to Renewal's main focus is on poverty in the United States, but this focus is definitively informed by the theological concerns raised in the pages of *Sojourners*, and Call to Renewal firmly believes that poverty in the United States is in part produced by America's policies regarding military affairs and the global economy. Accordingly, while *Sojourners* and Call to Renewal are distinct entities, in many cases articles that appear in the pages of *Sojourners* are representative of the concerns and positions taken by Call to Renewal.

I want to thank Duane Shank for clarifying the relationship between Call to Renewal and *Sojourners*. While Shank has made clear that the magazine "does speak for Call to Renewal," the articles from *Sojourners* that I discuss in this chapter demonstrate clear philosophical, theological, and political—if informal—commonalties between Call to Renewal and *Sojourners*. (Shank, November 9, 2001; personal conversation.)

11. To this end, Call to Renewal has also recently established a "public policy team" whose members include: John DiIulio, Ron Sider, Ron Thiemann, Mary Jo Bane, Richard Parker, William Julius Wilson, and Marshall Ganz. It is interesting to note that many of the members of the policy team (including the last five on the above list) are from Harvard University. One of the likely reasons is that Wallis spent the 1998–99 academic year at Harvard as a fellow at the Center for the Study of Values in Public Life. The presence of such academic policy activists takes on further significance when contrasted with the anti-intellectual rhetoric of Billy Sunday and Promise Keepers. William Julius Wilson's keynote address at the Call to Renewal 2000 conference—a statistic-riddled explanation of the causes and status of poverty in the United States—would be inconceivable at a Promise Keepers event.

12. The total number of attendees of course pales in comparison with those participating in Promise Keepers events. However, as an umbrella organization, Call to Renewal is less interested in attracting large numbers than it is in reaching out to leaders and activists in already existing faith-based organizations.

13. Signers include: David Beckmann, President, Bread for the World; Paul Bollwahn, Director, Social Services Department, Salvation Army; Peter Borgdorff, Executive Director of Ministries, Christian Reformed Church; Daryl Byler, Director, Mennonite Central Committee Washington Office; John Carr, Secretary, Department of Social Development and World Peace, U.S. Catholic Conference; Rich Cizik, Vice President for Governmental Affairs, National Association of Evangelicals; Marian Wright Edelman, President, Children's Defense Fund; James Forbes, Senior Pastor, Riverside Church; Leah Gaskin Fitchue, Associate Minister and Consultant, African Methodist

Episcopal Church; Millard Fuller, President, Habitat for Humanity International; Wes Granberg-Michaelson, General Secretary, Reformed Church in America; Frank Griswold, Presiding Bishop, The Episcopal Church; Richard Hamm, General Minister and President, Christian Church/Disciples of Christ; Steve Hayner, President, Inter-Varsity Christian Fellowship; Bishop Kenneth Hicks, United Methodist Council of Bishops; Bishop George McKinney, Church of God in Christ; Grant McMurray, President, Reorganized Church of Jesus Christ of Latter Day Saints; Mary Nelson, President, Bethel New Life, Inc.; Ron Nikkel, President, Prison Fellowship International; Glenn Palmberg, President, The Evangelical Covenant Church; Ron Sider, President, Evangelicals for Social Action; Bishop Melvin Talbert, United Methodist Church; Daniel Weiss, General Secretary, American Baptist Church.

14. Wallis, "Evangelical Social Conscience," *Sojourners* 33, no. 3 (March 2004): 5.

15. Wallis 1995, 151.

16. See Gundry-Wolf, *Sojourners* (September–October 1998). Mary Stewart Van Leeuwen (1998) offers a similar critique of the notion of "male headship" espoused by Promise Keepers as based on theology so shaky it amounts to "proof-text poker." "Proof-text," Van Leeuwen explains, is a manner of using isolated, a-contextual passages from the Bible in order to substantiate a theological or political argument. Such a method of using the Bible neglects—among other Scriptural complexities—internal contradictions within the Bible, the particularities of the authors and various audiences of the books of the Bible, the array of types of biblical writing (e.g., household codes, psalms, poetry, chronicles, narratives, parables are all read in the same literalist manner as the inerrant word of God). On the variety of biblical styles and texts, see, generally, Alter.

17. Wallis 2000, 72. See also Wallis 1995, 177ff.

18. In an essay on racism as a form of idolatry, for example, Call to Renewal Board member and *Sojourners* contributing editor Bill Wylie-Kellermann quotes George Kelsey: "'When [people] elevate any human or historical factor to so great a height that it has the power to give substance and direction to all cultural institutions . . . that human or historical factor has become a god.' Idolatry is perhaps the primary spiritual mechanism by which a glorious human diversity, created by God for praise and delight, becomes in the Fall a power of division, a device of injustice, a demonic servant of death" (10).

19. Wallis 1995, 101. Former Call to Renewal board member Eugene Rivers is explicit in his denouncing of the founding identification of America as a "New Israel," as a form of idolatry. What is particularly striking about Rivers' critique is that he employs one Exodus trope—the warning against idolatry—to challenge the use of another Exodus trope—the conviction that America is the "New Israel." "Girded with what were then new scriptural interpretations identifying America with the New Israel (and often peoples of color as the antagonists to God's chosen) . . . the name of God was invoked to justify white idols; the principalities and powers were given religious sanction" (1998, 16). That these conflicting historical and political assessments of the nation both take place within the figurative scaffolding of Exodus is but a further illustration of the continuing vitality of this American sacred story. In speaking of "principalities and powers," Rivers is grounding his argument in the political theology of William Stringfellow (a contributing editor of *Sojourners* prior to his death). Stringfellow argues that American churches were "notoriously and scandalously and complacently accommodating" to human constructions of racial identity and consumerism rather than the message of Jesus (Rivers 1998, 15).

20. Wallis 1996, 4. Consider, for example, the infamous conversation between Pat Robertson and Jerry Falwell about the causes of the attacks of September 11, 2001.

21. Of course, like Snow and Benford, I would suggest that storytelling is an integral component of social movements more generally. What sets Promise Keepers and Call to Renewal apart is the explicit assertion of the importance of storytelling to the

life of the organization. See the aforementioned opening of *Seven Promises of a Promise Keeper.* Indeed, one of the subtexts of this project is precisely the degree to which revivalist politics are energized and directed through compelling narratives.

22. Here we should recall Perry Miller's reminder that revivals are not so much directed toward unbelieving "heathen" as they are toward members of a religious community who have "forgotten" their beliefs (1965, 6ff.).

23. Heschel declares that this tension between despair and hope is central to the message of the biblical prophets. "Every prediction of disaster is in itself an exhortation to repentance. The prophet is sent not only to upbraid, but also to 'strengthen the weak hands and make firm the feeble knees' (Is. 35:3). Almost every prophet brings consolation, promise, and the hope of reconciliation along with censure and castigation. He begins with a *message of doom;* he concludes with a *message of hope*" (1969, 12).

24. The anecdotal evidence of crisis throughout Call to Renewal's works is buoyed by statistical data. See, for example, the litany of statistics offered by Wallis in *Faith Works* on the question of economic inequality (2000, 77ff.).

25. See Wallis 1995, 114ff.

26. See Wallis 1995, 65ff. See also *Who Is My Neighbor? Economics as if Values Mattered* and the January–February 2000 issue of *Sojourners* dedicated to the question of "Justice and Business Ethics."

27. See generally *America's Original Sin: A Study Guide of White Racism* and *Crossing the Racial Divide: America's Struggle for Justice and Reconciliation.*

28. In a short op-ed piece published in *The New York Times* on July 2, 2000, Beverly Daniel Tatum captures this difference quite nicely. If you think, Tatum writes, of "racism as a problem of individual bigotry and hatred . . . then the solution is individual acts of kindness—polite, respectful behavior, maybe even friendly outreach." However, if you understand racism as "an intricate web of individual attitudes, cultural messages, and institutional practices that systematically advantage whites and disadvantage people of color . . . then the solution is a concerted daily effort to interrupt that system . . . that requires more than being nice." Promise Keepers emphasizes the former conception of racism, while Call to Renewal preaches the latter.

29. Wallis 2000, xxvii. As Wallis asserts elsewhere, we face a serious religious and political problem in the United States when "personal piety become[s] an end in itself instead of the energy for social justice" (1995, 43).

30. In Isaiah's words: "they will be called the repairer of the breach" Is. 59:12. See Ricoeur 1995, 265ff.

31. As Ricoeur points out, and as is surely the case in the model of Martin Luther King Jr., the summoned subject in the prophetic tradition is a "suffering mediator" (1995, 263). If King or the biblical prophets are valid evidence, fulfilling such a role invariably involves the redemptive power of suffering.

32. This born-again notion of "conversion" is by no means the only—or even the traditional—understanding of the term. Conversion can indicate the adoption of a new religious faith, as in the case when a Christian converts to Judaism, for example. However, the understanding of conversion as a Christian faith commitment that is a sudden transformation includes not just Saul's becoming Paul, but also Augustine's account of his conversion in book 7 of his *Confessions.* This conception of conversion as a sudden transformative moment has an extensive legacy in revivalist history of America. The "altar calls" introduced in the Second Great Awakening by Charles Finney, the hitting of the sawdust trail inside Billy Sunday's tabernacles, and the stadium streaming altar calls of Promise Keepers, are all a part of this tradition of Christians being convicted and born anew in the name of Jesus. Most commonly this notion of conversion is conceived in privatized, personal terms. Consider the answer George W. Bush gave during a 2000 Republican presidential primary debate when asked to explain why Jesus Christ was his favorite political philosopher: "Well, if they don't know, it's going to be hard to explain. . . . When you turn your heart and your life over to Christ, when you accept

Christ as the Savior, it changes your heart. It changes your life. And that's what happened to me."

33. Call to Renewal's notion of prophetic politics is more schematic than the open definition of prophetic politics I use in this project. In fact, Call to Renewal's understanding of prophetic politics is quite akin to that of Riemer (1996). Compare with Wallis 1995, 47, 54–56.

34. See Wallis 2000, 258–60.

35. Ganz, CTR 2000. This portrayal of Moses as an organizer recalls the invocation of the story of Exodus by the labor organizer Mother Jones. Speaking to striking coal miners from the steps of the Capitol building in Charleston, West Virginia, on August 15, 1912, Jones proclaimed: "The labor movement was not originated by man. The labor movement, my friends, was a command from God Almighty. He commanded the prophets thousands of years ago to go down and redeem the Israelites that were in bondage, and he organized the men into a union and went to work. And they said, 'The masters have made us gather straw; they have been more cruel than they were before. What are we going to do?' The prophet said, 'A voice from heaven has come down to get you together.' They got together and the prophet led them out of the land of bondage and robbery and plunder into the land of freedom. And when the army of the pirates followed them the Dead Sea opened and swallowed them up, and for the first time the workers were free." http://www.pbs.org/greatspeeches/timeline//mother_jones_s.html.

36. Morris, 13. Speaking of the history of white supremacy in the United States, Wallis likewise declares:

> Our history has affected us all in profound ways. It still shapes our national experience and obstructs the fulfillment of our professed values. Its face is dramatically revealed in the continued devastation of native, black, and other communities of color; in the legacy of benefit still enjoyed by most white people; and in the fear and anger felt by many whites facing shrinking economic realities and the temptation to scapegoat racial minorities. The nation's original sin of racism must be faced in a way that we have never really done. Only then can America be rediscovered. (1995, 101)

37. While by no means celebrating America's past as the ideal of economic justice, Call to Renewal is quick to point out that whereas great strides have been made in matters of racial and gender equality, in terms of the distribution of wealth, the United States is becoming increasingly unequal. See Wallis 2000, 77ff.

38. This slippage can be read as illustrative of the "Americanism" implicit in all forms of prophetic politics in the United States. The conservative pattern of calling America to "live up to its principles"—without ever getting outside of those principles—is crucial to Bercovitch's critique of the tradition of the American jeremiad. I return to this point and elucidate what I take to be shortcomings of this line of analysis in the concluding chapter.

39. Whereas King returned time and again to the story of Moses leading the people out of Egypt, Call to Renewal draws its vision less from the initial stage of liberation and more from the prophetic vocation of giving people back their history and reminding them of their forgotten covenant. Admittedly, this differentiation between King and Wallis is more a matter of emphasis than a clear divide. King, of course, often cited Isaiah and Amos and, as I have just discussed, Call to Renewal is quite clear in its use of Moses as a particularly inspiring and accessible model. Nevertheless, the patterns of emphasis of King and Call to Renewal speak more to the political contexts in which they work than to a profound divergence in their beliefs that America was no Promised Land or their understanding of Moses and the prophets as part of the same Exodus story.

40. See Spencer Perkins, "Does Racial Pride Hinder Reconciliation?" *Sojourners Online* 27, no. 6 (November–December 1998): 25–27.

41. Wallis writes: "Let's remember that oppression is a biblical word, used by Amos, Isaiah, and Jeremiah long before the Bolshevik revolution of 1917, and it is clearly meant to describe the injustice of structures and institutions. Both political and economic institutions came under prophetic interrogation by the prophets of the Bible" (1996, 177).

42. An intriguing statement made by Wallis on the issue of sexism in America illustrates this point quite well—and is especially revealing in contrast to Promise Keepers' approach to gender issues. "We men will be converted by listening to our wives, lovers, mothers, sisters, friends, colleagues, and co-workers. Only by coming to see the world through their eyes will we have ours opened. Through the women with whom we live and work, we will come to understand justice, faith, and even power in more inclusive ways" (1995, 146).

43. I participated in such seminars at Call to Renewal 1999 and Call to Renewal 2000. For further information on Call to Renewal's lobbying and organizing strategies, see Call to Renewal's 1999 *Organizing Manual*, the 2000 Poor No More summit materials, especially the section "Organizing and Advocacy" and Call to Renewal's online guide, "Building Support for Advocacy," www.calltorenewal.org/public_policy/index.cfm/action/influence_policy.html.

44. The titles of these works are themselves revealing: *America's Original Sin: A Study Guide on White Racism, Recovering the Evangel: A Guide to Faith, Politics, and Alternatives to the Religious Right, Crossing the Racial Divide: America's Struggle for Justice and Reconciliation, Holy Ground: A Resource on Faith and the Environment,* and *Who is My Neighbor? Economics as if Values Matter, Putting Down Stones: A Faithful Response to Urban Violence.* Many of the essays in these study guides first appeared in the pages of *Sojourners.*

45. Moreover, each study guide generally includes plans on how to use them, lists of organizations concerned with the issues covered in the guide, and texts recommended for further study. The lists of these texts are often quite fascinating. For instance, the texts recommended in *Crossing the Racial Divide* include works by authors such as Manning Marable, Roberto Rodriguez, Cornel West, Taylor Branch, William Julius Wilson, and Glenn Loury.

46. There is, of course, an ironic twist to Delk's citation of King's defining of the immediate needs of the "racial times" in the United States—thirty years after his death.

47. So concerned was Call to Renewal to convey this message that this dialogue was adapted for publication in the January–February 1999 issue of *Sojourners.*

48. Campolo 1999.

49. On coalition politics, see the classic essay by Bernice Johnson Reagon, 1983.

50. Wallis, "Class Warfare," *Sojourners* 32, no. 5 (September–October 2003a): 7–8.

51. Wallis cites Walter Brueggemann on this point: " 'We may yet discern that the covenantal discourse of the Bible,' must be uncompromisingly bold but not sectarian, 'speaking the human agenda in a way that honors our social pluralism, in a way that honors our shared human requirements of love, mercy, justice, peace, and freedom. These are the property of no confessional truth and the monopoly of no confessional commitment' " (quoted in Wallis 1995, 40). This passage is taken from a piece by Brueggemann in the August–September 1991 issue of *Sojourners* titled "History on the Margins." *Sojourners* 20, no. 7 (August–September 1991): 19.

While Brueggemann and Wallis may be accused of being vague in with regard to the *content* of what "humans share," what is more important to them is that the covenant binds a people to collective participatory discourse, in other words, to the process of wooing.

52. Call to Renewal, "Covenant to Overcome Poverty," http://www.calltorenewal.org/about_us/index.cfm/about_us/what_is_ctr.html/about_us/index.cfm/action/covenant.html.

53. Quotations are from Promise Keepers' "D.C. Covenant."

54. The full text of the Campaign, including an elaboration on these seven moral priorities, can be found at "Campaign to Overcome Poverty," http://www.calltore-newal.org/about_us/index.cfm/action/campaign.html.

55. In its attention to the detail of public policy, its focus on the political engagement, in the language it uses to define its ambitions, Call to Renewal's current campaign contrasts quite sharply with Promise Keepers 2003–04 Platoon Challenge to bring a million men to Jesus.

56. This passage is the opening statement of Call to Renewal's "Building Support for Advocacy" guide, posted on the CAPOR website, http://www.calltorenewal.org/public_policy/index.cfm/action/influence_policy.html.

57. "Building Support for Advocacy," http://www.calltorenewal.org/public_policy/index.cfm/action/influence_policy.html.

## 6. *Politics in the Wilderness*

1. McCartney, "Promise Makers," http://www.policyreview.com/sept97/promise.html.

2. See Ex. 32:27 for counter reference.

3. Calvin, *Jeremiah*, lecture 2; 1:44. Cited in Walzer (1965).

4. Arendt expands on this point in her essay on Lessing (1968), in "Truth and Politics" (1977) and elsewhere.

5. See King, "A Time to Break Silence" (1986).

6. Ricoeur 1995, 206.

# Bibliography

Abraham, Ken. 1997. *Who Are the Promise Keepers? Understanding the Christian Men's Movement.* New York: Doubleday.

Alter, Robert. 1981. *The Art of Biblical Narrative.* New York: Basic Books.

*America's Original Sin: A Study Guide on White Racism.* 1995. Edited by Bob Hulteen and Jim Wallis. Washington, DC: Sojourners.

Anderson, David Earle. 2003. "Not a Just or Moral War." *Sojourners* 32, no. 1 (January–February): 26–29, 63.

Antczak, Frederick J. 1993. "When 'Silence Is Betrayal': An Ethical Criticism of the Revolution of Values in the Speech at Riverside Church." In *Martin Luther King, Jr., and the Sermonic Power of Public Discourse,* edited by Carolyn Calloway-Thomas and John Louis Lucaites, 172–46. Tuscaloosa: University of Alabama Press.

Arendt, Hannah. 1953. "Religion and Politics." *Confluence: An International Forum* 2, no. 3 (September): 105–26.

———. 1968. *Men in Dark Times.* New York: Harcourt Brace & World.

———. 1971. "Thinking and Moral Considerations: A Lecture." *Social Research* (Autumn): 417–46.

———. 1972. *Crises of the Republic.* New York: Harcourt Brace Jovanovich.

———. 1974a. *The Human Condition.* Chicago: University of Chicago Press.

———. 1974b. *Rahel Varnhagen: The Life of a Jewish Woman.* Translated by Richard Winston and Clara Winston. New York: Harcourt Brace Jovanovich.

———. 1977. *Between Past and Future: Eight Exercises in Political Thought.* New York: Penguin.

———. 1978a. *The Jew as Pariah: Identity and Politics in the Modern Age.* Edited by Ron H. Feldman. New York: Grove Press, 1978.

———. 1978b. *The Life of the Mind.* New York: Harcourt Brace.

———. 1979. *The Origins of Totalitarianism.* New York: Harcourt Brace and World.

———. 1982. *Lectures on Kant's Political Philosophy.* Edited by Ronald Beiner. Chicago: University of Chicago Press.

———. 1987a. *Amor Mundi: Explorations in the Faith and Thought of Hannah Arendt.* Edited by James Bernauer, S.J. Boston: Martinus Nijhoff.

———. 1987b. *Eichmann in Jerusalem: A Report on the Banality of Evil.* New York: Penguin.

——. 1990. *On Revolution*. New York: Penguin.

Aristotle. 1962. *Poetics*. Translated by S. H. Butcher. New York: Hill and Wang.

Augustine. 1961. *Confessions*. Translated by R. S. Pine-Coffin. New York: Penguin.

Bakhtin, M. M. 1981. *The Dialogic Imagination*. Translated by Caryl Emerson and Michael Holquist. Edited by Michael Holquist. Austin: University of Texas Press.

Baldwin, James. 1962. *The Fire Next Time*. New York: Random House.

Balmer, Randall. 1999. *Blessed Assurance: A History of Evangelicalism in America*. Boston: Beacon Press.

Barnouw, Dagmar. 1990. *Visible Spaces: Hannah Arendt and the German-Jewish Experience*. Baltimore: Johns Hopkins University Press.

Barthes, Roland. 1978. *Image Music Text*. Translated by Stephen Heath. New York: Hill and Wang.

Bartkowski, John P. 2000. "Breaking Walls, Raising Fences: Masculinity, Intimacy, and Accountability among the Promise Keepers." *Sociology of Religion* 61, no. 1 (Spring): 33–53.

Beiner, Ronald. 1989. "Interpretive Essay." In *Lectures on Kant's Political Philosophy*, by Hannah Arendt, edited by Ronald Beiner, 89–156. Chicago: University of Chicago Press.

Bellah, Robert. 1974. "Civil Religion in America." In *American Civil Religion*, edited by Russell E. Richey and Donald G. Jones, 21–44. New York: Harper & Row.

Benhabib, Seyla. 1994. "Hannah Arendt and the Redemptive Power of Narrative." In *Hannah Arendt: Critical Essays*, edited by Lewis P. Hinchman and Sandra K. Hinchman, 111–37. Albany: State University of New York Press.

Benjamin, Walter. 1968. *Illuminations: Essay and Reflections*. Edited by Hannah Arendt. New York: Schocken Books.

Bercovitch, Sacvan. 1978. *The American Jeremiad*. Madison: University of Wisconsin Press.

——. 1993. *The Rites of Assent: Transformations in the Symbolic Construction of America*. New York: Routledge.

Bernauer, James, S.J. 1987. "The Faith of Hannah Arendt: *Amor Mundi* and Its Critique—Assimilation of Religious Experience." In *Amor Mundi: Explorations in the Faith and Thought of Hannah Arendt*, edited by James Bernauer, S.J., 1–28. Boston: Martinus Nijhoff.

Bernstein, Richard J. 1996. *Hannah Arendt and the Jewish Question*. Cambridge: The MIT Press.

*The Best of Billy Sunday: 17 Burning Sermons From the Most Spectacular Evangelist the World Has Ever Known*. 1963. Edited by John R. Rice. Murfreesboro, TN: Sword of the Lord Publishers.

*The Bible and the Narrative Tradition*. 1986. Edited by Frank McConnell. New York: Oxford University Press.

Bickford, Susan. 1996. *The Dissonance of Democracy: Listening, Conflict and Citizenship*. Ithaca: Cornell University Press.

——. 1997. "Propriety and Provocation in Arendt's Political Aesthetic." In *Hannah Arendt and the Meaning of Politics*, edited by Craig Calhoun and John McGowan, 85–97. Minneapolis: University of Minnesota Press.

*Billy Sunday Speaks*. 1970. Edited by Karen Gullen. New York: Chelsea House Publishers.

Bishop, Bill. 2004. "The Schism in U.S. Politics Begins at Home." *Austin American-Statesman*, April 4. http://www.statesman.com/specialreports/content/specialreports/greatdivide/0404divide.html.

Blenkinsopp, Joseph. 1996. *A History of Prophecy in Israel*. Lousiville: Westminster John Knox Press.

Bloch, Ernst. 1972. *Atheism in Christianity: The Religion of the Exodus and the Kingdom*. Translated by J. T. Swann. New York: Herder and Herder.

——. 1991. *Heritage of Our Times*. Translated by Neville Plaice and Stephen Plaice. Berkeley: University of California Press.

Bloch, Ruth H. 1990. "Religion and Ideological Change in the American Revolution." In *Religion and American Politics: From the Colonial Period to the 1980s*, edited by Mark A. Noll, 44–59. New York: Oxford University Press.

Blumer, Hans. 1995. "Social Movements." In *Social Movements: Critiques, Concepts, Case-Studies*, edited by Stanford M. Lyman 60–83. New York: New York University Press.

Boone, Wellington. 1994. "Why Men Must Pray." In *Seven Promises of a Promise Maker*, 25–31. Colorado Springs: Focus on the Family Publishing.

——. 1996. *Breaking Through: Taking the Kingdom into the Culture by Out-Serving Others*. Nashville: Broadman & Holman.

Boyer, Paul S. 1992. *When Time Shall Be No More: Prophecy Belief in Modern American Culture*. Cambridge, Mass: Belknap Press.

Branch, Taylor. 1988. *Parting the Waters: America in the King Years, 1954–1963*. New York: Simon and Schuster.

——. 1999. *Pillar of Fire: America in the King Years, 1963–1965*. New York: Touchstone.

Brennan, Kristin. 1998. "Ways to Use This Resource." In *Crossing the Racial Divide: America's Struggle for Justice and Reconciliation*, edited by Jim Wallis and Aaron Gallegos, 76–80. Washington, DC: Sojourners.

Bright, Bill. 1995. *The Coming Revival: America's Call to Fast, Pray, and "Seek God's Face."* Orlando: New Life Publications.

Brown, Wendy. 1995. *States of Injury: Power and Freedom in Late Modernity*. Princeton: Princeton University Press.

Brueggemann, Walter. 1978. *The Prophetic Imagination*. Philadelphia: Fortress Press.

Bruns, Roger A. 1992. *Preacher: Billy Sunday and Big-Time American Evangelicalism*. New York: W. W. Norton.

Buber, Martin. 1949. *The Prophetic Faith*. New York: Harper Torchbooks.

——. 1965. *Moses: The Revelation and the Covenant*. New York: Torchbooks.

——. 1966. *Paths in Utopia*. Translated by R. F. C. Hull. Boston: Beacon Press.

——. 1967. *Kingship of God*. Translated by Richard Scheimann. New York: Harper Torchbooks.

Bush, George W. 1999. *A Charge to Keep*. New York: William Morrow.

Butler, Judith. 1990. *Gender Trouble: Feminism and the Subversion of Identity*. New York: Routledge, 1990.

Button, Mark. 2001. "Social Contract, Promising, and Political Order." Ph.D. diss., Rutgers University.

Calhoun, Craig. 1997. "Plurality, Promises, and Public Spaces." In *Hannah Arendt and the Meaning of Politics*, edited by Craig Calhoun and John McGowan, 232–59. Minneapolis: University of Minnesota Press.

*Call to Renewal Newsletter*. 1999. 4.1, First Quarter.

*Call to Renewal Organizing Manual*. 1999.

Campolo, Tony, and Peggy Campolo. 1999. "Holding It Together: A Dialogue on the Church and Homosexuality." *Sojourners* 28, no. 3 (May–June): 28–32.

Carr, David. 1986. "Narrative and the Real World: An Argument for Continuity." *History and Theory* 25, no. 2: 117–31.

Carson, Clayborne. 1997. "Martin Luther King, Jr., and the African-American Social Gospel." In *African-American Religion: Interpretive Essays in History and Culture*, edited by Timothy E. Fulop and Albert J. Raboteau, 341–63. New York: Routledge.

Carson, Clayborne, and Peter Holloran. 1988. Introduction to *A Knock at Midnight: Inspiration from the Great Sermons of Martin Luther King, Jr.* by Martin Luther King, Jr., edited by Clayborne Carson and Peter Holloran, vii–xx. New York: Warner Books.

Carter, Stephen L. 1993. *The Culture of Disbelief: How Law and Politics Trivialize Religious Devotion*. New York: Basic Books.

Carver, Terrell. 1996. *Gender Is Not a Synonym for Women*. Boulder: Lynne Rienner.

Cerbone, Mark. 1997. "Short on Scripture, Long on Ideology: The Paradox of the Religious Right." In *Recovering the Evangel: A Guide to Faith, Politics and Alternatives to the Religious Right*, edited by Jim Wallis, Bob Hulteen, and Aaron Gallegos, 10–13. Washington, DC: Sojourners.

Chafe, William H. 1998. *The Unfinished Journey: America since World War II*. New York: Oxford University Press.

Chappell, David L. 2004. *A Stone of Hope: Prophetic Religion and the Death of Jim Crow*. Chapel Hill: University of North Carolina Press.

Cherry, Conrad. 1971. *God's New Israel: Religious Interpretations of American Destiny*. Englewood Cliffs, NJ: Prentice-Hall.

*Citizen King*. 2003. Dir. Orlando Bagwell and Noland Walker. Transcript: http://www.pbs.org/wgbh/amex/mlk/filmmore/pt.html.

Collins, Joseph. 1915. "Revivals, Past and Present." *Harper's Weekly* 135, no. 810 (June 19): 580–82.

Cone, James. 1969. *Black Theology and Black Power*. New York: Seabury Press, 1969.

Congressional Record. 1918. 65th Congress, 2nd Session, Washington, DC, 56, 761.

Cooper, Rodney L. 1995. *We Stand Together: Reconciling Men of Different Color*. Chicago: Moody Press.

Cox, Harvey. 1995. *Fire from Heaven: The Rise of Pentecostal Spirituality and the Reshaping of Religion in the Twenty-first Century*. New York: Addison-Wesley.

Crites, Stephen. 1988. "The Narrative Quality of Experience." In *Why Narrative? Readings in Narrative Theology*, edited by Stanley Hauerwas and L. Gregory Jones, 65–88. Grand Rapids: William B. Eerdmans.

*Crossing the Racial Divide: America's Struggle for Justice and Reconciliation*. Ed. Jim Wallis and Aaron Gallegos. Washington, DC: Sojourners.

Curtis, Kimberley F. 1997. "Aesthetic Foundations of Democratic Politics in the Work of Hannah Arendt." In *Hannah Arendt and the Meaning of Politics*, edited by Craig Calhoun and John McGowan, 27–52. Minneapolis: University of Minnesota Press.

——. 1999. *Our Sense of the Real: Aesthetic Experience and Arendtian Politics*. Ithaca: Cornell University Press.

Darsey, James. 1997. *The Prophetic Tradition and Radical Rhetoric in America*. New York: New York University Press.

Davidson, Osha Gray. 1996. *The Best of Enemies: Race and Redemption in the New South*. New York: Scribner.

Delk, Yvonne V. 1998. "A Time for Action: A Five-Part Strategy to Dismantle Racism." In *Crossing the Racial Divide: America's Struggle for Justice and Reconciliation*, edited by Jim Wallis and Aaron Gallegos, 68–69. Washington, DC: Sojourners.

D'Emilio, John, and Estelle B. Freedman. 1989. *Intimate Matters: A History of Sexuality in America*. New York: Harper & Row.

Diamond, Sara. 1989. *Spiritual Warfare: The Politics of the Religious Right*. Boston: South End Press.

———. 1996. *Facing The Wrath: Confronting the Right in Dangerous Times*. Monroe, ME: Common Courage Press, 1996.

Dienstag, Joshua Foa. 1997. *Dancing in Chains: Narrative and Memory in Political Theory*. Stanford: Stanford University Press.

Disch, Lisa Jane. 1996. *Hannah Arendt and the Limits of Philosophy*. Ithaca: Cornell University Press.

———. 1997. "'Please Sit Down, but Don't Make Yourself at Home': Arendtian 'Visiting' and the Prefigurative Politics of Consciousness-Raising." In *Hannah Arendt and the Meaning of Politics*, edited by Craig Calhoun and John McGowan, 132–65. Minneapolis: University of Minnesota Press.

Dolan, Frederick M. 1994. *Allegories of America: Narratives, Metaphysics, Politics*. Ithaca: Cornell University Press.

Dorsett, Lyle W. 1991. *Billy Sunday and the Redemption of Urban America*. Grand Rapids: William B. Eerdmans.

Dowd, Maureen. 1997. "Promises, Promises, Promises." *New York Times*, October 4, A15.

———. 1999. "Playing the Jesus Card." *New York Times*, December 15, A23.

DuBois, W. E. B. 1989. *The Souls of Black Folk*. New York: Bantam Books.

Dyson, Michael Eric. 1995. *Making Malcolm: The Myth & Meaning of Malcolm X*. New York: Oxford.

———. 2000. *I May Not Get There with You: The True Martin Luther King, Jr*. New York: Free Press.

Eck, Diana L., et al. 1997. *On Common Ground: World Religions in America* (Interactive Multimedia). New York: Columbia University Press.

Edwards, Jonathan. 1971. "The Latter-Day Glory Is Probably to Begin in America." In *God's New Israel: Religious Interpretations of American Destiny*, edited by Conrad Cherry, 55–59. Englewood Cliffs, NJ: Prentice-Hall.

Elazar, Daniel J. 1998. *Covenant and Constitutionalism: The Great Frontier and the Matrix of Federal Democracy (The Covenant Tradition in Politics*, vol. 3). New Brunswick: Transaction Publishers.

Ellin, Abby. 2004. "Seeing Overeating as a Sin, and God as the Diet Coach." *New York Times*, May 29. http://www.nytimes.com/2004/05/29/national/29religion.html.

Ellis, William T. 1914. *"Billy" Sunday: The Man and His Message*. Philadelphia: L. T. Myers.

Emerson, Michael O., and Christian Smith. 2001. *Divided by Faith: Evangelical Religion and the Problem of Race in America*. New York: Oxford University Press.

Erskine, Noel Leo. 1994. *King among the Theologians*. Cleveland: Pilgrim Press.

Evans, Tony. 1994. "Spiritual Purity." In *Seven Promises of a Promise Keeper*, 73–81. Colorado Springs: Focus on the Family Publishing.

Fairclough, Adam. 1987. *To Redeem the Soul of America: The Southern Christian Leadership Conference and Martin Luther King, Jr*. Athens: University of Georgia Press.

"Faith-Based Funding Backed, but Church-State Doubts Abound." 2001. Pew Research Center for the People and the Press. April 10. http://people-press.org/reports/display.php3?ReportID=15.

Farrar, Steve. 1999. "Understanding the Times & Knowing What to Do About It: Lack of True Leaders Is Killing America." 1999 Promise Keepers Conference, Indianapolis, Indiana. http://www.otherside.net/farrar/htm.

Finke, Roger, and Rodney Stark. 1992. *The Churching of America, 1776–1990: Winners and Losers in Our Religious Economy.* New Brunswick: Rutgers University Press.

Finney, Charles G. 1988. *Revivals of Religion.* Minneapolis: Bethany House.

Fish, Stanley. 1994. *There's No Such Thing as Free Speech: And It's a Good Thing, Too.* Oxford: Oxford University Press.

Foucault, Michel. 1980. "Two Lectures." In *Power/Knowledge: Selected Interviews and Other Writings, 1972–1977,* edited by Colin Gordon, 78–108. New York: Pantheon Books.

Fowler, Robert Booth, and Alan D. Hertzke. 1995. *Religion and Politics in America.* Boulder: Westview Press.

Frank, Douglas W. 1986. *Less than Conquerors: How Evangelicals Entered the Twentieth Century.* Grand Rapids, MI: William B. Eerdmans.

Fraser, Nancy. 1996. *Justice Interruptus: Critical Reflections on the "Postsocialist" Condition.* New York: Routledge.

Freud, Sigmund. 1939. *Moses and Monotheism.* Translated by Katherine Jones. New York: Vintage Books.

*Frontiers in Social Movement Theory.* 1992. Edited by Aldon D. Morris and Carol McClurg Mueller. New Haven: Yale University Press.

Gabel, John B., Charles B. Wheeler, and Anthony D. York. 1996. *The Bible as Literature: An Introduction.* Oxford: Oxford University Press.

Gallagher, Steve. 2003. "Be Strong and Very Courageous: Emerging from the Prison of Pornography." http://www.promisekeepers.org/arti/arti118.htm.

Gallegos, Aaron McCarroll. 1998. "Following the Path of Grace: Spencer Perkins' Long Road to Reconciliation." *Sojourners* 27, no. 6 (November–December): 24–28.

Garrow, David J. 1988. *Bearing the Cross: Martin Luther King, Jr. and the Southern Christian Leadership Conference.* New York: Vintage Books.

Geertz, Clifford. 1973. *The Interpretation of Cultures.* New York: Basic Books.

Genovese, Eugene D. 1976. *Roll, Jordan, Roll: The World the Slaves Made.* New York: Vintage.

"Go the Distance." 2000. Promise Keepers Promotional Brochure.

Gomes, Peter J. 1998. *The Good Book: Reading the Bible with Mind and Heart.* New York: Bard.

Good, Paul. 1975. *The Trouble I've Seen: White Journalist/Black Movement.* Washington, DC: Howard University Press.

Gorski, Eric. 2003. "Promise Keepers to Shift Direction Under New Chief." *Denver Post,* October 6, B1.

Granberg-Michaelson, Wesley. 1999. "Many Members, One Body." *Sojourners* 28, no. 3 (May–June): 24–27.

Green, John C., James L. Guth, Corwin E. Smidt, and Lyman A. Kellstedt. 1996. *Religion and the Culture Wars: Dispatches from the Front.* Lanham, MD: Rowman & Littlefield.

Gundry-Wolf, Judith. 1998. "Neither Biblical Nor Just: Southern Baptists and the Subordination of Women." *Sojourners* 27, no. 5 (September–October): 12–13.

Gutterman, David S. 2000. "Prophetic Narratives of Hope and Identity: The Promise Keepers and the Theology of Masculinity." In *The Promise Keepers:*

*Essays on Masculinity and Christianity*, edited by Dane Claussen, 133–52. Jefferson, NC: McFarland.

——. 2001. "Presidential Testimony: Listening to the Heart of George W. Bush." *Theory & Event*, 5:2, July.

——. 2005. "A Nation of Sinners: Narratives of Identity in America." In *Religion, Politics and the American Experience after September 11: New Perspectives, New Directions*, edited by David S. Gutterman and Andrew Murphy. Lanham, MD: Lexington Books.

Ha-'Am, Ahad. 1981. *Selected Essays of Ahad Ha-'Am*. Translated and edited by Leon Simon. New York: Atheneum.

Hammer, Dean C. 1997. "Incommensurable Phrases and Narrative Discourse: Lyotard and Arendt on the Possibility of Politics." *Philosophy Today* 41, no. 4 (Winter): 475–90.

Hanson, Paul D. 1996. "The Origin and Nature of Prophetic Political Engagement in ancient Israel." In *Let Justice Roll: Prophetic Challenges in Religion, Politics and Society*, edited by Neal Riemer, 1–22. Lanham, MD: Rowman & Littlefield.

Harris, Frederick C. 1995. "Religious Institutions and African-American Religious Mobilizaton." In *Classifying by Race*, edited by by Paul E. Peterson, 278–310. Princeton: Princeton University Press.

Hartz, Louis. 1955. *The Liberal Tradition in America: An Interpretation of American Political Thought since the Revolution*. New York: Harcourt & Brace.

Hatch, Nathan O. 1989. *The Democratization of American Christianity*. New Haven: Yale University Press.

Hayford, Jack. 1994. "Setting a Sure Foundation." In *Seven Promises of a Promise Keeper*, 17–23. Colorado Springs: Focus on the Family Publishing.

Hendricks, Howard. 1994. "A Mandate for Mentoring." In *Seven Promises of a Promise Keeper*, 47–55. Colorado Springs: Focus on the Family Publishing.

Herzog, Annabel. 2001. "The Poetical Nature of Political Disclosure: Hannah Arendt's Storytelling." *Clio* 30:2, 169–94.

Heschel, Abraham J. 1969. *The Prophets: An Introduction*. New York: Harper Torchbooks.

——. 1975. *The Prophets*. Vol. 2. New York: Harper Torchbooks.

Higginbotham, A. Leon, Jr. 1996. *Shades of Freedom: Racial Politics and Presumptions of the American Legal Process*. New York: Oxford University Press.

Hill, Melvyn A. 1979. "The Fictions of Mankind and the Stories of Men." In *Hannah Arendt: The Recovery of the Public World*, edited by Melvyn A. Hill, 275–300. New York: St. Martin's Press.

Hofrenning, Daniel J. B. 1995. *In Washington But Not of It: The Prophetic Politics of Religious Lobbyists*. Philadelphia: Temple University Press.

*Holy Ground: A Resource and Faith and the Environment*. 1997. Edited by Jim Wallis, Aaron Gallegos, and Bob Hulteen. Washington, DC: Sojourners.

Honig, Bonnie. 1993. *Political Theory and the Displacement of Politics*. Ithaca: Cornell University Press.

——. 2003. *Democracy and the Foreigner*. Princeton: Princeton University Press.

Howard-Pitney, David. 1990. *The Afro-American Jeremiad: Appeals for Justice in America*. Philadelphia: Temple University Press.

Huntington, Samuel P. 1981. *American Politics: The Promise of Disharmony*. Cambridge: Belknap Press.

Jackson, Jesse L., Jr. 1997. "Promise Keepers: Watch as Well as Pray," http://www.now.org/issues/right/promise/jackson/html.

Jacobson, Norman. 1983. "On Revolution." *Salmagundi*, no. 60 (Spring–Summer): 123–40.

——. 1987. *Pride and Solace: The Functions and Limits of Political Theory.* New York: Methuen.

James, Bill. 2001. *The New Bill James Historical Baseball Abstract.* New York: Free Press.

Jelen, Ted. 1991. *The Political Mobilization of Religious Beliefs.* New York: Praeger.

Johnson, Curtis. 1993. *Redeeming America: Evangelicals and the Road to Civil War.* Chicago: Ivan R. Dee.

Kaminer, Wendy. 1992. *I'm Dysfunctional, You're Dysfunctional: The Recovery Movement and Other Self-Help Fashions.* New York: Addison-Wesley Publishing Company.

Kant, Immanuel. 1986. *The Critique of Judgment.* Translated by James Creed Meredith. New York: Oxford University Press.

Kateb, George. 1990. "Hannah Arendt: Alienation and America." In *Raritan: Reading,* edited by Richard Poirier, 196–221. New Brunswick: Rutgers University Press.

Kateb, George. 1984. *Hannah Arendt: Politics, Conscience, Evil.* Totowa: Rowman & Allanheld.

Kerby, Anthony Paul. 1991. *Narrative and the Self.* Bloomington: Indiana University Press.

Kermode, Frank. 2000. *The Sense of an Ending: Studies in the Theory of Fiction.* New York: Oxford University Press.

King, Martin Luther, Jr. 1981. *Strength to Love.* Philadelphia: Fortress Press.

——. 1986. *A Testament of Hope: The Essential Writings and Speeches of Martin Luther King, Jr.* Edited by James M. Washington. San Francisco: HarperCollins.

——. 1988. *The Measure of a Man.* Philadelphia: Fortress Press.

——. 1998. *A Knock at Midnight: Inspiration from the Great Sermons of Martin Luther King, Jr.* Edited by Clayborne Carson and Peter Holloran. New York: Warner Books.

Kintz, Linda. 1997. *Between Jesus and the Market: The Emotions that Matter in Right-Wing America.* Durham: Duke University Press.

Kosmin, Barry A., and Seymour P. Lachman. 1993. *One Nation Under God: Religion in Contemporary American Society.* New York: Harmony Books.

Kramnick, Isaac. 2003. Introduction to *Democracy in America and Two Essays on America* by Alexis de Tocqueville. New York: Penguin.

Kristeva, Julia, 1984. *Powers of Horror.* Translated by Leon S. Roudiez. New York: Columbia University Press.

Kundera, Milan. 1996. *The Book of Laughter and Forgetting.* New York: Harper-Collins.

Larson, Edward J. 1997. *Summer for the Gods: The Scopes Trial and America's Continuing Debate Over Science and Religion.* New York: Basic Books.

Lewis, Gregg. 1995. *The Power of a Promise Kept: Life Stories.* Colorado Springs: Focus on the Family Publishing.

Lienesch, Michael. 1993. *Redeeming America: Piety and Politics in the New Christian Right.* Chapel Hill: University of North Carolina Press.

Lincoln, Abraham. 1953. *The Collected Works of Abraham Lincoln, Volume IV.* Edited by Roy P. Basler. New Brunswick: Rutgers University Press.

Lincoln, Bruce. 2003. *Holy Terrors: Thinking about Religion after September 11.* Chicago: University of Chicago Press.

Lindsey, Hal. 1970. *The Late Great Planet Earth.* Grand Rapids, MI: Zondervan.

Locke, Jill. 2004. "Unashamed Citizenship." Feminist Theory Workshop, Western Political Science Association.

London, H. B., Jr. 1994. "The Man God Seeks." In *Seven Promises of a Promise Maker,* 141–50. Colorado Springs: Focus on the Family Publishing.

Longinow, Michael A. 2000. "The Price of Admission? Promise Keepers' Roots in Revivalism and the Emergence of Middle Class Language and Appeal in Men's Movements." In *The Promise Keepers: Essays on Masculinity and Christianity,* edited by Dane Claussen, 42–55. Jefferson, NC: McFarland.

Machiavelli, Niccolò. 1950. *The Prince and The Discourses.* New York: Modern Library.

MacIntyre, Alasdair. 1984. *After Virtue.* Notre Dame: University of Notre Dame Press.

*Man of His Word: The New Testament, NIV Version.* 1996. Colorado Springs: International Bible Society.

Markell, Patchen. 2003. *Bound by Recognition.* Princeton: Princeton University Press.

Marsden, George M. 1991. *Understanding Fundamentalism and Evangelicalism.* Grand Rapids, MI: William B. Eerdmans.

Marsh, Charles. 1997. *God's Long Summer: Stories of Faith and Civil Rights.* Princeton: Princeton University Press.

Marty, Martin E. 1997. *The One and The Many: America's Struggle for the Common Good.* Cambridge: Harvard University Press.

McCartney, Bill. 1993. *Men of Action Newsletter,* Winter.

———. 1994. "A Call to Unity." In *Seven Promises of a Promise Keeper.* Colorado Springs: Focus on the Family Publishing.

———. 1997. Interview on Meet the Press, NBC, October 5.

———. 1997. Promise Keeper letter, January 20.

———. 1997. "Promise Makers," *Policy Review* no. 85 (September–October), Heritage Foundation. www.policyreview.com/sept97/promise.html.

———. 1997. "To Save the Nation." Interview in *The Washington Post,* October 4, C7.

McCartney, Bill, et al. 1992. *What Makes a Man? Twelve Promises That Will Change Your Life.* Colorado Springs: Navpress Publishing Group.

McCollough, Thomas E. 1991. *The Moral Imagination and Public Life: Raising the Ethical Question.* Chatham, NJ: Chatham House.

McLaren, Angus. 1997. *The Trials of Masculinity: Policing Sexual Boundaries, 1870–1930.* Chicago: University of Chicago Press.

McLoughlin, William G., Jr. 1955. *Billy Sunday Was His Real Name.* Chicago: University of Chicago Press.

———. 1959. *Modern Revivalism: Charles Grandison Finney to Billy Graham.* New York: Ronald Press.

———. 1978. *Revivals, Awakenings and Reform: An Essay on Religion and Social Change in America, 1607–1977.* Chicago: University of Chicago Press.

McWilliams, Wilson Carey. 1973. *The Idea of Fraternity in America.* Berkeley: University of California Press.

———. 1984. "The Bible in the American Political Tradition." In *Religion and Politics,* edited by Myron Aronoff. New Brunswick: Transaction.

*Men's Study Bible (New International Version).* 1997. Grand Rapids, MI: Zondervan.

Melville, Herman. 1981. *White-Jacket; or, The World in a Man-of-War.* Evanston: Northwestern University Press.

Metz, Johann Baptist. 1974. *Religion and Political Society.* New York: Harper & Row.

Miller, Keith D. 1992. *Voice of Deliverance: The Language of Martin Luther King Jr. and Its Sources.* New York: Free Press.

Miller, Perry. 1956. *Errand into the Wilderness.* Cambridge: Belknap Press.

——. 1965. *The Life of the Mind in America: From the Revolution to the Civil War.* New York: Harcourt, Brace & World.

——. 1967. *Nature's Nation.* Cambridge: Belknap Press.

Moltmann, Jürgen. 1967. *Theology of Hope: On the Ground and the Implications of a Christian Eschatology.* New York: Harper & Row.

——. 1975. *The Experiment Hope.* Philadelphia: Fortress Press.

——. 1984. *On Human Dignity: Political Theology and Ethics.* Translated by M. Douglas Meeks. Philadelphia: Fortress Press.

Morone, James A. 2003. *Hellfire Nation: The Politics of Sin in American History.* New Haven: Yale University Press.

Morris, Aldon. 1984. *The Origins of the Civil Rights Movement: Black Communities Organizing for Change.* New York: Free Press.

Morris, Calvin S. 1995. "We, the (White) People." In *America's Original Sin: A Study Guide on White Racism,* edited by Bob Hulteen and Jim Wallis, 12–15. Washington, DC: Sojourners.

Mosse, George. 1996. *The Image of Man: The Creation of Modern Masculinity.* New York: Oxford University Press.

Murphy, Andrew. 2005. "One Nation under God, September 11, and the Chosen Nation: Moral Decline and Divine Punishment in American Public Discourse." *Political Theology* 6, no. 1 (March): 9–30.

Myers, Ched. 2000. "Stories to Live By." *Sojourners* 29, no. 2 (March–April): 32–35, 51.

Neuhaus, Richard John. 1984. *The Naked Public Square: Religion and Democracy in America.* Grand Rapids, MI: William B. Eerdmans Press.

"The News Hour with Jim Lehrer." 1997. Public Broadcasting Systems, October 7.

Niebuhr, H. Richard. 1954. "The Idea of Covenant and American Democracy." *Church History* 23, no. 2 (June): 126–35.

Nietzsche, Friedrich. 1969. *On the Genealogy of Morals and Ecce Homo.* Translated and edited by Walter Kaufmann. New York: Vintage Books.

——. 1974. *The Gay Science.* New York: Random House.

——. 1980. *On the Advantage and Disadvantage of History for Life.* Translated by Peter Preuss. Indianapolis: Hackett.

——. 1988. *The Portable Nietzsche.* Translated and edited by Walter Kaufmann. New York: Penguin Books.

Noah, Timothy. 2004. "Mister Landslide's Neighborhood." April 7. *Slate.* http://slate.msn.com/id/2098387.

Noll, Mark A. 1982. "The Image of the United States as a Biblical Nation, 1776–1865." In *The Bible in America: Essays in Cultural History,* edited by Nathan O. Hatch and Mark A. Noll. New York: Oxford University Press.

Nye, Russell. 1966. *The Almost Chosen People: Essays in the History of American Ideas.* East Lansing: Michigan State University Press.

Oldfield, Duane Murray. 1996. *The Right and the Righteous: The Christian Right Confronts the Republican Party.* New York: Rowman & Littlefield.

Orlie, Melissa. 1997. *Living Ethically, Acting Politically.* Ithaca: Cornell University Press.

Osborn, Michael. 1993. "The Last Mountaintop of Martin Luther King, Jr." In *Martin Luther King, Jr., and the Sermonic Power of Public Discourse,* edited by

Carolyn Calloway-Thomas and John Louis Lucaites, 147–61. Tuscaloosa: University of Alabama Press.

Oliver, Gary. 1994. "Black-and-White Living in a Gray World." In *Seven Promises of a Promise Keeper*, 83–90. Colorado Springs: Focus on the Family Publishing.

Palau, Luis. 1994. "The Great Commission." In *Seven Promises of a Promise Keeper*, 193–202. Colorado Springs: Focus on the Family Publishing.

Palmer, Benjamin R. 1971. "National Responsibility before God." In *God's New Israel: Religious Interpretations of American Destiny*, edited by Conrad Cherry, 177–94. Englewood Cliffs, NJ: Prentice-Hall.

Parker, Jennifer. 1997. "No Cheap Reconciliation." *Reconcilers* (Summer): 4–6.

Perkins, Spencer. 1998. "Does Racial Pride Hinder Reconciliation?" *Sojourners* 27, no. 6 (November–December): 25–27.

Perry, Michael J. 1997. *Religion in Politics: Constitutionalism and Moral Perspectives*. New York: Oxford University Press.

Phillips, Holly. 1995. "Costly Promises." New Man. http://www.strang.com/nm/stories/nm296s.htm.

Phillips, Randy. 1994. "Seize the Moment." In *Seven Promises of a Promise Keeper*. Colorado Springs: Focus on the Family Publishing.

———. 1995. "Introduction: The Power of a Promise Kept." In *The Power of a Promise Kept: Life Stories*, by Gregg Lewis, 1–4. Colorado Springs: Focus on the Family Publishing.

Pitkin, Hanna Fenichel. 1972. *Wittgenstein and Justice: On the Significance of Ludwig Wittgenstein for Social and Political Thought*. Berkeley: University of California Press.

———. 1998. *The Attack of the Blob: Hannah Arendt's Concept of the Social*. Chicago: University of Chicago Press.

*The Politics of Manhood*. 1995. Edited by Michael S. Kimmel. Philadelphia: Temple University Press.

Polter, Julie. 1999. "A Civil Discourse: Seeking Common Ground on Abortion Clinic Activism." *Sojourners* 28, no. 3 (May–June): 11.

Price, Reynolds. 1997. *A Palpable God*. Pleasantville, NY: Akadine Press.

*Promise Builders Study Series*. 1995. Edited by Bob Horner, Ron Ralston, David Sunde. Boulder: Promise Keepers.

*The Promise Keeper*. 2000. 3, no. 1 (July/August ):5.

Prothero, Stephen. 2003. *American Jesus: How the Son of God Became a National Icon*. New York: Farrar, Straus and Giroux.

Putney, Clifford. 2001. *Muscular Christianity: Manhood and Sports in Protestant America, 1880–1920*. Cambridge: Harvard University Press.

*Putting Down Stones: A Faithful Response to Urban Violence*. 1996. Edited by Aaron Gallegos and Kelly M. Green. Washington, DC: Sojourners.

Raboteau, Albert J. 1978. *Slave Religion: The "Invisible Institution" in the Antebellum South*. New York: Oxford University Press.

Reagon, Bernice Johnson. 1983. "Coalition Politics: Turning the Century." In *Homegirls: A Back Feminist Anthology*, edited by Barbara Smith, 357–68. New York: Kitchen Table/Women of Color Press.

*Recovering the Evangel: A Guide to Faith, Politics and Alternatives to the Religious Right*. 1997. Edited by Jim Wallis, Bob Hulteen, and Aaron Gallegos. Washington, DC: Sojourners.

Reed, Ralph. 1996. *Active Faith: How Christians Are Changing the Face of American Politics*. New York: Free Press.

Reichley, A. James. 1985. *Religion in American Public Life*. Washington, DC: Brookings Institution.

Ricoeur, Paul. 1983. "Action, Story, History." *Salmagundi*, no. 60 (Spring–Summer): 60–72.

———. 1984–1988. *Time and Narrative, Volumes 1–3*. Translated by Kathleen Blarney and David Pellauer. Chicago: University of Chicago Press.

———. 1986. *Lectures on Ideology and Utopia*. Edited by George H. Taylor. New York: Columbia University Press.

———. 1991. "Life in Quest of Narrative." In *On Paul Ricoeur: Narrative and Interpretation*. Edited by David Wood, 20–33. New York: Routledge.

———. 1992. *Oneself as Another*. Translated by Kathleen Blamey. Chicago: University of Chicago Press.

———. 1995. *Figuring the Sacred: Religion, Narrative, and Imagination*. Translated by David Pellauer. Edited by Mark I. Wallace. Minneapolis: Fortress Press.

Riemer, Neal. 1996. Preface to *Let Justice Roll: Prophetic Challenges in Religion, Politics and Society*, edited by Neal Riemer, ix–xi. Lanham, MD: Rowman & Littlefield.

Ring, Jennifer. 1991. "The Pariah as Hero: Hannah Arendt's Political Actor." *Political Theory* 19, no. 3 (Aug.): 433–52.

Rivers, Eugene F., III. 1998. "Blocking the Prayers of the Church: The Idol of White Supremacy." In *Crossing the Racial Divide: America's Struggle for Justice and Reconciliation*, edited by Jim Wallis and Aaron Gallegos, 15–19. Washington, DC: Sojourners.

Rivers, Eugene F., III, and Jackqueline C. Rivers. 2000. "The Fight for the Living: AIDS, Orphans, and the Future of Africa." *Sojourners* 29, no. 4 (July–August): 18.

Roof, Wade Clark, and William McKinney. 1992. *American Mainline Religion: Its Changing Shape and Future*. New Brunswick: Rutgers University Press.

Rorty, Richard. 1999. "Religion as Conversation-stopper." In *Philosophy and Social Hope*, 168–74. New York: Penguin.

Rudy, Kathy. 1997. *Sex and the Church: Gender, Homosexuality, and the Transformation of Christian Ethics*. Boston: Beacon Press.

Ruether, Rosemary Radford. 1996. "Prophetic Tradition and the Liberation of Women: A Story of Promise and Betrayal." In *Let Justice Roll: Prophetic Challenges in Religion, Politics, and Society*, edited by Neal Riemer, 59–70. Lanham, MD: Rowman & Littlefield.

Schlafer, Dale. 1994. "Honoring and Praying for Your Pastor." In *Seven Promises of a Promise Keeper*, 133–40. Colorado Springs: Focus on the Family Publishing.

———. 1997. *A Revival Primer*. Denver: Promise Keepers.

*Seven Promises of a Promise Keeper*. 1994. Colorado Springs: Focus on the Family Publishing.

Shulman, George. 1996. "American Political Culture, Prophetic Narration, and Toni Morrison's *Beloved*." *Political Theory* 24, no. 2, (May): 295–314.

Sizer, Sandra. 1979. "Politics and Apolitical Religion: The Great Urban Revivals of the Late Nineteenth Century." *Church History* 48, no. 1 (March): 81–98.

Smalley, Gary, and John Trent. 1994. *The Hidden Value of a Man: The Incredible Impact of a Man on His Family*. Colorado Springs: Focus on the Family Publishing.

Smith, Theophus H. 1994. *Conjuring Culture: Biblical Formations of Black America*. New York: Oxford University Press.

Snow, David A., and Robert D. Benford. 1992. "Master Frames and Cycles of Protest." In *Frontiers in Social Movement Theory*, edited by Aldon D. Morris and Carol McClurg Mueller, 133–55. New Haven: Yale University Press.

*Social Movements and American Political Institutions.* 1998. Edited by Anne N. Costain and Andrew S. McFarland. Lanham, MD: Rowman and Littlefield.

Solomon, Martha. 1993. "Covenanted Rights: The Metaphoric Matrix of 'I Have a Dream.'" In *Martin Luther King, Jr., and the Sermonic Power of Public Discourse,* edited by Carolyn Calloway-Thomas and John Louis Lucaites, 66–84. Tuscaloosa: University of Alabama Press.

Somers, Margaret R., and Gloria D. Gibson. 1994. "Reclaiming the Epistemological Other: Narrative and the Social Constitution of Identity." In *Social Theory and the Politics of Identity,* edited by Craig Calhoun, 37–99. Oxford: Blackwell.

*Standing on Promises: The Promise Keepers and the Revival of Manhood.* 2000. Edited by Dane S. Claussen. Cleveland: Pilgrim Press.

Stark, Rodney, and Kevin J. Christiano. 1992. "Support for the American Left, 1920–1924: The Opiate Thesis Reconsidered." *Journal for the Scientific Study of Religion* 31: 62–75.

Stevens, Jacqueline. 1993. "Leviticus in America: The Politics of Sex Crimes." *Journal of Political Philosophy* 1, no. 2 : 105–36.

Stout, Jeffrey. 1988. *Ethics After Babel: The Languages of Morals and Their Discontents.* Boston: Beacon Press.

Sunday, Billy. 1882–1974. *The Papers of Billy Sunday.* Collection at New York Public Library.

Tarrow, Sidney. 1998a. *Power in Movement: Social Movements and Contentious Politics.* Cambridge: Cambridge University Press.

———. 1998b. "'The Very Excess of Democracy': State Building and Contentious Politics in America." In *Social Movements and American Political Institutions,* edited by Anne N. Costain and Andrew S. McFarland, 20–38. Lanham, MD: Rowman and Littlefield.

Taylor, Charles. 1992. *Multiculturalism and "The Politics of Recognition": An Essay.* Princeton: Princeton University Press.

Terkel, Studs. 1992. *Race: How Blacks & Whites Think & Feel about the American Obsession.* New York: New Press.

Thiemann, Ronald F. 1996. *Religion in Public Life: A Dilemma for Democracy.* Washington, DC: Georgetown University Press.

Thomas, Cal, and Ed Dobson. 2000. *Blinded By Might: Why the Religious Right Can't Save America.* Grand Rapids, MI: Zondervan.

Thomas, George M. 1989. *Revivalism and Cultural Change: Christianity, Nation Building, and the Market in the Nineteenth-Century United States.* Chicago: University of Chicago Press.

Tocqueville, Alexis de. 1988. *Democracy in America.* Translated by George Lawrence. Edited by J. P. Mayer. New York: HarperPerennial.

Tracy, David. 1987. *Plurality and Ambiguity: Hermeneutics, Religion, Hope.* San Francisco: Harper & Row.

Tuveson, Ernest Lee. 1968. *Redeemer Nation: The Idea of America's Millennial Role.* Chicago: University of Chicago Press.

*United by Faith: The Multiracial Congregation as an Answer to the Problem of Race.* 2003. Edited by Curtiss Paul Deyoung et al. New York: Oxford University Press.

*Unsecular America.* 1986. Edited by Richard John Neuhaus. Grand Rapids: William B. Eerdmans.

Van Leeuwen, Mary Stewart. 1998. "Promise Keepers: Proof-text Poker." *Sojourners* 27, no. 1 (January–February): 16–21.

Villa, Dana. 1992. "Beyond Good and Evil: Arendt and Nietzsche on the Aesthetics of Political Action." *Political Theory* 20, no. 2 (Spring): 274–305.

Wagner, E. Glenn, with Dietrich Gruen. 1994. *Strategies for a Successful Marriage: A Study Guide for Men.* Colorado Springs: Navpress.

Wallis, Jim. 1992. *The Call to Conversion: Recovering the Gospel for These Times.* San Francisco: HarperCollins.

———. 1995. *The Soul of Politics: Beyond "Religious Right" and "Secular Left."* New York: Harcourt, Brace.

———. 1996. *Who Speaks for God? An Alternative to the Religious Right—A New Politics of Compassion, Community and Civility.* New York: Delacorte Press.

———. 2000. *Faith Works: Lessons from the Life of an Activist Preacher.* New York: Random House.

———. 2003a. "Class Warfare." *Sojourners* 32, no. 5 (September–October): 7–8.

———. 2003b. "Nothing Shall Make Them Afraid," June 9. http://www.calltorenewal.org/resources/index.cfm/action/display_theological/item/Pentecost_2003_MR_Sermon.htm.

———. 2003c. "Prophetic Leadership," *Sojourners* 32, no. 1 (January–February): 7–8.

———. 2004. "Evangelical Social Conscience." *Sojourners* 33, no. 3 (March): 5.

Walzer, Michael. 1965. *The Revolution of the Saints: A Study in the Origins of Radical Politics,* Cambridge: Harvard University Press.

———. 1985. *Exodus and Revolution.* New York: Basic Books.

———. 1996. "Prophecy and Social Criticism." In *Let Justice Roll: Prophetic Challenges in Religion, Politics and Society,* edited by Neal Riemer, 22–37. Lanham, MD: Rowman & Littlefield.

West, Cornel. 1982. *Prophecy Deliverance! An Afro-American Revolutionary Christianity.* Philadelphia: Westminster Press.

Weber, Max. 1976. *The Protestant Ethic and the Spirit of Capitalism.* Translated by Talcott Parsons. New York: Charles Scribner's Sons.

Weber, Stu. 1995. *Locking Arms: God's Design for Masculine Friendship.* Sisters, OR: Multnomah Books.

Weisbrot, Robert. 1991. *Freedom Bound: A History of America's Civil Rights Movement.* New York: Penguin Books.

Wertenbaker, Thomas Jefferson. 1963. *The Founding of American Civilization: The Middle Colonies.* New York: Cooper Square.

Weyrich, Paul M. 1999. "A Moral Minority? An Open Letter to Conservatives." February 16. http://www.freecongress.org/fcf/specials/weyrichopenltr.htm.

White, Hayden. 1983. "The Question of Narrative in Contemporary Historical Theory." *History and Theory* 23, no. 1: 1–33.

———. 1985. *Tropics of Discourse: Essays in Cultural Criticism.* Baltimore: Johns Hopkins University Press.

*Who Is My Neighbor? Economics As If Values Matter.* 1994. Edited by Bob Hulteen and Jim Wallis. Washington, DC: Sojourners.

*Why Narrative? Readings in Narrative Theology.* 1988. Edited by Stanley Hauerwas and L. Gregory Jones. Grand Rapids, MI: William B. Eerdmans.

Wilcox, Clyde. 1996. *Onward Christian Soldiers? The Religious Right in American Politics.* Boulder: Westview Press.

Wildavsky, Aaron. 1984. *The Nursing Father: Moses as a Political Leader.* Tuscaloosa: University of Alabama Press.

Wilkerson, Bruce H. 1997. *Personal Holiness in Times of Temptation* (Video and Course Workbook). Atlanta: Walk Thru the Bible Ministries.

Wills, Garry. 1990. *Under God.* New York: Simon & Schuster.

Wilson, William Julius. 1997. *When Work Disappears: The World of the New Urban Poor.* New York: Vintage Books.

Winthrop, John. 1971. "A Modell of Christian Charity" In *God's New Israel: Religious Interpretations of American Destiny,* edited by Conrad Cherry, 39–43. Englewood Cliffs, NJ: Prentice-Hall.

Wolf, Naomi, and Frederica Mathewes-Green. 1999. "Getting to Disagreement." *Sojourners* 28, no. 1 (January–February ): 32–35.

Wolfe, Alan. 1998. *One Nation After All: What Middle-Class Americans Really Think About: God, Country, Family, Racism, Welfare, Immigration, Homosexuality, Work, The Right, The Left, and Each Other.* New York: Viking.

Wolin, Sheldon S. 1983. "Democracy and the Political." *Salmagundi,* no. 60 (Spring–Summer): 3–19.

——. 1989. *The Presence of the Past: Essays on the State and the Constitution.* Baltimore: Johns Hopkins University Press.

Wood, Gordon S. 1969. *The Creation of the American Republic, 1776–1787.* Chapel Hill: University of North Carolina Press.

Wuthnow, Robert. 1994. *Producing the Sacred: An Essay on Public Religion.* Urbana: University of Illinois Press.

——. 1998. *After Heaven: Spirituality in America since the 1950s.* Berkeley: University of California Press.

Wylie-Kellermann, Bill. 1998. "Exorcising an American Demon." In *Crossing the Racial Divide: America's Struggle for Justice and Reconciliation,* edited by Jim Wallis and Aaron Gallegos, 9–12. Washington, DC: Sojourners.

Young, James P. 1996. *Reconsidering American Liberalism: The Troubled Odyssey of the Liberal Idea.* Boulder: WestviewPress.

Zakai, Avihu. 1992. *Exile and Kingdom: History and Apocalypse in the Puritan Migration to America.* New York: Cambridge University Press.

Zerilli, Linda M. G. 1994. *Signifying Woman: Culture and Chaos in Rousseau, Burke, and Mill.* Ithaca: Cornell University Press.

Zemike, Kate. 2000. "Serving the Community?" *Boston Globe,* February 22, B1.

# Index